MW01001947
to the office
of the holy ministry
of Word and
with joy and hope!
Barry +

Keeping Time

Keeping Time

The Church's Years

Using *Evangelical Lutheran Worship*
Volume Three

Gail Ramshaw
Mons Teig

Augsburg Fortress

Using *Evangelical Lutheran Worship*
Volume 1, *The Sunday Assembly*
Volume 2, *The Christian Life: Baptism and Life Passages*
Volume 3, *Keeping Time: The Church's Years*

Other *Evangelical Lutheran Worship* Leader Guides
Indexes to Evangelical Lutheran Worship
Musicians Guide to Evangelical Lutheran Worship
Hymnal Companion to Evangelical Lutheran Worship

KEEPING TIME: The Church's Years
Using Evangelical Lutheran Worship. Volume Three

Manufactured in the U.S.A.

ISBN 978–0–8066–7016–4

15 14 13 12 11 10 09 1 2 3 4 5 6 7 8 9 10

CONTENTS

Preface to the *Evangelical Lutheran Worship* Leader Guides

Evangelical Lutheran Worship includes a number of related print editions and other resources developed to support the worship life of the Evangelical Lutheran Church in America and the Evangelical Lutheran Church in Canada. The core print editions of *Evangelical Lutheran Worship*, released in 2006, include the following:

Pew (Assembly) Edition [AE]
Leaders Edition and Leaders Desk Edition [LE]
Accompaniment Edition: Liturgies
Accompaniment Edition: Service Music and Hymns

An encounter with these core editions and their introductions is important to an understanding of the goals and principles embodied in *Evangelical Lutheran Worship.*

In addition to the core materials, *Evangelical Lutheran Worship* includes other published resources that are prepared to extend the usefulness of the core editions and to respond to the developing needs of the church in mission. The *Evangelical Lutheran Worship* leader guides, which include the present volume, supplement the core editions in a variety of ways.

These resources are intended to provide worship leaders and planners with support for *Evangelical Lutheran Worship* in ways that would not be possible within the core editions themselves. Although the assembly edition includes more interpretive material than its predecessors, such as the annotated patterns for worship that complement the notes within the services, it provides only minimal guidance for leading worship in a variety of settings. Although the leaders edition includes a more extensive section titled Notes on the Services, it is not designed to accommodate deeper historical context, theological reflection, or extensive practical counsel for those who want to lead worship with understanding and confidence.

The leader guides include a set of three volumes, Using *Evangelical Lutheran Worship*. This set addresses as its primary audience pastors, seminarians, and church musicians—people who together take the lead in preparing the assembly's worship week by week. In a time when many congregations have implemented a broader sharing in worship leadership and planning, however, the contents of these three volumes will be valuable also for assisting ministers with various roles, altar guilds and sacristans, worship committees, and worshipers who are seeking deeper understanding.

The Sunday Assembly, the first book in the set of three volumes, includes a general introduction to worship that is evangelical, Lutheran, and ecumenical. That is followed by in-depth historical, theological, and practical reflections on the service of Holy Communion and the Service of the Word. *The Christian Life: Baptism and Life Passages* is the second volume in the set and takes up the service of Holy Baptism and related services such as Affirmation of Baptism, together with the services of Healing, Funeral, and Marriage. This book, *Keeping Time: The Church's Years,* the third volume in the set, addresses the church's calendar of Sundays, festivals, and seasons; the place of the lectionary and other propers; and the cycle of daily prayer.

The leader guides series includes two volumes focused on assembly song. *Musicians Guide to Evangelical Lutheran Worship* presents essays on the musical leadership of assembly song in a variety of styles and genres, and offers music performance helps for each piece of liturgical music and every hymn in *Evangelical Lutheran Worship.* The *Hymnal Companion to Evangelical Lutheran Worship* includes detailed background on the words and music of the hymns, together with an overview of the role of hymnody in the church's worship. Both of these volumes, while having particular appeal to church musicians, will be useful also to pastors, seminarians, worship committees, choir members, and other worshipers.

Other reference and interpretive resources will be included among the leader guides as needed. *Indexes to Evangelical Lutheran Worship* is one such volume, with an extensive list of suggested hymns for the church year and an expanded set of other indexes.

Many of the church's gifted teachers have contributed to the writing and assembling of the leader guides. They have sought to discern and give additional focus to the vision for worship among Lutherans that emerged from the five-year Renewing Worship process (2001–2005) that engaged thousands of people across the Evangelical Lutheran Church in America and the Evangelical Lutheran Church in Canada in encountering provisional materials, sharing creative gifts, and evaluating various stages of the proposal. To be sure, this vision is one marked by a great diversity of thought and practice, a diversity the contributors seek to reflect in these volumes. Yet these gifted teachers also bring to this work their own distinctive points of view, shaped by their own experiences and by their encounters with other teachers, rostered leaders, and worshiping communities around the world.

The *Evangelical Lutheran Worship* leader guides thus do not intend to provide definitive answers or official positions in matters related to worship among Lutherans. In these volumes, however, we are invited to engage in conversation with teachers of the church, to consider how their insights and guidance may best inform and inspire the many different contexts in which local leaders guide the worship life of their communities. In so doing, these leader guides in their own ways seek to do what also the core editions set out to do: "to make more transparent the principle of fostering unity without imposing uniformity," so that ultimately all these resources might "be servants through which the Holy Spirit will call out the church, gather us around Jesus Christ in word and sacrament, and send us, enlivened, to share the good news of life in God" (*Evangelical Lutheran Worship,* Introduction, p. 8).

PART ONE

1

The Church's Year

CHAPTER ONE

My Times Are in Your Hands

Time, the fourth dimension of earthly existence, is both blessing and bane. It allows for measured progress, for the joys of watching a child's development, for anticipation of holidays, weddings, reunions. It also allows for the dread of less happy future events: a risky surgery, a confrontation. Time gives order to our lives, so that matters don't just come at us randomly, but it also can take over to such an extent that we may feel we are serving the clock, the calendar.

Think of how our lives are bound to appointments. It is time for school or work. It is time for a meeting. It is time for teeth cleaning. Our lists go on and on. Clocks measure seconds, minutes, and hours but do not speak to the significance or content of events that fill time. Calendars list appointments and important dates but can only hint at the deeper realities those events may contain. For all its centrality in our daily existence, chronological time or clock time is empty, moving space waiting—even demanding—to be filled. When we don't fill that time we sometimes say that we are "killing time" or "wasting time."

The church certainly knows *chronos,* or clock time. We use calendars, we announce services and other activities at certain times, and the schedules of church professionals are as crammed as anyone's. But the church also knows another kind of time. Biblical time—*kairos*—is filled with God's gracious actions and presence. Time is viewed as a gift of God and filled with grace. Beginning his ministry, Jesus proclaims that "the *time* is fulfilled, and the kingdom of God has come near" (Mark 1:15). After Jesus' sermon in the Nazareth synagogue, he amazed the worshipers when he said, "*Today* this scripture has been fulfilled in your hearing" (Luke 4:21). In a similar way, the apostle Paul says to the Corinthian congregation that has heard the gospel proclamation: "See, now is the acceptable time; see, now is the day of salvation!" (2 Cor. 6:2). The promises of God are now fulfilled: "When the fullness of time had come, God sent his Son . . ." (Gal. 4:4). God's will for the world in the entry of Jesus into the world's history is viewed "as a plan for the fullness of time" (Eph. 1:10). This is not just "once upon a time" but perpetually: Jesus "is able for all time to save those who approach God through him, since he always lives to make intercession for them" (Heb. 7:25). And we trust the promise and anticipate that Christ "will appear a second time . . . to save those who are eagerly waiting for him" (Heb. 9:28). So Christians not only mark the days on the calendar or fill in the boxes in our appointment books (chronos), but we discover in the patterns of biblical time (kairos or "pregnant" or "life-giving" time) the rich meaning of time filled with God and time fulfilled in Jesus.

A classic biblical description of times and seasons is given us by the writer of Ecclesiastes: "For everything there is a season, and a time for every matter under heaven: a time to be born, and a time to die; a time to plant, and a time to pluck up what is planted . . ." (3:1-8). This reinforces for us the wisdom of not forcing events at unsuited times, a tendency to which we often fall prey under the influence of the clock and the calendar. Rather, this writer advises, pay attention to God-given times and seasons and enjoy the blessings of the right thing done at the right time.

In one of his sermons, the apostle Peter urged: "Repent therefore, and turn to God so that your sins may be wiped out, so that times of refreshing may come from the presence of the Lord" (Acts 3:19-20). Times of refreshing! What a marvelous description of Sunday worship and daily prayer! Because we are "in Christ," now our time is bound up with God's mission in Christ in the power of the Spirit: "Be careful then how you live . . . making the most of the time" (Eph. 5:15-16). Christian living values the time we spend with others: "Conduct yourselves wisely toward outsiders, making the most of the time" (Col. 4:5).

About our present time as the gospel is proclaimed, the apostle Paul says, "You know what time it is, how it is now the moment for you to wake from sleep" (Rom. 13:11). So there can be urgency in kairos, though this urgency is underscored not by a deadline but by a holy need.

We teach children to tell time. Our appointment books and electronic calendars keep us aware of commitments and schedules of time. Even the church's schedule organizes times daily, weekly, and yearly around gospel and mission content. But in an era when we have specialists in time management, the church year provides a complementary way of understanding and making use of time. Working through kairos offers a pattern for the church's ordering of time in service of the gospel and a way to let our time be in God's hands.

The Church Keeps Time

Sunday. Easter. Like the planets orbiting the sun, the six days of the week orbit or revolve around Sunday. Likewise, the days and festivals of the year orbit or revolve around Easter. This basic pattern has been followed since the earliest days of the Christian church.

The common point for Sunday and Easter, and the reason for their centrality, is the resurrection of Jesus from the dead. Jesus was raised from the dead on the first day of the week, on the day within the calendar year that we now celebrate as Easter. The same day points us both backward and forward. Jesus' resurrection on the first day of the week echoes the beginning of the creation of the cosmos in the first chapter of Genesis. Within the Judeo-Christian tradition, that account of creation is what has given shape to the seven-day week that ends with the seventh-day sabbath. Luke's gospel (24:1) makes the connection between the resurrection and this counting of days: "On the first day of the week, at early dawn, [the women] came to the tomb. . . ." And Paul reminds us of the connection between the first creation and the world remade through Christ's resurrection: "If anyone is in Christ, there is a new creation" (2 Cor. 5:17). This sense of the new covenant and the new creation in Christ that invites all the baptized to "walk in newness of life" (Rom. 6:4) sometimes has been expressed by dubbing Sunday the *eighth day*. That is, this is the day that breaks the confines of normal life, the day every week that we remember and celebrate the Easter good news of Christ's death and resurrection to make all things new in the world. As early as the late first or early second century, *The Epistle of Barnabas* presented God as speaking of Sunday as the eighth day:

> The present sabbaths are not acceptable to me, but that which I have made, in which I will give rest to all things and make the beginning of an eighth day, that is the beginning of a new world. Wherefore we also celebrate with gladness the eighth day in which Jesus also rose from the dead, and was made manifest, and ascended into heaven.[1]

When one considers that the early Christians had been formed by the long tradition among Jews of keeping the Sabbath (our Saturday), one realizes that a powerful reason or event must have influenced the emerging church's practice of gathering for worship on the first day of the week (later named Sunday) instead of on the Sabbath. Because of the Easter or Paschal gospel, this first day of the week, or eighth day, came to be called "the Lord's day" (Rev. 1:10). In the book of Acts, Luke implies a weekly practice when he gives a time reference for a worship gathering: "On the first day of the week, when we met to break bread . . ." (Acts 20:7).

Therefore the first day of the week (later called Sunday), or the eighth day, has been central to the church's and individual lives for two thousand years. It was the day that the Christian community gathered eagerly around word and sacrament, together with prayers, praise, fellowship, and offerings for the poor. Gerhard Frost, a 20th century theologian, described Sunday's gathering for worship as the dinner bell of the soul.[2]

Sunday has been the way most Christians observe the third commandment of the Decalogue. Luther's explanation of the third commandment in the Small Catechism (AE p. 1160) stresses that this day provides and preserves time for the proclamation of God's gracious gospel. It is time, as Luther stressed, for receiving God's Word in both audible and visible (edible/drinkable) forms. Sunday is time for communal sharing in worship. That central action every Sunday in worship renews our communal and personal lives. The challenge of the church is to claim the life offered in the risen Christ: "The church of Christ, in every age beset by change, but Spirit-led, must claim and test its heritage and keep on rising from the dead" (ELW #729).

Keeping the Day Holy

The two statements of the commandment to keep the sabbath (our Saturday) holy (Exodus 20 and Deuteronomy 5) suggest not oppressive law but festivity, freedom, deliverance, refreshment, and renewal. In the Exodus account, the sabbath is a time for refreshment and renewal, a time to reflect on the good gift of creation and life itself.

> Remember the sabbath day, and keep it holy. Six days you shall labor and do all your work. But the seventh day is a sabbath to the LORD your God; you shall not do any work—you, your son

> or your daughter, your male or female slave, your livestock, or the alien resident in your towns. For in six days the LORD made heaven and earth, the sea, and all that is in them, but rested the seventh day; therefore the LORD blessed the sabbath day and consecrated it. [Exod. 20:8-11]

In Deuteronomy, sabbath is a festival of freedom that celebrates the deliverance of God's people from bondage and slavery.

> Observe the sabbath day and keep it holy, as the LORD your God commanded you. Six days you shall labor and do all your work. But the seventh day is a sabbath to the LORD your God; you shall not do any work—you, or your son or your daughter, or your male or female slave, or your ox or your donkey, or any of your livestock, or the resident alien in your towns, so that your male and female slave may rest as well as you. Remember that you were a slave in the land of Egypt, and the LORD your God brought you out from there with a mighty hand and an outstretched arm; therefore the LORD your God commanded you to keep the sabbath day. [Deut. 5:12-15]

One might say that the sabbath is, for Moses' descendants, the weekly religious version of the United States' annual secular Independence Day.

But what does it mean to keep the day holy? Much of the vigor of Judaism comes from rabbinic interpretations of the Torah's teachings. Also in the case of the sabbath commandment, many layers of interpretation built up, some of which Jesus saw as obscuring, even sometimes contradicting, the intent of the commandment. Over against the restrictions that fenced in life on the sabbath, Jesus brought a new vision of what sabbath meant. Jesus observed the third commandment and did attend the synagogue regularly: "When [Jesus] came to Nazareth . . . he went to the synagogue on the sabbath day, as was his custom" (Luke 4:16). However, he also broke many interpretations that had grown up around this holy day. Challenging the extensive rules about what religious authorities considered work and not rest, Jesus proclaimed that "the sabbath was made for humankind, and not humankind for the sabbath; so the Son of Man is lord even of the sabbath" (Mark 2:27-28). In effect, the message is: the sabbath is meant as a blessing, but finally, Jesus is our rest.

Another challenge was addressed to the restriction on healing or helping someone on the sabbath. Jesus said, "So it is lawful to do good on the sabbath" (see Matt. 12:9-14). Again the message may be that Jesus is our health and healing. Further, the sabbath is not only for one's self but for the neighbor in need. In another sabbath synagogue event, of healing a woman of a long-term disease, Jesus sets her free from her eighteen-year bondage to ill health. This spirit of sabbath keeping recalls God's deliverance from Egyptian bondage.

Because of Christ's resurrection on the first day of the week, Christians have transferred their observance of the sabbath to that day, Sunday. For Christians' weekly remembering of that one day, the new sabbath, brings all the days of the week into focus around what God was doing in Jesus, what God has been up to in the history of the world, and what God promises to do for the healing and health of the nations.[3] Since their beginnings, both Jews and Christians have seen the week through the eyes and focus of sabbath or Sunday. Sunday gives a new vision for our ordinary days. For Christians, Sunday proclaims and reminds us that Jesus is our life, our new creation, our deliverance, our rest, our hope. Our gathering on the Lord's day reminds the baptized that we belong to Christ; and because we belong to Christ, we belong to one another. The theologian Jürgen Moltmann suggests that "the sabbath opens creation to its true future."[4]

But as the prophet Amos reminds us, sabbath or Sunday worship that does not work for justice, does not care for the poor and the oppressed, does not live out God's care for the earth during the days of the week, is not acceptable. In fact, Amos says God will not listen to our music or take delight in our solemn liturgies if our worship on that one day is not lived out in the days of the week. What happens in church does not stay in church but is lived out in all our days. Far from being separate entities, regular keeping of Sunday gives a gospel rhythm to all our days and to our entire lives. Then we can say with the psalmist about every new day: "This is the day that the LORD has made; let us rejoice and be glad in it" (Ps. 118:24).

Biblical accounts reflect times when God acts on behalf of the creation and all people. There are times of deliverance, redemption, salvation, and blessing that give all time significance, meaning, and hope. This leads the psalmist to pray, "So teach us to number our days that we may apply our hearts to wisdom" (Ps. 90:12). The writer of

Lamentations asserts, in the midst of a great national tragedy, the gift of each day lived in faith in the faithfulness of God: "The steadfast love of the LORD never ceases, his mercies never come to an end; they are new every morning; great is your faithfulness" (Lam. 3:22-23). This promise for each day is grasped by many who sing with such gusto Thomas Chisholm's hymn (#733) based on this text; they claim in all circumstances "strength for today and bright hope for tomorrow."

A good visual image of the way the church year works in the community of faith is the spiral. The circle may suggest simple repetition, like the squirrel cage, without going anywhere. But the spiral can suggest bringing the past with its revelatory, saving, and blessing acts of God into the present moment, even as we are thrust into God's promised future. This suggests the continuity and change that God works in the church and in our individual lives. That sort of "time across time" is just what kairos seeks to express.

As pastors, musicians, and lay planners/leaders prepare worship for their local worshiping assemblies, a hard reality faces them. In the Evangelical Lutheran Church in America, nearly 70 percent of congregational members are absent from Sunday worship in the average week. (The proportion is similar for other mainline denominations.) The challenge for leaders is to find ways to communicate the centrality and the gift of Sunday, the eighth day, the day for communities of faith to focus and refocus their lives around the resurrection message of the crucified and risen Lord Jesus Christ for the sake of the world.

Even when widespread persecution could have kept them away from worship, early Christians were committed to this weekly gathering for fellowship, for sharing the proclaimed word, and joining in "the cup of blessing . . . [and] the bread that we break" (1 Cor. 10:16). The martyrs of Abitina said, "We have to celebrate the Lord's Day. It is our rule. . . . we could not live without celebrating the Lord's Day."[5] The challenge for our day is to again grasp and celebrate the great gift of grace that can center individual and congregational life around the Easter gospel in each Sunday's gathering for communal worship.

A three-year daily lectionary, new to *Evangelical Lutheran Worship* (AE pp. 1121–1153), also supports the centrality of Sunday for all the days of the week. Daily texts for Monday through Wednesday draw out implications of the *previous* Sunday's texts and themes, while daily texts for Thursday through Saturday point us toward *next* Sunday's assembly and its appointed biblical texts and themes. In order to make these texts available to worshipers, it is helpful if the citations are printed in the Sunday worship folder and included in the congregation's newsletter or Web site.

The Year Centered on Easter

As the days of the week orbit around Sunday for Christians, so the days of the year orbit around Easter (or the Three Days, with its focus on Christ's suffering, death, and resurrection). This annual feast of feasts centers the whole year.[6] As we can speak of every Sunday as a "little Easter," so we can speak of Easter as a "big Sunday." Easter and Sunday reinforce each other as Christians seek to keep all their days focused in the gospel of the God who is from everlasting to everlasting and who encounters us through Jesus Christ in the power of the Holy Spirit. Time is encompassed in this crucified and risen Jesus Christ who gives meaning to all our days: "I am the Alpha and the Omega, the first and the last, the beginning and the end" (Rev. 22:13).

Although we do not know exactly when an *annual* celebration of Easter began to occur throughout the early Christian communities, its *weekly* observance on the first day of the week, when Jesus was raised from the dead, certainly gave focus to the life and mission of the earliest Christian communities. Indeed, still today "Sunday is the principal festival day of Christians" (*The Use of the Means of Grace* 6A, printed as Appendix C in *The Sunday Assembly*). The development of the church year is layered on top of this fundamental, weekly celebration.

As a yearly pattern started to form, the annual Easter festival was a logical beginning, a reflection of the center of the Christian faith that focused in the life, death, and resurrection of Jesus Christ. It also grew naturally out of the Christian church's origins within Judaism. A center of Jewish temporal life is the celebration of the Passover and God's deliverance of Israel from death into new life.

> The blood shall be a sign for you on the houses where you live: when I see the blood, I will pass over you, and no plague shall destroy you when I strike the land of Egypt. This day shall be a day of remembrance for you. You shall celebrate it as a festival to the LORD; throughout your generations you shall observe it as a perpetual ordinance. [Exod. 12:13-14]

Associated from the beginning with the Passover celebration and its annual observance, Easter proclaimed the paschal gospel of God's deliverance and salvation in the death and resurrection of Jesus Christ. Very early it also became the preferred time for baptisms, as converts were baptized into Christ's death and raised in Christ to newness of life.

The Three Days (Triduum) and Holy Week clearly and emphatically draw out and focus the church's attention on the crucial core of the Christian gospel. In its focus on the Three Days and Holy Week, the church or liturgical year takes its cue from the four biblical gospels. If Jesus' life on this earth was thirty-three years, then he lived among us for a bit over 1,700 weeks. However, the four biblical gospels devote 25 to 40 percent of their accounts to this one week, the last week of his life, which focused on final teaching, the institution of holy communion, his death on the cross, and the resurrection. This Holy Week shines its saving message on all the other fifty-one weeks of the year. The message is that there is good news from all the graveyards of life. It reminds all worship planners of the central core of the church's faith, which illumines and holds in orbit the worship of the whole year. Later, Lent and the Easter season filled out what we now call the Easter cycle.

The origins of the Lenten season of fasting, its duration, and scheduling are a subject of much scholarly debate. What can safely be said is that at least in some areas, such a period of fasting developed within the first few centuries after Christ. It was variously promoted as a time of mourning, of cleansing, and of preparation for the Three Days to come. At first, the length of this fast varied; it was only in the Middle Ages that the idea of a forty-day fast became common. The choice of that length probably had various reasons, including Jesus' post-baptismal time in the wilderness, which in turn echoed the Israelites' forty-year wandering in the desert. Another source of some consternation has been how to make that forty-day number match the calendar. Some do that by counting all the days except Sundays from Ash Wednesday through Saturday of Holy Week. Others count the Sundays but drop the Three Days as well as the days before the first Sunday in Lent. Such numerical gymnastics are, finally, unimportant. The forty-day count is less important than the concept of setting aside the time.

But set aside for *what*? The oldest traditions seem to reflect a practice of preparation for adult baptisms during this time before Easter.

An intensive instruction into the basics of the Christian faith, and examination of the candidates to make sure they were truly ready to become part of the Christian community, would culminate in their baptisms at the Vigil of Easter. Later, in medieval times, the number of adult baptisms had waned, so the nature of the Lenten season became more penitential, more focused on Christ's suffering and death and on human sinfulness as the cause of that. In recent times, the church has tried to achieve a balance—not losing the richness of hymns and other resources that built up around the passion-centered Lent, but lifting up again the baptismal emphasis that resonates with Luther's concept of ongoing baptismal renewal, of daily dying and rising with Christ.

As we have seen, Easter—the Resurrection of Our Lord—is the principal feast in the Christian year. The day, Easter Sunday, is also a *hinge*, as the church celebrates the culmination of the Three Days while also beginning the great fifty days. For centuries, the church has acknowledged that Christ's resurrection from the dead is too important an event to be limited to a single-day observance. Rather, Easter is celebrated over fifty days, from Easter Sunday through the Day of Pentecost. Sometimes this is referred to as a week of weeks—seven times seven—with the Day of Pentecost seen as not standing on its own but as the "capper" to this grand festival. For it is on that day that we recall the resurrection promise fulfilled as the Holy Spirit comes to enable the church to be the risen body of Christ here on earth.

The next annual festival relating to Christ that developed after Easter was probably Epiphany. This was the opportunity for the church to reflect on the meaning of the incarnation, God's Word made flesh in Jesus, becoming the "light for revelation to the Gentiles" (Luke 2:32). Later, the Western church added the December 25 celebration of Jesus' birth in Bethlehem, though the Epiphany on January 6 remained the Eastern church's primary celebration. Between the doublet of Christmas and Epiphany we have the twelve days of Christmas. Because of school vacations and the ending of the frantic preparations for this festival both in secular society and the church, perhaps more attention can be given during these days to the significant meaning of God's offer of light and life to the world in Jesus Christ. For Christians Christmas is not over after December 25.

The lesser festivals that fall during the twelve days of Christmas bring a realistic perspective to what often can be a sentimental mask covering the clash caused by God's challenge to the principalities and powers of the world. On December 26, we remember the first Christian martyr, Stephen. He reminds us that Christians have been willing to make their witness to Christ even under threat of death. They understood that Christ could not be isolated as a helpless, harmless baby.

The festival of St. John, apostle and evangelist, on the next day exemplifies the great cloud of witnesses who took the good news of the child grown to be Savior and spread it abroad through word and deed.

The third lesser festival, on December 28, commemorates the Holy Innocents, martyrs. The gospel text for this commemoration recounts how the person in power, King Herod, sought to exterminate any threat to his position and power by executing all the children around Bethlehem two years old and under. Perhaps this reminds the church and individuals to stand up against child abuse in our society, to help feed the children who are threatened with death by lack of food and all the forces that militate against the possibilities inherent in each human life.

Finally, the festival of the Name of Jesus, falling on New Year's Day, demonstrates among other things how kairos intersects with and plays off of chronos.

These four commemorations are outlined here as an example of the way, here within the twelve days of Christmas but also in other times, that the major days and seasons of the year can be supplemented and enhanced through creative use of the lesser festivals and commemorations. In that calendar we have endless material for contemplating the Christian life. These commemorations will be taken up in more detail in chapter 4.

By the fourth century, the season of Advent had been added before the celebrations of Christ's nativity: a preparatory and anticipatory period that considers God's faithful promises in times past, God's fulfillment in the fullness of time, and the hope of God's presence that opens up a new future offered to the whole world. Advent came to mark the beginning of the church year. Together with the time after Epiphany that ends with the feast of the Transfiguration, we have what is often called the Christmas cycle.

These two cycles centered on the nativity and the resurrection cover approximately half the church or liturgical year. In the other half of the year, the time after Pentecost (as well as the time after

Epiphany), Sunday reasserts its primacy without any overlay of particular seasons or feasts. During these times, readings draw out the significance of God's mission in Jesus Christ for the world and Jesus' prayer for and charge to the church: "As the Father has sent me, so I send you" (John 20:21).

Chapter three in this volume spells out in more detail the centrality of Sunday and dimensions of the festivals of the church year for worship planners and leaders. As we consider the whole sweep of the liturgical year, it is wise to remember that "the Lord's day is the original feast day . . . the foundation and nucleus of the whole liturgical year."[7]

The Gift of Keeping Time Today

For two thousand years Sunday has been a day to celebrate the crucified Christ's resurrection and receive God's promised grace around word and sacrament. The weekly celebration of holy communion keeps the church walking in newness of life as we eat this bread and drink the cup and "proclaim the Lord's death until he comes" (1 Cor. 11:26).

However, until the imperial decree by Emperor Constantine in 321, the first day of the week (our Sunday) was not a day off from work, so Christians either worshiped at sundown on our Saturday, which was the start of the first day of the week, or early on Sunday morning before work started. In most areas today, the work day is no longer an impediment to gathering for worship on Sunday; political and public support for Sunday as a day for worship has been in place for nearly seventeen centuries. Today, though, other forces come into play. As the church has become less dominant in society, Sunday has been claimed as a day for shopping, for leisure, for sleeping in, for youth and spectator sports, and many other things. We know that most congregations only have one-fourth to one-third of their members in worship on the average Sunday. These challenges suggest a reconsideration of the meaning of Sunday as the Christian sabbath. This is a place where congregations and individual Christians may need to be countercultural in purposely receiving the gift of Sunday and discovering how all the days of the week can be blessed by observing and keeping Sunday time.

One excellent and realistic attempt to do so in our contemporary context is Dorothy Bass's book *Receiving the Day,* a worthy resource for people seeking to observe God's gift of time amid the busyness of life and its hectic schedules. Bass notes:

> Trying to keep sabbath for one full day each week goes against the grain of how most of us live, and it is possible that further social change will soon make this Christian practice even more difficult than it already is. Even so, holding up a sabbath day as an ideal is important. This gift of time is not meant to be nibbled at in bits and pieces as our convenience allows. It is a gift that has ancient roots, and it is a gift best received in community. Opening it, we find not only time but also the stories, the meals, the gatherings, and the songs that prepare us to cherish creation, to resist slavery in all its forms, and to proclaim new life all week long.[8]

As Sunday goes, so to an extent go the remaining days of the week. The domination by the calendar shows no sign of abating. Too often we are servants of our schedules, not the other way around. And if Sunday cannot reserve a place for worship, what chance do other days have? But the worship traditions of the church provide help for reordering priorities and reclaiming time as a gift, not a burden. Psalm 51:15 prompts us: "O Lord, open my lips, and my mouth shall proclaim your praise." That verse, retained as one option for beginning Morning Prayer in *Evangelical Lutheran Worship* (AE p. 298), works well to begin the day, even outside the context of corporate worship. It could be combined with Martin Luther's advice: "In the morning, as soon as you get out of bed, you are to make the sign of the holy cross and say: 'God the Father, Son, and Holy Spirit watch over me. Amen' " (AE p. 1166). That helps to establish a frame for the day—this day, like all of life, will be lived under God's caring and watchful eye, and the purpose of today's speech and action is the praise of God.

If that is the context of the day, then how will we approach our calendar, our schedule? What was mere chronos now takes on something of what could be called a kairotic (rather than chaotic!) character. Yes, we still need to attend this meeting, meet that deadline. But can we look more deeply for God's presence in what we are doing? Can we seek out the opportunity to turn what was just another box on the calendar into a moment pregnant with God's unexpected gifts—for us, perhaps, but even more for others? Can we find God redeeming time itself? Such a transformation in perception doesn't happen easily or quickly, but it can come about, with the help of the Holy Spirit.

Of course, it isn't only readers of this volume who need help with understanding time as God's purposeful gift. Nearly everyone in today's society is afflicted by the subversion of that gift. Those who administer the gospel, then, are called to be aware and upfront about meeting that challenge. The period around the beginning of Advent, with its texts about the theme of time, can provide an opening for conversations about time as a grace. When clock time awareness seems to be dominating worship planning, a word of judgment about idolizing the clock may be in order, followed again by a gospel word that lays out God's gracious intent. Such conversations are often uneasy, so deeply have we bought into chronos's tyranny. But because of the very depth of that subjugation, the relief from the word of freedom can be all the greater.

Daily times of worship can be a wonderful part of such a freed approach to time. Beginning and ending the day with prayer is a good start. Some congregations, at least in some seasons, provide opportunities for daily prayer, often modeled after monastic patterns (see chapter 5). Back in the home setting, grace at the table is a way of bringing worship into the daily routine, as are devotions in the evening and prayer upon rising and before sleep. All of these give great benefits. Helps are widely available, including the daily prayer section in *Evangelical Lutheran Worship* (AE pp. 295–331), the psalms, and Luther's Small Catechism (AE pp. 1166–1167).

Resources for a fuller understanding and observance of the various times and seasons of the church can come from many sources. The planning and educational resources gathered by Augsburg Fortress around the title *Sundays and Seasons* provide both broad view and detailed help for pastors, musicians, and lay worship planners. Other publishers provide similar materials. The worship offices of denominations that work with the Revised Common Lectionary are often good sources to turn to, and their Web sites generally provide entrance points. Resources for help in sermon preparation are of varied usefulness for the liturgical preacher, but the best can assist in creating worship in which the sermon and the liturgy are not discrete emphases but are creatively woven together.

As we search for resources to enhance appreciation for the church year, the poetry and music of hymns in *Evangelical Lutheran Worship* should not be overlooked. They can contribute richly to the proclamation of the gospel through the particular times and saving events of God's activity in Jesus Christ for the sake of all people. Not only can the hymns be sung in worship, but their texts can be fruitful for devotion and preparation, often sparking related ideas.

Some hymns relate specifically to particular times and seasons; others focus more on topical concerns. To demonstrate the wealth of support available in hymns and songs, we can look at some that celebrate the gifts God has given us in time, from creation to consummation. About the fulfillment of God's saving action on the cross of Christ, one hymn writer bids us "mark that miracle of time, God's own sacrifice complete" (#347). Another hymn writer celebrates the coming of Christ as a day full of grace: "O day full of grace, O blessed time, our Lord on the earth arriving" (#627). The cross of Christ now pervades all our time and provides "joys that through all time abide" (#324). The birth of Jesus points to the time when the whole world will sing with the angels: "For lo! The days are hastening on, by prophets seen of old, when with the ever-circling years shall come the time foretold, when peace over all the earth its ancient splendors fling, and all the world give back the song which now the angels sing" (#282). While "time, like an ever-rolling stream, bears all our years away," yet we pray to the God of our past and our future: "O God, our help in ages past, our hope for years to come, still be our guard while troubles last and our eternal home" (#632). This perspective invites us to exclaim with the psalmist: "My times are in your hand" (Ps. 31:15).

The liturgical year focuses our eyes, ears, and hearts on God's grace proclaimed in the gospel. What better way to describe the purpose of the development and practice of the church year down through the centuries? At its center is the proclamation of the gospel of Jesus Christ, the present tense of God in the Holy Spirit, and the providence and plan of our creator God and Father. The church year is the way we Christians keep time for God and practice the presence of God in Jesus Christ in the power of the Holy Spirit—as communities of faith and in our individual lives. While we may speak of our doing the pattern of the liturgical year, it may be more accurate to say that through the means of grace and the patterns of proclaiming the gospel, God *does us*, forms us, saves us, shapes us, and blesses us.

Having considered the weekly, yearly, and daily patterns of the Christian life, is there something to be said about even smaller segments of time? Unfortunately, the tyranny of chronos extends even down to this level. Self-imposed sixty-minute (or even forty-five-minute) limits on worship services tend to buy into the idea that clock time is and should be preeminent. But what if we are so caught up in the event that time is filled with such significance (kairos) that clock time is not counted? Perhaps it is like the exciting game that goes into overtime or the concert that calls for encores. Some ethnic and religious traditions let the event of worship determine the time of worship. A West Coast radio station devoted entirely to news advertised: "Give us twenty minutes and we will give you the world." Perhaps the church advertisement should be more audacious: "Give us sixty minutes (or more!) every Sunday and we will give you the world renewed by its Creator, redeemed by its Savior, and empowered by the Holy Spirit. Your life will be caught up in God's history from creation to consummation." In this way all our time, all of life is sanctified.

Changing Ways of Understanding Worship Space

The church worships not only in time but also in space. What is the mission of the building as it serves the church's worship? Because the space and the appointments (form) are meant to serve the church's various liturgies (function), worship planners and leaders must reflect creatively on how their present space hinders or helps the mission of worship. Often we need to think imaginatively about how we can overcome the limitations many buildings place on the worshiping assembly.

As an example, in many older buildings, a gathering space for worshipers to welcome and interact with one another before and after worship is minimal. The entry (narthex) in many churches was designed to be very small, for it served chiefly as a quick passage from outside to the worship room (nave); it allowed for a place for ushers to hand out bulletins and the pastor to greet exiting worshipers, but little else. Present needs have evolved and are in conflict with a space that was not planned for hospitable welcoming and gathering space. In many of our communities today, worshipers only interact with each other as they gather for worship on Sunday mornings. Larger gathering places are often added to older buildings and incorporated into newer structures so that we "welcome one another . . . just as Christ has welcomed you" (Rom. 15:7) and provide hospitality to all who gather for worship. This larger gathering space also provides gathering space for participants in processions, families and friends who surround and accompany the coffin at funerals, and other entrance rites associated with various liturgies, such as the Easter Vigil.

Because of pews that restrict movement or limit varied arrangements for seating, microphones that tie clergy and lay leaders to stationary spaces, and the controlling idea that all leadership roles happen "on stage" up front on a raised platform, worship leaders and planners need to think creatively to avoid having the building form them into its mold.[9]

Winston Churchill remarked at the dedication of a remodeled government building that "first we shape our buildings and afterwards our buildings shape us." This happens in our worship spaces. The relationship between the theology expressed in our worship and the theology expressed by our buildings can be positive and mutually reinforcing, or negative and contradictory. Put another way, the form and configuration of our worship space can shape the worship we do in it in good or bad ways. The history of church architecture demonstrates this tension; many of the buildings in which we worship insert worshipers into this tension between the theology set in stone in the past and the present theological dimensions of worship. Worship and worship space are necessarily linked in a vital relationship.[10]

Following are some themes emphasized in worship today, plus some thoughts on how the space accommodates those perspectives.

The worshiping assembly is central. A core dimension shared by most churches today is that "all the faithful be led to that full, conscious, and active participation in liturgical celebrations which is demanded by the very nature of the liturgy. Such participation by the Christian people as a 'chosen race, a royal priesthood, a holy nation, a purchased people' (1 Peter 2:9), is their right and duty by reason of their baptism. . . . This full and active participation by all the people is the aim to be considered above all else."[11] The emphasis on the priesthood of all believers in Lutheran theology underlines this dialogical interaction that we call participatory worship. The question for worship planners is: Given our present space, how can we more fully draw all the worshipers into this full and active participation?

Many church buildings tend to give the impression of two rooms, one for the clergy and lay leaders of worship (the chancel), the other for worshipers (the nave). This separation of clergy who celebrated the drama of the liturgy while the people alternately watched the drama and did their private devotions in the second room was even more pronounced in the medieval period. In calling for active involvement of all worshipers in the liturgy, many Reformers urged a recovery of the one-room space where clergy and leaders were actively engaged. One of those Reformers, Martin Bucer, said: "That the choir (or chancel) should be so distantly separated from the rest of the temple, and the service, which pertains to the whole people and the clergy, be set forth in it alone, is anti-Christian."[12]

Many churches have moved the altar-table closer to the people to partially overcome this distancing from the worshipers. This also allows the worship leaders to face the congregation instead of turning their backs to the worshiping assembly. Instead of focusing on the transcendent God out beyond us, this arrangement invites us to address the God in our midst. It reflects the incarnation, the Word become flesh and dwelling in our midst. It also reclaims a point of theology all but lost in the Middle Ages, that when we gather for communion, the body of Christ is present in the form of the assembly at least as much as it is in the sacramental bread. The assembly is not mere audience but is essential to the action of worship.

How else can the walls between leaders and assembly be broken down? Having a cantor lead the Kyrie from the midst of the congregation can startle the worshipers next to the cantor, but worshipers sense more dramatically that this is indeed the prayer of the whole congregation. On festive occasions, at least, a gospel procession can bring the proclamation of the gospel reading into the midst of the congregation. Perhaps the prayers of intercession, the prayers of the people, can be led from the midst of those people, which in turn might encourage individuals whose hearts are joyful or sad to add their own petitions.

Along with such positive steps, it is worthwhile paying attention to factors that can take away from the assembly's central role. The parts of the liturgy assigned to the assembly (hymns, psalm, hymn of praise, and so forth) should in most cases not be given to others. Appropriate lighting and sound reinforcement need careful attention. Note, however, that even something as simple and commonplace as a microphone can, if overamplified, be a megaphone that silences singing or communicates power on the part of the leaders.

The centers of action need to be clear. We have all been in situations where the visual environment is so cluttered that it is hard to know where to look. Conversely, we have experienced well-designed arenas in which it is graciously clear where our attention needs to be focused. To function well as a center for corporate worship, our church spaces need to reflect the second of those models. What are the centers of action? The font, the table, the place of the word, and the assembly itself. If the choir, the song leaders, the organ, the ministers, or anything else detracts visually from the proper centers, it will make the space less effective for worship.

Church buildings can be difficult and expensive to modify. If that is a factor, sometimes creative solutions can be employed. Often through use of fabric or lighting, attention can be drawn away from distracting sights and toward the more important centers. Sometimes it is as simple (if not always easy!) as deciding that as much as people enjoy watching, say, the handbell choir up front, their contribution to worship might be greater if they were less visible.

A particular challenge that is becoming more prevalent is the projection screen. While the use of projection does have its advantages, such as reducing the amount of paper used and getting people's heads up and into the action, it easily leads to the syndrome often seen at sporting events where many people pay more attention to the projection screen than to the live action. Again, the focus becomes misplaced. In some buildings, especially those that are newer, the skillful placement of the screens can lessen the problem. But it remains something to be carefully considered before moving wholesale into projection: If it is employed, can the worship still retain the sense of the family of God, the body of Christ, gathered personally around the means of grace, or will it rather contribute to the idea that worship in that place is a semi-detached spectator activity?

Probably the single most important way to keep the visual focus on the centers of worship is to work tirelessly on simplifying the space. Remove clutter wherever possible, even if it is a treasured banner the women's guild made thirty years ago. Ask strangers to the building to tell you what they see when they walk in for worship. If it is something other than the table, the font, the place of the word, the gathered assembly, can something more be taken out or made less prominent? Such efforts, graciously done, will enhance the worship in the place.

Ideals are adapted for local use. The service of word and sacrament has been done in grand Gothic cathedrals, prairie churches, hospital rooms, and led from the hood of a jeep on the battlefield. There is no one perfect design for a worship space, but when we do put our theology in stone, the building can contradict or shape worship in ways that are hard to overcome. For example, a long narrow building with the altar at the far end of a deep chancel against the east wall speaks of the transcendence of God but makes it harder to communicate the priesthood of all believers. A room in which the altar-table is exactly in the center helps address that issue but can make ritual action more challenging, since the ministers may have worshipers behind them.

Shelters or buildings in many cultures tended to invite people into a circular communal arrangement, but missionaries often sought to replace those with buildings modeled after the tradition they came from. The missionaries' experience, dating back to medieval times, was that of a longer rectangular shape divided into two spaces, chancel and nave. One message communicated by this form was that there was a division between clergy leaders and the laity or a sense of the "holy of holies" at the altar space—a concept that was foreign to those cultures. Over time, adaptations were made.

Similar adaptations have happened in the United States and Canada over the past decades as churches have rethought ideas that had shaped church architecture for centuries. Among the more important changes have been:

- a larger area for gathering and sending (formerly called the narthex);
- a more prominent and centrally located baptismal font;
- a chancel area is closer to the assembly, with a freestanding altar-table;
- a single place for the word, rather than both lectern and pulpit.

These changes respond to concepts that have come to the fore:

- The times of gathering and sending, both within and outside of the service itself, are important. They are when the individuals come and form an assembly, and later move out to become the church in mission. A good-sized space facilitates these transitional times.

- The font is the place where new Christians are added to the body of Christ. This is such an important moment, not just for the individual but for the whole assembly, that it calls for more than a small bowl of water off in a corner. Then, following Martin Luther's advice, we return to our baptism daily, and often within our corporate worship. A centrally located font can remind us of that need simply by its visibility and also can ease worship moments in which baptismal remembrance occurs. More will be said about this shortly.
- We have come increasingly to understand the human side of worship not as something to be done by clergy for laity but rather as something done by the assembly as a whole, with some members of the assembly designated (or ordained) to have specific roles. It makes a lot of sense, then, to reflect that in the way the worship space is set up, having the assembly close to, even gathered around, the presiding and assisting ministers as they lead the worship. Similar benefits come from following Luther's advice and having the presiding minister face the assembly across the table.
- The sermon is not an entity separate from the scripture readings. They are, rather, different ways of proclaiming the word of God. There is no reason, then, to maintain different places for reading and for preaching the word. A single place of the word (ambo, pulpit), of equal prominence to the table and font, will eloquently communicate the unitary nature of the word and the blessings we gain from all the means of grace.

These are trends in worship, somewhat recent adaptations, though well-founded. Within the Lutheran tradition, no authority dictates that congregations must adopt such changes, either immediately or long-term. It is often difficult and expensive to make changes to existing worship spaces, so such adaptations tend to happen gradually. Each congregation needs to assess its own situation and determine its best course. However, the concepts—the ideals—reflect the emerging wisdom not of experts alone but of the whole church. As such, they invite consideration and creative engagement.

The Body at Worship

In a book such as this, we commonly speak of the corporate body of Christ, the gathered assembly at worship. While that is appropriate, it is helpful as well to remember that each of us takes up space, and our individual bodies have their own architecture and symbolic movement. The liturgy invites movement and different foci during worship. Our bodies will stand, sit, and kneel. Hands may be folded or raised in prayer. We will reach out to others as we share the peace of Christ. Bodies will be signed with the cross. Oil may be applied in baptism as a sign of the sealing of the Holy Spirit, and oil may accompany prayer for those who are distressed in relationships, spirit, and body.

Body language in communion. Consider the possible movement in holy communion. Contrast it with the actors in a play. In a drama, the actors never stand in only one place. Yet this is often what leaders of worship do because of the placement of the microphone or the tendency to do everything from the altar-table.

As a way to emphasize the various central actions of worship, consider ways that movement of leaders help the worshipers focus on the various movements of the liturgy. There is a time of welcome and hospitality as the worshiping assembly gathers for communal worship. The order for confession and forgiveness or the thanksgiving for baptism reflects the daily baptismal pattern of our lives, so this is appropriately conducted wherever the baptismal font or pool is located. The sign of the cross may be made over our bodies as we hear the name of God in which we were baptized. The gathering song or hymn invites a parade or procession to the front of the worshiping assembly. This whole gathering rite is ideally done close to the congregation and argues against the idea of moving into the second room if your space suggests that division. When the Kyrie is sung from the midst of the people, there is an immediate sense that this is the community's prayer.

At the word section, the focus shifts to the place of proclamation, the pulpit or ambo. As mentioned earlier, it is suggested that all the readings be proclaimed from this place of the word. If the first two readings are read from a lectern by lay lectors and the gospel reading from the pulpit or ambo, the two-room division is perpetuated in a separation of clergy and laity. Announcements of the congregation's life and mission and the prayers of the people could be done from the lectern if the worship room has a lectern.

To emphasize the movement in the liturgy, leaders will ideally wait to go to the altar until bread and wine are brought to the table at the offering. The table is the focus for the meal of holy communion.

Before the blessing and dismissal, the presiding and assisting ministers may move out from behind the table toward the congregation. This movement stresses the sending of the community out to their daily baptismal vocation and mission in the world.

Body language at baptism. While the amount of water does not condition the validity of baptism, an ample amount of water and generous use of water in baptism serves as a more vivid and expressive symbol. Many baptismal fonts are very small, capable of holding only a minimal amount of water. This can be remedied by putting a larger bowl on the stand where the water can be seen and heard. The visual reminder of baptism is stronger when baptismal covers or lids are removed whenever worship occurs. This allows individuals to remember and affirm their baptismal identity and vocation as they dip their fingers in the water and retrace the sign of the cross made over them in their baptisms.

In contrast with some past practices, one of the most important "body language" communications for our day is that baptisms are not done in private or apart from the communal worship of the church, the body of Christ.[13] Not only do we belong to Christ, in baptism we belong to each other as well. In baptism we are initiated into Christ's missionary community and fellowship. Because the worshiping assembly is actively involved as witnesses, in welcome, as prayer sponsors, and encouragers, baptisms ideally are visible to the whole congregation.

Placement of the font at the entrance can serve as a symbol of entry into the community of faith and also a reminder of our baptismal vocation and mission in our daily lives when we leave. Some have placed the font in the middle of the assembly. Others place the font at the front. If in front, ideally, it is accessible to worshipers who wish to dip their hands in the water as a remembrance of baptism.

In many newer worship rooms or remodeled spaces for worship, the smaller font has been replaced by a baptismal pool or larger font that may have running or *living* water.

Pews and chairs. Pews came to be added to worship spaces over the fifteenth to seventeenth centuries. Although pews provide orderly seating, they also make the worship room more rigid and restrictive of movement. They also do not allow variations such as antiphonal seating where two parts of the congregation face each other. This is an ideal arrangement for the daily prayer liturgies. Chairs allow for removal of seats when there are smaller gatherings for worship or addition of seats when there is a large festival worship or larger funeral service. Flexibility of chairs and moveable altar-table and ambo (pulpit) allow for various seasonal arrangements that may reflect the seasonal texts and themes.

Such arrangements also provide flexible space for the various music, dance, instrumental, or dramatic groups that share in the gospel proclamation in worship. If one's space is not flexible, leaders and planners must think imaginatively about how they can overcome that inflexibility. Because many of us have been shaped by more rigid and nonflexible spaces, we may find ourselves using a new flexible space in rigid ways.

This discussion suggests that in planning for new or renovated spaces, much thought needs to be given to the varied needs of the church's various liturgies. Form (the worship space) needs to follow function (the dynamic of communal worship).

Incarnation and Architecture

The poet John Donne mused about "immensity cloistered in [Mary's] womb." Notice the three "space" words. This phrase senses the wonder of the incarnation, the Word become flesh.

In a profound way, this provides a perspective on our worship and the spaces in which we worship. Our worship sings of the wonder of the immensity of our Creator God and the wonders of the world and also the amazing grace of this great God in the child Jesus, born of the virgin Mary. Both God and human. The Sanctus catches this. Isaiah's great vision in worship is in awe of the "holy, holy, holy . . . Lord of hosts." Isaiah trembles before this holiness and his own sin. But the Sanctus goes on to a very boisterous parade as Jesus comes riding into the Holy City, Jerusalem, on a donkey, where the people welcome him with palm branches and with shouted hosannas. Holy and hosanna. This great immensity that we name God now comes with the promise of grace cloistered in the earthly elements of a meal of bread and wine. There is a sense of both wonder and welcome. It is about God both beyond us and yet among us. It is both the grandeur of the Gothic cathedral and the intimacy of the house church.

In our worship and in our worship spaces, we do well to keep in mind the creative tension of the incarnation. There is a vertical and a horizontal dimension to worship spaces that proclaim the incarnation, the Word become flesh. Our spaces and our liturgies serve us well when they proclaim and give us the experience of the immensity of the Creator of all things and the grace of the man Jesus, "Emmanuel, God with us." Good spaces and liturgies will help us live in the wonderful tension implicit in that *immensity cloistered in Mary's womb.*

CHAPTER TWO

The Lectionary and the Propers

A mere eighteen pages into the assembly edition of *Evangelical Lutheran Worship* we come to the listing of propers—those assigned elements in worship that change from week to week or season to season. This listing assumes use of a lectionary—leading naturally to the questions What is a lectionary? and Why should we use one?

Because Christians believe that God speaks to us through the words of the Bible, Christians read from the Bible when they gather to worship. However, no Christian community reads the entire Bible in public worship. The list of biblical *selections* that a church adopts is called its lectionary. The word *lectionary* also refers to the volume, sometimes beautifully bound and including liturgical art, in which all the readings are printed sequentially, week after week. In the following discussion, the word *lectionary* generally refers to the list rather than to the book.

To appreciate more fully the use of a lectionary, it is important first to consider how the Bible was formed. Many Israelite and Jewish believers wrote about their faith in God and their life in the religious community. In some passages in what Christians call the Old Testament, we can hear the voices of several different authors. In the creation poem in Genesis 1, God is called "God" in English ("Elohim" in Hebrew), human beings are created last, and everything is good. In the narrative of Genesis 2–3, God is called "the LORD" in English ("YHWH" in Hebrew), the male is created before the other animals and separate from the female, and a divine command indicates that there is such a thing as evil. The editors of this material decided to place these two versions one after another, the good news first, then the bad, so that the sacred scripture includes both versions of the origin of humankind. A third version of the creation story is found in the later Jewish book *Jubilees*. According to this more complicated narrative, not only did God create seven different kinds of angels on day one, but God condemns to death anyone who violates the sabbath.

During the exile the Jewish religious leaders began the process, not completed until late in the first century C.E., of selecting from among their many writings those that should receive authorization as the books from which to read in the synagogue each Sabbath. In assembling the Hebrew Bible, the Tanakh, Genesis was authorized for synagogue use but *Jubilees* was not. From the canon of approved books, the weekly readings were selected. Thus the formation of the Tanakh was itself a lectionary decision: these books, but not those, are to be read in the gathering at the synagogue.

The process was similar in early Christianity. Many more gospels than the four canonical gospels of Matthew, Mark, Luke, and John were written, and some of these noncanonical gospels have received considerable scholarly and popular attention. Perhaps some of these other gospels became authoritative in branches of the church that died out. Christians whose names and works have been forgotten wrote histories, letters, and extended homilies that circulated around the Mediterranean world. It is likely that Paul wrote more letters than the ones that have survived. Much of this history has been lost to us: for example, we do not know who traveled around from one Christian community to another, gathering copies of Paul's dispersed letters. Colossians 4:16 indicates that after the Christians in that city read their letters, they were to exchange apostolic letters with the Christians in Laodicea: unfortunately, no such letter to the Laodiceans has survived. But it is clear that already in the first century, revered Christian writings were passed around from one Christian community to another to be read aloud when the assembly gathered.

Just as in Judaism, so then in Christianity the time came to decide which of the many texts written by believers should be designated as appropriate for proclamation when the community assembled for weekly worship. Again, we do not know as much about this process as we wish we did. There was a debate in the second century as to whether Christians should continue to read from the Old Testament, but we know that in about the year 150, Justin wrote that when Christians met together on Sunday, they read from "the records of the apostles and the writings of the prophets for as long as there is time," in other words, from books in what we call the New and Old Testaments. Lists of which books are to be read in church circulated from the second century on, but it was not until 367 that Bishop Athanasius provided the authoritative list of what books constituted the New Testament. Four gospels, some letters, and one apocalyptic piece were judged to be "apostolic," that is, they represented most accurately the testimony of the generation closest to Christ.

In the second century, a prominent bishop named Irenaeus explained that Christians needed Matthew, Mark, Luke, and John, since each presented Christ in a somewhat different light. He joined with other church leaders in judging that the works written by gnostic Christians erred by describing Jesus as a kind of divine spirit and salvation as a secret granted only to insiders. Thus, what are now called the Gnostic gospels were excluded from the canon. Only certain writings were judged as proclaiming in the fullest way the good news of God's mercy in Christ and God's power in the Spirit, and the worshiping assembly can trust these words. It is best for us to think of the Bible as not a single book, but rather a library of books, selected over time by Jewish and Christian authorities and their communities as those writings most appropriate to be read at the weekly gathering for worship.

We know little about exactly when and how specific lectionary systems developed. It appears that in the practice of the early churches in Western Europe, Christians selected from the biblical books their weekly lectionary choices using a pattern called *lectio continua,* or continuous reading. Biblical books, or sections from them, were read through continuous, long passages each week. However, for major festivals, it was not long before preachers were relying on a circulated list of texts as being especially appropriate. Sermons by Augustine in the fourth century make clear that at least sometimes he relied on such a list of selected texts, what is called *lectio selecta.* When in the late fourth century the pilgrim Egeria traveled from France to Jerusalem and there worshiped during Holy Week, she wrote, "The Easter Vigil is observed here exactly as we observe it at home." Yet she reported that sometimes passages of scripture different from those familiar to her were tied to a certain day. So it seems that by the year 400 there was both agreement and variation across the Mediterranean world concerning the selection of biblical texts for worship.

Interaction among church leaders led to a growing consensus as to which texts were best proclaimed on which Sundays and festivals. By the Middle Ages, the Western church had a one-year cycle of two readings each Sunday. The gospel readings came from Matthew twenty-four times, from Mark four times, from Luke twenty-one times, and from John fifteen times. An epistle reading was selected to fit with the gospel. At the beginning of the service, a psalm text, sometimes called an introit, was chosen for the choir or cantor to sing—although there is a story that sometime along the way the psalm list got off by one Sunday, with the result that some introits fitted better with the gospel of the adjacent week! No texts from the Old Testament were regularly proclaimed, although sermons surviving from early centuries are filled with references to Old Testament passages that preachers used to expound the meaning of the New Testament readings. Such a one-year/two-readings lectionary is still used in Eastern Orthodox churches throughout the world. These churches pride themselves that their contemporary lectionary is similar to their lectionary of the seventh century.

Martin Luther judged the medieval lectionary to be perfectly acceptable. Rather than change the lectionary, he urged the clergy to preach more profoundly on the appointed texts. Since he agreed with Augustine that the Bible was "of mountainous difficulty and enveloped in mysteries," the faithful needed to hear the texts interpreted for them. Luther also demanded that preaching focus on the good news of God's mercy in Christ, rather than on the preacher's whims or popular fables, which Luther ridiculed when, in the *Deutsche Messe,* he criticized sermons that were about "blue ducks" (*LW* 53:78). Lutherans have tended to maintain rigorous attention to the content of preaching, and many Lutheran preachers through the centuries have based their sermons on the biblical readings as designated in the lectionary.

Most Lutherans and Anglicans continued to use a version of the one-year/two-readings medieval system until the middle of the twentieth century. These churches judged the traditional pattern a good one and the coordination with other Christians a useful sign of the unity of the church. Following the medieval practice that had developed in the monasteries and convents, especially Anglicans used the standard *lectio selecta* on Sunday morning but *lectio continua* in their services of daily prayer. In those Protestant countries in which the government regulated worship, for example, England or Sweden, clergy were required by law to use the approved lectionary. England's Act of Uniformity, promulgated under Queen Elizabeth I, stipulated harsh punishments for clergy who ignored the legally mandated lectionary, and it was against such requirements that groups such as the Puritans and the

Norwegian Pietists rebelled, and when emigrating to North America many brought along their resentment against authorized lectionaries.

Some prominent Reformers rejected the medieval lectionary as too limited, too associated with Roman Catholic theological emphases, and, since the readings were taken out of their biblical context, too liable to be misinterpreted. Inspired by Ulrich Zwingli, Martin Bucer, and John Calvin, most Reformed churches developed two separate systems for Sunday worship. An entire chapter of the Old Testament and an entire chapter of the New Testament were read, moving through the biblical books Sunday by Sunday—thus *lectio continua*—but the preacher was to choose "as he shall see fit" the passage upon which he preached—thus a pattern we might call *lectio individua*. In later centuries the discipline of reading entire chapters of the Bible was abandoned in these Reformed churches, and in its place remained only the preacher choosing which biblical text was read as the basis of the sermon. This must have been an attractive option for many clergy, since even fifty years ago in some Lutheran churches, the two stipulated lectionary readings were proclaimed, then the pastor announced from the pulpit a third biblical passage upon which his sermon was based. The one-year lectionary currently used by many Protestants in Germany includes a six-year cycle of preaching texts to which clergy are expected to adhere.

In the twenty-first century, some Protestant churches maintain that the clergy's free choice is the best procedure to use, and thus their lectionary is the pastor's individual creation. Some churches suggest that Sunday's selection from the Bible must be extremely short, perhaps only a single sentence, because the people are biblically illiterate and cannot handle anything more. On the other hand, some denominations that had been nonlectionary churches are now incorporating a churchwide lectionary into their practice, their seminaries are teaching the lectionary in worship courses, and their publishing houses are producing a wide variety of lectionary resources for local use.

Currently, nearly all Lutheran church bodies around the world defend the disciplined use of an authorized lectionary as the best pattern for Sunday proclamation. In the Evangelical Lutheran Church in America the lectionary principle is articulated in *The Use of the Means of Grace*, a 1997 document on worship and the sacraments. Principle 7 states:

> *The Scriptures are read aloud*
> The public reading of the Holy Scriptures is an indispensable part of worship, constituting the basis for the public proclamation of the Gospel.

The document then enumerates three reasons why the ELCA has an approved lectionary for congregational use.

The first reason cited is that the use of a lectionary serves the unity of the church. By committing ourselves to the discipline of the lectionary, preachers acknowledge that they are not Lone Rangers riding around on their own horse. Rather we are joined with Christians around the world in a common identity and a common purpose. We relinquish personal preferences for the greater goal of common practice. We stand together, whenever we meet, hearing the same gospel each week. When we are away from our home congregation and worshiping with a different assembly of Christians, we know what biblical readings to expect. In some locales, clergy from various church bodies meet together for lectionary study of their common texts, and they can benefit from exposure to the interpretive patterns of other Christians.

The church is both local and universal. As a sign that the church is local, some parts of Sunday worship are selected and prepared by each specific assembly. The sermon is written for that assembly on that Sunday, and the hymns and intercessions reflect the specific assembly's time and place. Art and music are offered by the members of the local congregation to enrich each Sunday service. Thanks to this specificity, worship reflects the presence of God within each weekly assembly of the church.

Meanwhile, other parts of the church's worship signify the universality of the church. These parts of the liturgy are deeper and wider than any specific congregation; they connect us with Christians long dead and unite us with the millions who are worshiping this week. The Lord's Prayer is greater than the creativity of an individual worship committee or the needs of a specific assembly. We join together in these ancient words, Christians all around the world every Sunday. Our use of the Lord's Prayer binds us together with the evangelists Matthew and Luke and with countless faithful women and men praying across the ages. There is value in each individual congregation crafting its own intercessions, and there is value in all the baptized uniting in praying the Lord's Prayer. Christians who advocate the use of the lectionary maintain that the biblical readings each week can be more like the Lord's Prayer than like the intercessions: there is value in unity in our worship.

Many Christian congregations present to their newly baptized or confirmed members a copy of the Bible. This practice expresses the conviction of the church that God's word is not the private property of the clergy, some kind of secret writing managed by the religious elite. Rather, the Bible is to be known and treasured by all the people of God. In the late medieval church, Sunday worship was to great degree enacted by only the clergy. Much of its Latin would not have been understood by most lay people. In most churches with fine music programs—cathedrals, convents, and monasteries—the music was presented to the assembly by a small, select group. The practice of ringing a bell at the time of the elevation of the bread and wine developed so that people would know that the priest had come to an important part of the service.

Martin Luther urged liturgical reforms that would encourage full and active participation of the entire worshiping assembly. The regular use of a lectionary, printed in the book of worship in the pews, responds to this concern of Luther's by uniting the entire congregation in the biblical readings. Congregational committees can work together on music and art for worship. Congregational leaders can plan for education that complements the biblical readings. Sunday-school children can draw pictures of the gospel of the day. Worshipers can prepare themselves for the Sunday service by reading and praying over the biblical texts beforehand. One way for the entire assembly to prepare for the Sunday readings is by using the Daily Lectionary that is included in *Evangelical Lutheran Worship* (AE pp. 1121–1153). Many Lutherans maintain the habit of daily Bible reading, and the selections suggested in the daily lectionary in one way or another complement the Sunday lectionary. Those who know the readings each week can accompany the preacher into the sermon, attending more deeply to what they already have, embracing what they already own. We agree to be united.

The second reason cited in *The Use of the Means of Grace* is that a lectionary assists us in encountering the breadth of the scriptures. When preachers choose their own texts, those choices will naturally be limited by many things, such as the educational background of that particular preacher, the amount of time the preacher can dedicate to the selection process, the preacher's judgment of the assembly's inclinations, and the preacher's theological preferences. Lutherans are among those denominations that judge that because of these limitations, personal text selection likely would expose an assembly to only a small portion of the Bible. Furthermore, some preachers might choose only passages that concur with their personal inclinations; thus the Bible might come to function as a proof-text for the pastor's ideas, with the sermon more expressive of the preacher than of the Bible. The lectionary included in *Evangelical Lutheran Worship* exposes regular worshipers to more than five hundred biblical passages, plus the weekly use of the psalms. This pattern proclaims more of the Bible than has any lectionary that we know about throughout Christian history. Lutherans, with all others who use the Revised Common Lectionary, especially can rejoice over this wide and deep exposure to the Bible on Sundays and festivals.

The third reason cited in *The Use of the Means of Grace* is that the approved lectionary proclaims the evangelical meaning of the liturgical year. Without carefully chosen biblical texts, the liturgical year might be misinterpreted or even misunderstood by a Christian assembly. An example is the four Sundays of Advent. According to American consumer culture, the month of December is dedicated to attending Christmas parties and purchasing presents for everybody. Many Christian churches, however, exemplify a radically different view of December. Advent is recognized as an essential part of the liturgical year: we live in hope, waiting for the Lord, standing with all those in need, and we pray fervently that God will arrive to bring light to our darkened world. The church relies on its lectionary selections to direct our focus to this truth of the faith. Without Advent and the cries of the prophets and the preaching of John the Baptist, an American Christmas could ignore the sorrowful human conditions that are the reasons for God's incarnation among us.

The lectionary readings enlarge us in many ways. Not only do we join with Christians of various denominations all around the world to hear the word of the Lord. We put ourselves into each of the biblical characters about whom we hear, listening for God's word to us as simultaneously sinners and saints. If as individuals we are either sad or happy, the readings may call us to the opposite emotion, asking us to stand with those who suffer and with those who rejoice. Since each set of readings contains so many possibilities for thought and reflection, we are glad that as the spiral continues to circle forward, we will hear each set of readings once again with new ears in another time.

The three readings of the lectionary draw us into the very life of the triune God. The first readings, from the Old Testament and from Acts, tell us of God's creative might and mercy throughout all times and places. The second reading, from an epistle, inspires us with the Spirit of God, for it is within the assembly of the faithful that we receive the spirit of the resurrection. In the gospel, we hear the proclamation of the incarnation, the preeminent event in our history, God living as Jesus Christ, who died and rose for us. Each week the three readings proclaim that the God we know in Jesus Christ continually creates the world and inspires the church, and the template provided by the lectionary can become more and more the map for the journey of our life.

The Development of the Revised Common Lectionary

Both believers and nonbelievers read the Bible for many different reasons: for personal comfort, for remarkable poetry, for ancient Near Eastern history, for study of comparative religion. Yet many Christians agree that during the Sunday worship, the primary purpose for the reading of the scriptures is "the proclamation of the gospel." This proclamation is not the same thing as Bible study, although of course some Bible study will be involved. The proclamation of the gospel is the weekly announcement to the assembly that God embraces them, that Christ has saved them, and that the Spirit enlivens them to be Christ's body in the world. In describing preaching, Lutherans usually use the terms "law" and "gospel." That is, we need to hear the Bible both as it shows us sin and death and as it announces to us God's mercy and grace. Some parts of the Bible are more suited to this task than others, and the selection of the most appropriate passages toward these goals is a core reason for the formation of a lectionary.

About some texts, most Christians have agreed. For example, the Levitical directions for animal sacrifices are not proclaimed on Sunday morning. Yet one group or one generation of Christians might construct a different lectionary than another. For example, before the Civil War, some American Christians routinely included in their Sunday proclamation the third section of the household codes, found in Ephesians 6:1-9 and Colossians 3:18—4:1, in which slaves and masters are instructed in their duties to one another. After the Civil War, most Christians omitted this section, judging that although the biblical worldview did assume slavery, we no longer see that economic system as ethical for Christ's body in the world. Since the teaching that slaves should obey their masters was no longer heard as God's word for the assembled believers, it was deleted from the Sunday proclamation. Such editing of lectionaries continues as the church works to have its Sunday proclamation include the best possible choices for communal worship. Some Christians include the passages that regulate women's hairstyles and jewelry, others include the passages that order wives to obey their husbands, and some include neither, depending on each church's biblical hermeneutic. Since there are only a given number of Sundays and festivals annually, we must make choices, and these decisions must consider many issues and attitudes.

Among the many reforms undertaken by the Roman Catholic bishops when they gathered in Rome in the 1960s for the Second Vatican Council was the question of lectionary. The council decided that the medieval one-year/two-readings lectionary was not as good as it might be, for it did not expose the faithful to enough of the Bible. A committee was charged with the task of constructing an entirely new lectionary, one in which, as the document stated, "the treasures of the Bible are opened up more lavishly, so that a richer share in God's word may be provided for the faithful." Inspired by this stirring request, a committee designed the three-year/three-reading lectionary, first promulgated for Roman Catholic use in 1969. The new lectionary was to make clear that the central theme of the Christian faith is Christ's death and resurrection for us. Clearly, some parts of the Bible are essential in proclaiming the death and resurrection of Christ, while other parts are of minimal use for that specific purpose.

This three-year/three-reading lectionary became an ecumenical hit and has been judged by many the most significant Christian ecumenical achievement of the twentieth century. Over the subsequent decades, first Anglicans, then other churches, and then a consortium of Protestants adapted the Roman Catholic lectionary for their own use, making whatever alterations they found necessary so that the selections reflected more closely their own hermeneutic and theological emphases. The Lutheran emendation of the Roman Catholic lectionary was published in *Lutheran Book of Worship* (AE pp. 13–41). Eventually church leaders judged that too many versions of the original three-year lectionary were in use. Especially, ecumenical study groups and church publishing houses saw the benefit of a lectionary shared by a number of churches. As well, high interest at that time in the ecumenical movement made natural the search for worship resources shared in common.

The Consultation on Common Texts, a committee dedicated to the tasks of worship renewal and comprised of representatives from nearly twenty Christian denominations and church agencies, set out to produce a single ecumenical lectionary. By making choices among the several variants of the three-year lectionary, the Consultation hoped to present a truly common lectionary that at least all Protestant churches, and perhaps also Roman Catholics, could use. The Common Lectionary was first published in 1983 and in response to comments and criticisms was later revised. In 1992, the Revised Common Lectionary (RCL) was published and offered to any church bodies and communions that chose to use it.

In practice, entire denominations typically make a decision about lectionary usage. As in the century after the Reformation, some churches mandate a specific lectionary, others advise its use, others suggest its use, while still others do not engage in these kinds of worship decisions. The Evangelical Lutheran Church in America and the Evangelical Lutheran Church in Canada have joined with many other church bodies in North America and throughout the world by choosing the RCL as the preferred system for Sunday proclamation. It is printed in *Evangelical Lutheran Worship* (AE pp. 18–53). Other variants of this three-year/three-reading lectionary system remain in use by some churches around the world.

In preparing the RCL, the Consultation on Common Texts did not stipulate any specific biblical translation for use by the churches. In practice, entire denominations show a preference for one of the many biblical translations available. Lutherans are pulled in two opposite ways in choosing among translations. Since they value beloved passages of scripture that are treasured in the memory, they might retain a familiar translation. Yet Martin Luther was a biblical scholar who promoted vernacular translation, so Lutherans also see the need to update their translations with current biblical scholarship and contemporary linguistic usage. Although the ELCA does not mandate any particular biblical translation, the English language translation currently used in ELCA publications is the New Revised Standard Version of 1989.

Three Years, Three Readings

A single liturgical year has about fifty-two Sundays and six to ten non-Sunday liturgies. Granting the length and complexity of the Bible, this limited annual number presents a challenge to the church. A three-year lectionary at least triples the number of sets of an annual system. It is interesting that nearly two thousand years ago, Palestinian Jews also used a three-year lectionary in their synagogues.

Biblical studies, as practiced in the twentieth century, were foundational to the development of a three-year scheme. The primary task of the Christian lectionary is to proclaim the life, death, and resurrection of Christ within the believing community. To accomplish this, a reading from one of the gospels is most important. Until the last several centuries, most Christians intertwined the four gospels in their minds, their teaching, and their preaching. Preachers often were not trained to see the differences between the testimonies to Jesus as recorded by the communities of Matthew, Mark, Luke, and John. In our day, illustrated children's Bibles exemplify this entwined use of the New Testament. Those Christians who during Lent or on Good Friday attend to the "seven last words of Christ" continue this manner of merging the gospels into one composite picture. The medieval one-year lectionary handled the four gospels in this composite way.

However, because the biblical scholars who designed the three-year lectionary were trained in seminaries and universities in the twentieth century, a different biblical hermeneutic was operative. It is now common for Christians to study each gospel separately and to recognize and appreciate the differences in each portrayal of Jesus. That Mark's community remembered Jesus on the cross as saying, "My God, why have you forsaken me?" shows a different side of Jesus—a different Christology—than Luke's community, which remembered Jesus as forgiving the soldiers. Although each gospel is unique, Matthew, Mark, and Luke are called "the synoptics" because they share a way of seeing. They narrate more or less the same outline of Christ's ministry. These three synoptic gospels made a three-year lectionary a natural suggestion. John's gospel, quite different from the other three, describes seven "signs" that Jesus enacts. These signs are accompanied by lengthy discourses, and the gospel is not amenable to being divided up into sixty individual units. Thus John's gospel is designated especially at festivals, functioning in its unique way in the three-year lectionary.

In about the year 150, Justin wrote that each Sunday Christians gathered to read from "the writings of the prophets and the memoirs of the apostles," thus, at least two readings. There are several reasons why it makes sense for lectionaries to appoint more than one biblical reading. For one thing, the Bible is so long, so complex, so filled with significant scriptural material that we want more than one reading. Because preachers and theologians realized that one part of the Bible informed another part, Christians are helped through one section of the Bible by consulting another passage of scripture. Luke says that when Jesus was proclaiming his crucifixion and resurrection to the disciples on the road to Emmaus, he began "with Moses and all the prophets," interpreting to them "the things about himself in all the scriptures" (Luke 24:27). Theologians refer to this as "scripture interpreting scripture." Much of the New Testament would not make Christian sense to persons who do not know the history, language, and religion of the Old Testament. Thus, from the second century Christians read at least two biblical selections, in which the opening reading, what Justin calls "the writings of the prophets," in some way complemented the gospel reading.

But the Bible also includes what we call the epistles, the letters written by Paul, his associates, and other early church leaders, proclaiming the Christian faith and encouraging the communities in their participation in the life of the Spirit. While some of these passages have value primarily for the historian, other passages convey a breathtaking timelessness. Paul's description of how the Spirit enables the many ministries in the church needs to be heard by each generation of Christians. So in the medieval lectionary, the reading that complemented the gospel reading was chosen from the epistles.

Thus, like a few other Christian groups before them, the Roman Catholic lectionary committee of the 1960s decided to combine both of these historic practices. The primary reading each week comes from the gospels. Two other readings, one usually from the Old Testament and one usually from the epistles, accompany the gospel reading. The proclamation of three readings each Sunday and festival has an essential hermeneutical purpose. It is often easy to suggest the meaning of a single, short biblical quotation or an isolated brief narrative. But examining one passage in the light of another may well suggest a different interpretation. Juxtaposing several citations enriches the meaning, renders the portrayal more nuanced, and gives us yet more upon which to reflect. The three-reading lectionary calls us away from oversimplifying the word of the triune God and the call to Christian life. Because the Bible records so many different voices, nearly any ethical position can be supported by citing one short sentence from somewhere in the Bible. But if one keeps reading, one may well discover that the opposite position can be supported by a different biblical passage. Three readings each Sunday acknowledges the magisterial complexity of the Bible. It is as if we are surrounded by the three-part song of God.

Four Gospels Proclaimed over Three Years

On each Sunday and festival the church gathers to celebrate the presence of Jesus Christ. One of the primary events through which Christians experience the risen Christ is in the proclamation of the gospel. The Word of God is speaking, not only then, but also now. So it is that Western churches have appropriated the etiquette common in our culture, that when someone important enters the room, we stand. We rise for the gospel reading, and we announce the gospel by singing Alleluia, the Greek form of the Hebrew Hallelujah, meaning "Praise the LORD." By this acclamation, Christians praise the risen Christ as Lord and God, and we laud Christ come among us in the Word. In some congregations or situations, Christians follow ancient religious practice by chanting the gospel reading. It is as if the words of the gospels are too magnificent for mere speech, and so our voice breaks into song. Others process down the aisle with the gospel book, flanking the lector with candles, thus symbolizing that Christ comes among us with the light of mercy.

In contrast to the Western medieval lectionary that functioned somewhat like a children's Bible, blending the four gospels together into one single narrative, the three-year lectionary helps the church to value each gospel for its specific theological emphasis. Matthew, Mark, and Luke are proclaimed in successive years, but we need to begin by examining why John is proclaimed at most festivals and through much of Easter.

In granting this priority to John, the church follows the inclination of Irenaeus, a bishop in ancient France, who in about 180 argued that each Christian community needed all four canonical gospels to hear the whole truth of Christ. He wrote that, for example, those who used only Mark's gospel would stress too much Jesus as a suffering man. Some of Irenaeus's arguments are quite alien to us: for example, he stated that there must be four gospels because there are four corners of the earth. However, the many Lutheran churches that display liturgical art of Matthew, Mark, Luke, and John as, respectively, a winged man, a lion, an ox, and an eagle are using the same imagery that Irenaeus cites in his defense of the unique riches found in the four different gospels.

These images of the winged man, the lion, the ox, and the eagle are first cited in the book of Ezekiel (1:5-11). That Jewish visionary probably borrowed them from neighboring religions that imagined such mythical beasts as guarding the divine throne in the heavenly sphere. In Revelation (4:6b-8), the Christian visionary John reuses these same images. Irenaeus likens these four beings to the four evangelists. Because Matthew begins with the human genealogy of Jesus, Matthew is the winged man. Because Mark 1:2 refers to Isaiah's prophecy that Christ comes with prophetic power, the lion signifies Mark. Because Luke commences with the priest Zechariah, the ox, an animal often sacrificed, represents Luke. The eagle depicts John, who soars on high on the wings of the Spirit. Those churches that have designed their lectern to resemble a great bronze or golden eagle mean to suggest that for Christians, the entire Bible rests on the back of John. The same can be argued for Christian doctrine, and thus also for the lectionary.

In the New Testament the church encounters early answers to the question that Jesus posed to the disciples: Who do you say that I am? As the decades progressed, the theology of the primitive church deepened. The New Testament book in which is found the "highest" Christology, that is, the book that expresses most fully the divinity of Christ, is the Gospel of John, the last of the four canonical gospels written, perhaps reaching its present form in about 100. Throughout John, Jesus is described as fully divine. For example, according to the prologue of John, Christ is not only born the son of God; Christ is God from before time. The synoptics report that Jesus predicted the destruction of the temple. But according to John, "he was speaking of the temple of his body" (2:21). The theology of John's community has developed from a memory of the sayings of Jesus to the Christian conviction that in Christ we encounter God. Because of the primary Christian belief that Jesus Christ is God incarnate, it is appropriate that on the most important festivals, the gospel reading comes from John.

The three-year lectionary employs two different techniques in assigning biblical passages to Sundays and festivals. Sometimes a biblical section is chosen because it is particularly appropriate in celebrating an event in the life of Christ. So we read the story of the Jerusalem palm procession on the Sunday of the Passion/Palm Sunday before we parade around the church with our palms. The other technique is called semicontinuous reading. On these Sundays passages from the gospels are chosen more or less one after another, as if we are reading straight through the book. The semicontinuous technique is used on standard or "green" Sundays throughout much of the year for the gospel selections, Matthew during year A, Mark during year B, and Luke during year C.

The Gospel of Matthew, written with an especially Jewish audience in mind, describes Jesus as the fulfillment of the promises made by the prophets, the Messiah born of the Davidic line of royalty, the new Moses who speaks the word of God for us. Matthew's gospel emphasizes the ethical life expected of those who follow Christ. "Be perfect, therefore, as your heavenly Father is perfect," says Jesus in Matthew's Sermon on the Mount (5:48). Matthew includes directions for how the community should discipline itself and stern parables and allegories about the need for us to live out our faith in everything we do.

Mark was probably the earliest gospel written of the four, perhaps about the year 65. Mark portrays Christ as the hidden Messiah who alters our religious expectations. In Mark, it is usually the outsiders who recognize who Jesus is. In Mark's gospel, parables can be short and enigmatic, and the disciples do not understand them. A year of hearing Mark calls the Christian assembly to a life of faith, to the realization that, like the disciples, also we miss the hidden God. God is beyond our knowing, and the gospel calls us to a life other than we might expect.

In the opening verses of the Gospel of Luke, the evangelist states that he is not an eyewitness but is in the third generation of believers. His gospel is the source of the church's canticles, those treasured biblical songs such as the Song of Mary and the Song of Zechariah, sung at Evening and Morning Prayer. Perhaps the best storyteller of the evangelists, Luke wrote probably for a Gentile audience and describes Jesus as the living savior of all peoples in the world. "Be merciful, just as your

Father is merciful," says Jesus in Luke's Sermon on the Plain (6:36), calling us to a life of justice for the poor. In many beloved parables found only in Luke, God is always ready to forgive everyone who seeks God's mercy.

The three-year, three-reading lectionary invites the church to attend to each of the four gospels. Each of the three synoptic gospels stands in conversation with John and with one another. Irenaeus said that the church needs all four gospels: the winged man, the lion, the ox, and the eagle. The mystery of Christ is so vast that we want to probe the message of all four gospels. Jesus Christ is the new Moses, the hidden Messiah, the forgiving Savior, and the incarnate God, and hearing each gospel, we stand in reverence and gratitude.

The Proclamation of the Old Testament

A debate arose in the second century as to whether Christians should continue to read from the Old Testament. Indeed, one still sometimes encounters the notion that the God of the Old Testament is somehow a different deity from the God incarnate in Jesus. Other Christians, sensitive to the church's grim history of anti-Semitism, have suggested that the Hebrew scriptures ought to be interpreted only through a Jewish worldview rather than with Christian eyes. Yet the dominant theological opinion of our time proposes that the ancient Israelite scriptures provide the foundation for two contemporary religious traditions. One is the Judaism that developed after the destruction of the Jerusalem temple in the year 70, which required the Jews, since they could no longer offer sacrifices, to reinterpret much in their ancient scriptures. The other trajectory, occurring about the same time, found Christians offering their own reinterpretation of the Hebrew scriptures. Christians saw Christ, rather than the family meal, the synagogue, and strict observance of Torah, as the replacement of the temple. The hope is that Jews and Christians can deepen their honor for each other, recognize one another as cousins in religion, and appreciate the different ways that an ancient faith in God took root and thrived in new situations.

Mainstream Christian theology continues to assert that the Old Testament is essential for the church's understanding of Jesus Christ. Without knowledge of the Hebrew scriptures, its vocabulary, narratives, and imagery, Christians cannot understand their own creedal statements concerning Jesus (a reuse of the name of Joshua) as Lord (a version of the Hebrew title for God) and Christ (which means Messiah). In continuing to cite the Old Testament, Christians are continuing a tradition ascribed to Jesus, who is quoted as likening his own death and resurrection to Jonah's three days in the sea monster, and to Paul, who described Christ as the paschal lamb. When Paul wrote that Christ was raised "in accordance with the scriptures" (1 Cor. 15:3-4), he was referring to the Hebrew scriptures, since the New Testament had not yet been written. The primary example of Christians proclaiming the resurrection of Christ "in accordance with the [Hebrew] scriptures" occurs in the Easter Vigil. Many Lutheran churches include imagery from the Old Testament on their walls. Indeed, every crèche that includes an ox and an ass is citing Isaiah 1:3. The prophet says that the ox and the donkey are the first to recognize their maker, and so Christian tradition has placed Isaiah's barnyard animals at the stable, adoring the baby Jesus.

Stated theologically, "scripture interprets scripture." This principle is embodied in the three-year/three-reading lectionary by designating that throughout the festival half of the year, the first reading from the Old Testament is chosen to complement the gospel. For the time after Pentecost, that is, the nonfestival half of the year, the lectionary offers two options for the first reading. In the first series, the festival pattern continues, with the Old Testament chosen to complement the gospel. This option, often called the complementary series, is the one recommended for the ELCA, preferred in the publications of Augsburg Fortress, and printed first in the *Evangelical Lutheran Worship* listing (AE pp. 38–53). When the Old Testament reading complements the gospel, the choice has been made for one of three reasons: to reference a citation in the gospel reading, to deepen our understanding of the gospel reading, or to provide a contrast to the gospel reading. By receiving first the Old Testament, we are ready to hear the New. Some Old Testament readings are narratives, some poems, some a prophetic speech, but according to the complementary principle, they always cast light on the gospel reading.

The most obvious use of the principle of complementarity is for the Old Testament selection to include a passage cited with the gospel reading. For example, on the second Sunday in Advent in year B, the gospel records the preaching of John the Baptist, who cites the prophet Isaiah. Thus the first reading is from Isaiah 40, the precise passage that John the Baptist cited: "In the wilderness prepare the way of the LORD." On the fourth Sunday of Lent in year B, the gospel refers to the story of Moses lifting up the serpent in the wilderness, and the first reading is from Numbers 21, the narrative of the poisonous serpents. Without knowledge of the Old Testament, we would have a difficult time understanding the New Testament narratives, for the evangelists assumed considerable familiarity with the Hebrew scriptural tradition.

In a second pattern of complementary selection of the Old Testament, the reading deepens our understanding of the gospel. In Lectionary 24, year A, when the gospel is Matthew 18:21-35, the parable of the unforgiving servant, the first reading is the narrative from Genesis 50 of Joseph forgiving his brothers. Here we see the biblical pattern of divine forgiveness in both Old and New Testaments. In Lectionary 17, year C, to complement the gospel in which Jesus urges his disciples to pray with persistence, the first reading is the wonderful, even comic, tale of Abraham begging God not to destroy the cities of Sodom and Gomorrah. Here the Old Testament narrative illustrates the persistent prayer that Jesus commends. The two readings enhance each other, scripture interpreting scripture. During five weeks in the summer in year B, when the lectionary interrupts Mark for the discourse on the bread of life in John 6, the first readings are the Old Testament narratives of God's miraculous feeding of the people. The first readings enflesh the proclamation of John's gospel.

The third technique of complementarity contrasts the Old and the New Testament so we can grasp more fully the implications of the evangelist's message. For example, on the first Sunday of Lent, year A, the narrative of Jesus successfully withstanding the devil's temptations is heard next to the legend from Genesis 3 of the woman and the man giving in to temptation. This pattern of opposites occurs seldom in the lectionary, since the ministry of Jesus is far more a continuation of, rather than a contrast to, God's actions in the Old Testament. The church sees similarity, rather than substantive differences, between God's covenants throughout time.

The Revised Common Lectionary provides an alternate way to pursue the principle of complementarity. This option is preferred by those Protestants in the tradition of John Calvin, who mandated that the Old Testament books be read straight through during public worship. For the Sundays May 29–June 4 to Christ the King, *Evangelical Lutheran Worship* lists this series second, under the heading "Semicontinuous reading and psalm." The Evangelical Lutheran Church in Canada has recommended this series for its use, primarily because this choice allowed for a common practice with the majority of the Protestant and Anglican churches in Canada, which prefer the semicontinuous Old Testament series.

According to this option, since Matthew relies so consistently on the Mosaic tradition, semicontinuous passages from especially Genesis and Exodus are read in year A. Since Mark describes Christ as the hidden Messiah, the court histories that tell of the anointed kings of Israel are heard in year B. Thus, for example, the first readings for June–August in year B follow monarchical history from the call of Samuel through the saga of the reign of David up through Solomon's dedication of the temple. In year C, since Luke's gospel shows such concern for justice to the poor, writings from the prophets are proclaimed. The complementarity functions not within each Sunday, but in a more comprehensive way through the half year.

The primary argument in support of this practice is that by reading more or less through the Old Testament in this way, people who attend church regularly will learn more of the sweep of the biblical story. The challenge is to maintain a Christian focus on each Sunday as the celebration of Christ's resurrection. Since using this series results in three readings each Sunday that bear no clear relationship to one another, some churches that use this series select from the lectionary's list only one biblical reading each Sunday, which might even be the Old Testament passage. In practice, entire church bodies have chosen one series over the other and support this preference by the publications and calendars issued by their publishing house. In order that the lectionary make coherent sense over the half year, one or the other series with its related psalm should be consistently followed.

There is the Eastertide exception to the reading of the Old Testament each Sunday. During the fifty days of Easter, the first readings come from the book of Acts. Early Christians saw the ministry of Jesus Christ as continuing beyond Easter Day into the life of the church. Following their resurrected Lord, now Peter and Paul are calling disciples, proclaiming the kingdom, traveling the countryside, performing miracles, suffering rejection, and anticipating their own executions.

The readings from Acts are selected to complement the gospel reading. For example, on the fourth Sunday of Easter, the gospel is from John 10, the discourse on the Good Shepherd. The first reading in year A, from Acts 2, describes the church as following Christ by caring for one another. In year B, the reading from Acts 4 speaks of Christ as the one who laid down his life. In year C, Tabitha hears the voice of Peter and rises from the dead, just as the sheep in John 10 hear the voice of the shepherd. The mission of Christ lives on in the apostles and within the inspired community.

The Proclamation of the Epistles

About half of the New Testament is comprised of letters written by Paul and other church leaders to communities of Christians or to individuals about the life of faith. Although none of the epistles is precisely dated, most biblical scholars judge that the earliest one was written by Paul to the church in Thessalonica shortly after the year 50. Some epistles that purport to be written by Paul discuss church situations that did not develop until decades after his execution in 63 or 64. Perhaps, as was common in the ancient world, one of Paul's disciples wrote under Paul's name, as if the student inherited the authority of the teacher. The final epistles were written around 100, perhaps later. The content of the epistles range from timeless theological homilies about the meaning of Christ's resurrection to regulations about women's clothing, from confidence in the coming of the end of time to organizational flowcharts for Christian communities. Theological emphases vary depending on the author. The epistles are the biblical evidence that the gospel proclamation is always contextualized in a specific time and place. From this wealth of first-century material, the lectionary appoints one passage each Sunday, not primarily as Bible study but rather as the proclamation of the God's good news to the assembled church.

In Advent, from Christmas through Epiphany, in Lent, and through Easter Day, the Sunday's epistle reading either illumines the liturgical season or follows the principle of complementarity by fitting the epistle with the gospel. For example, during Advent, the epistle readings speak of our preparation for the coming of God. On Christmas Eve, the reading from Titus speaks of the appearance of the glory of God, and on Christmas Day the reading from Hebrews articulates a high Christology that parallels the gospel from John 1. The epistle for Epiphany from Ephesians praises the mystery of God made manifest in Christ. The epistles through Lent speak of sin and law, forgiveness and grace, obvious Lenten themes. At the Easter Vigil we hear from Paul about Christ's resurrection and ours.

For some of the year, the second readings are semicontinuous passages chosen from epistles that are especially appropriate to the liturgical season. So during the fifty days of Easter, the Sunday epistles come from books particularly appropriate for the Easter season. In year A, 1 Peter is read from because of its emphasis on the life of the newly baptized. In year B, the Easter epistles come from 1 John, a letter that speaks of believers as illumined by God, living as God's children, loving one another, and being born of God. An exception to the rule that second readings come from the epistles occurs in year C when during Eastertide the second readings come from Revelation. Although much of Revelation envisions the great conflict between evil and good at the end of time, the passages selected for the Easter epistles are those in which the community encounters the risen Christ and sings hymns of praise.

Following Holy Trinity Sunday, the second readings are semicontinuous selections from the epistles. During year A, readings come from 1 Corinthians, Romans, Philippians, and 1 Thessalonians; during year B, more from 1 Corinthians, 2 Corinthians, Ephesians, James, and Hebrews; and during year C, the remainder of 1 Corinthians, Galatians, Colossians, more from Hebrews, and from Philemon, 1 Timothy, 2 Timothy, and 2 Thessalonians. The hope is that the assembly, inserted into the life of the early church, will hear from the Bible a proclamation appropriate to our own time. The gospels are essential to the church, since they tell the story of Jesus, but the epistles instruct the church in what to make of the life of Christ in our midst. The gospels tell the church to baptize, yet the epistles explain how baptism incorporates us into the death and resurrection of Christ. The epistles model the liturgical hermeneutic: God's word is proclaimed to the whole assembly, each week the eternal word is spoken within a unique community of the faithful.

Philosophers and psychologists of the twentieth century explored the ways that the human mind is always seeking coherence. From the toddler's puzzle to the astrophysicist's picture of the cosmos, humans try to order chaos and to find a pattern in what might first appear random.

A lectionary is a superb example of the human search for meaning and our hope for coherence. Of course, other lectionary systems have their advantages. To promulgate one lectionary need not be to disdain another. Yet the three-year/three-reading lectionary is now serving Christians of many denominations in churches around the world, and *Evangelical Lutheran Worship* calls us into the joy of participation and the depth of its discipline.

How to Serve as Reader

A century ago or less, Lutherans expected only the pastor to proclaim the readings in worship. It has now become common for lay people to participate in this leadership role. This is a welcome pattern among us. Even in the second century, Justin, in describing how Christians worshiped in Rome, wrote of "the reader" proclaiming the scriptures. Having lay people serve as readers symbolizes that the word of God belongs to and is cherished by all the people of God, and it insures that several different individual voices will be heard in the assembly's worship.

In some assemblies, the readings are proclaimed from a large pulpit Bible. In other churches, lectors read from a ceremonial volume, itself called "a lectionary," in which all the biblical selections are printed sequentially, week after week. In some assemblies, or at festival services, the reading of the gospel is given special honor. The reader processes into the middle of the nave, perhaps half way down a center aisle, and stands flanked with candles, while the assembly rises to show reverence to the presence of Christ in and as the Word. These practices enact our profound respect for God's word.

Several practices that have become common need to be reexamined. Just as many people who are musical are not qualified to be the week's organist, so many people who are literate are not excellent public speakers. It is good for assemblies to identify those members who are skilled at public proclamation and ask them to serve in this role. It is helpful to schedule annual training sessions for those readers. Lectors do well to be faithful Bible readers, so they know and love what they are reading, and to study the lectionary texts beforehand, so that they understand complex sentences and check pronunciation of difficult words. Readers need to practice the readings before the service, perhaps standing in place at the reading desk, speaking slowly, with sufficient pauses, in full voice. While the practice of allowing any member to serve as lector may meet the need to encourage lay participation, if the result is that the reading is poorly presented, we have failed in the necessity to proclaim God's word with beauty and understanding.

One method used in training readers advocates that they look at the assembly during the announcement of the reading and the concluding call, but that they focus their eyes on the book during the reading, making it clear that these are scriptural sentences, not those of the reader. Another method suggests that lectors know the reading so well that they can look up at the assembly as often as possible during the reading. With either technique, readers are advised to avoid either extreme of a flat, uninflected monotone or of an over-inflected theatrical performance. Yet a biblical narrative, a prophetic poem, and an excerpt of Pauline theology each call for a somewhat different style of public proclamation, an appropriate tone of voice.

In many assemblies, poor public reading has become accepted because everyone is following along on a printed text of the readings that was provided in the bulletin. Congregations would do well to reexamine this practice. If the readers are excellent, even competent, there will be no need for everyone to have a printed text. We do not read along with the sermon. Relying on printed texts suggests, perhaps erroneously, that everyone in the assembly is literate. It ignores the fact that small children are members of the assembly. It conveys the notion that worship is an exercise in reading, rather than a communal action during which we hear the living word of the Lord. Everyone will have heads down, reading from a piece of paper, rather than heads up, attentive to the reader. If a congregation continues to judge that printing out the readings is a good use of paper, handing out next week's readings at the close of the service is one practice that encourages everyone to have read the biblical passages as part of their preparation for worship. Such handouts, in larger print, could also be made available on request before the service for those whose hearing impairments prevent them from understanding the readings, though again, that will not help with the sermon. And one final, related observation: The practice of the reader carrying up to the reading stand a sheet of paper on which the readings are printed suggests to the assembly that the Bible reading is disposable and unimportant. Such seemingly harmless habits do communicate, even if unintentionally.

How the Lectionary Influences the Entire Service

In most Christian practice, an order of service has standard parts that are included each week, for example, the Lord's Prayer. These parts are sometimes called *the ordinary*, related to *ordo,* or the customary pattern of the service. Surrounding these standard parts are more or fewer variable parts, sometimes called *propers.* Some of these variable parts are proper to a given day, and others are proper to a liturgical season. A simple service has fewer variable propers, while a more elaborate service has many. Churches that use a lectionary base their decisions about many of the propers on the appointed Bible readings. Thus the lectionary readings influence the entire service. The propers that relate to the readings include many of the prayers, the psalm, the sermon, the hymns, any contributions by the choir, and any art printed or projected for the assembly. The variables in the service that correspond to the entire liturgical season rather than to a specific Sunday's readings may include the color of fabric adornments and some of the prayers.

Gathering

In deciding whether to begin the Sunday service with the confession and forgiveness, the thanksgiving for baptism, or neither, planners will want to reflect on the liturgical season and the Sunday's lectionary readings to make an appropriate choice. Whether either or both the Kyrie or a hymn of praise follows also may be influenced by the lectionary or the season.

Prayer of the Day

To conclude the gathering of the assembly for worship, the presiding minister prays the prayer of the day. This prayer, traditionally called the collect, encapsulates the readings that are designated by the lectionary and unites the minds of all the assembly in prayer. The texts of these prayers (AE pp. 18–63), like the texts of the prayers of thanksgiving, have been crafted for a single, practiced voice to speak aloud. Prayers that everyone joins in speaking together are printed in sense lines and crafted in more simple syntax.

The prayer of the day is a key that opens the door to the three readings. Since the prayer of the day always corresponds with the readings, *Evangelical Lutheran Worship* provides three years' worth of these prayers. The sources of the *Evangelical Lutheran Worship* prayers of the day include the following: traditional prayers, many translated from medieval Latin and some from Reformation times, and assigned over the centuries to a specific gospel; prayers familiar from *Lutheran Book of Worship*; prayers borrowed from several different twentieth-century collections of new Sunday prayers; prayers adapted from famous writings of revered Christians of the church's past; and prayers newly composed for *Evangelical Lutheran Worship*. See Appendix B for a specific listing of sources. Most prayers of the day follow this outline: God is named and described; God is praised for specific acts of mercy; we ask God for a continuation of these gifts; and we conclude by asking God to hear us because we are baptized into Christ.

Psalm

For each Sunday and festival, the three-year lectionary stipulates not only three biblical readings but also a passage from a psalm. The appointed psalm is meant to be not a fourth Bible reading but rather the communal response to the first reading. Having heard the Old Testament reading, the assembly enters into the word with the words of a psalm. We might think of the psalm following the first reading as something like the hymn of the day that follows the gospel and sermon.

The psalms have a long history of use. Although it was traditional to say that King David composed all the psalms, they were in fact composed over hundreds of years by many different authors. Some were poems written by anonymous poets. Some psalms were written for learned academic circles; some were used in the court, in praise of the king; some refer to Israelite liturgical rites; several psalms are Israelite adaptations of Canaanite hymns. These ancient praises and laments came to be used by the entire community to sing of its joys or sorrows to God, the specifics of the original situation functioning as metaphors of the contemporary situation. The psalms were compiled into something like a hymnal and were among the liturgical songs that Jesus sang.

In the Anglican Church following the Reformation, the committees that translated the Bible into English wanted the translation of the psalms to be crafted in such a way as to make them accessible and even lyrical for public prayer and praise. Miles Coverdale was the talented translator whose psalter was first published in 1535, and many English-speaking Christians have continued use of his work. Over the centuries and again in *Evangelical Lutheran Worship*, committees received the current version of Coverdale's work and revised it yet again, in some places rendering the English closer to the Hebrew and in other places making the translation more appropriate for contemporary communication.

One principle undergirding the *Evangelical Lutheran Worship* version of our inherited psalter was to minimize the number of times that God is referred to with masculine language. Although in previous centuries the English language used masculine terminology to include also females, increasingly in American English masculine nouns and pronouns are used only when indicating male gender. Because Christian theologians have consistently taught that God is not sexually male, contemporary translations of historic texts that are intended for use in worship call for nuanced translation.

Many different methods, including the five outlined here, are available for the singing of the psalm, and variety in usage is encouraged.

(1) *Evangelical Lutheran Worship* provides simple psalm tones (AE pp. 337–338) and instructions for their use (pp. 335–336). Using these or similar tones, the full psalm can be chanted by the assembly, singing directly from the printed text in *Evangelical Lutheran Worship*. There is no need to reprint these texts in a bulletin. The small vertical red line placed mid-verse indicates when the psalm tone moves from the reciting tone (the note on which most of the text is sung) to the termination (the notes that close off that portion of the psalm tone).

(2) Using these psalm tones, another method is to alternate verses, between a cantor and the assembly, between the choir and the assembly, or between one side of the room and the other.

(3) The psalm verses can be chanted by a cantor or the choir, with the assembly singing a refrain. This refrain, which is one verse of the psalm, is the key to why that psalm has been appointed for the day. The designated verse is indicated in red parentheses in the *Evangelical Lutheran Worship* lectionary listing, though the actual refrain text may only be a portion of that verse. The exact assigned refrain text is provided with the propers in the Leaders Edition. The refrain can be sung at the beginning and the end or at several times throughout the psalm.

(4) The assembly can sing a versification of the psalm that is provided in a hymn. Some versifications remain close to the psalm text, although in other hymns the Christian text has deviated significantly from the psalm itself.
(5) The choir can sing a choral rendition of the psalm. However, even were the assembly to have no active part in singing the psalm, the psalm intends to be the people's response to the first reading, and it means to engage our hearts and minds, if not also our voices.

The lectionary appoints which psalm is appropriate as a response to the first reading. One example of the application of a psalm to the first reading is Lectionary 17, year B. The gospel is John 6, the feeding of the five thousand. The first reading is the parallel story from 2 Kings of Elisha's feeding the multitude with twenty loaves. The appointed psalm is nine verses of Psalm 145, which praises God for the gift of food, and the refrain is the line we know from the beloved table prayer: "You open wide your hand and satisfy the desire of every living thing." Sometimes the psalm is quoted in the readings. For example, for Good Friday, the lament of Psalm 22 is echoed in the gospel's description of the crucifixion of Jesus. Yet even on Good Friday, we join in the concluding praise in verses 25–31 by recalling God's saving deeds. Sometimes the psalm contains an image that is central to the readings. The frontispiece of the *ELW* psalms (AE p. 333) depicts images especially significant for Christian use of these Hebrew poems: the river, the rock, sheep, deer, the sun, moon, and stars, the fruitful tree, and the lyre.

Gospel Acclamation

Not until the seventeenth century were Christian churches routinely equipped with seating. Although for the last four hundred years naves generally have had chairs or pews, at some points during worship we stand. Current practice urges worshipers who are able to rise for the reading of the gospel to honor the presence of Christ in the word. Traditionally the gospel is introduced by the singing of the Alleluia. To enrich this singing of the gospel acclamation, a proper verse, sometimes selected from the coming gospel reading, can be sung by a cantor or choir. It is as if the assembly is singing to Christ himself as he speaks to us through the gospel reading. The proper gospel acclamation texts are printed in the leaders edition (pp. 60–137). Since it has been Christian tradition to refrain from saying or singing the word Alleluia during Lent, *Evangelical Lutheran Worship* provides an alternate acclamation for use during the Lenten season.

Sermon

It is the intention of the liturgy that the sermon be based on the lectionary readings. In the sermon the preacher expounds on the word of God that has been proclaimed, rendering it more accessible to the assembly and commenting upon its meaning for today. More than simply personal reflections on the biblical texts, the sermon proclaims both "law," that is, the truth of our sin and death, and "gospel," the good news of the salvation of the world through the life, death, and resurrection of Christ. Such a proclamation of the faith of the church means to enliven the faithful with the word of God and to inspire the entire assembly for continued service in the world.

Hymn of the Day

A primary way that the lectionary readings influence the service is through the selection of hymnody. At least the hymn of the day, usually placed after the sermon, is chosen in light of the lectionary's readings. A rich hymn tradition allows the assembly to experience what other Christians around the world, in past centuries and in our time, have written about the emphases in the day's readings. In this way the assembly not only hears its own preacher but also sings along with Ambrose in the fourth century, Fortunatus in the sixth, Hildegard of Bingen in the twelfth, Martin Luther in the sixteenth, Isaac Watts in the eighteenth, Catherine Winkworth in the nineteenth century, and many authors of our own time—all the dozens of Christian hymn writers whose reflections on the biblical readings enhance our worship. The Topical Index of Hymns (AE pp. 1178–1188) assists in locating appropriate hymns. The text and mood of any choir selections also reflect the lectionary's readings.

Prayers of Intercession

One of the central actions of the assembled church is to pray to God for all the needs of the world. These intercessions usually occur at the conclusion to the service of the word and each Sunday are to include petitions for the church, the earth itself, the nations, the community, all in any need, and the congregation. The prayer concludes with a remembrance of the dead and a thanksgiving for their lives of faith. It is not intended that this intercessory prayer be a review of the readings, as if the prayer were another sermon; nor is the prayer to be "law," a list of the ways we are to live. However, as the intercessions beg God to act in the world, the readings offer guidance as to how on that specific Sunday or festival we might pray for the church, the earth, governments, and all the world's needy people. Perhaps images of God or memorable phrases from the readings fit into each petition. Perhaps the readings suggest a specific petition, so that, for example, on a Sunday of the feeding of the five thousand we pray for those who are starving.

Whoever prepares the intercessions needs to attend to the lectionary, to the concerns of the assembly, and to the week's news. The suggestion that the intercessions be both prepared and delivered by a trained lay person is another instance of encouraging many ministries to collaborate in the assembly's worship, and this practice helps the intercessions from becoming no more than an echo of the sermon. In the early centuries of the church it was part of the ministry of the deacon to prepare the intercessions, for it was expected that the deacon was committed to the relief of the afflicted and so was most aware of the specific needs of those in need.

Other Prayers

Other prayers throughout the holy communion service may also respond to the lectionary or to seasonal accents. *Evangelical Lutheran Worship* provides several examples of the optional prayer at the offering (AE pp. 107, 64) and of the prayer after communion (AE pp. 114, 65), and the lectionary's readings may suggest which option is preferred on a specific Sunday or festival. If yet another prayer is crafted for these purposes on a specific Sunday or festival, the prayer may reflect even more precisely the language of the readings. The presiding minister's thanksgiving at the table includes a preface that is specific to the day or the season (LE 224–237).

Evangelical Lutheran Worship includes the full text of ten thanksgivings at the table (AE pp. 108–111, 65–70). Thanksgivings III and IV are specifically seasonal. Because the great thanksgivings differ in biblical references, theological emphasis, and rhetorical tone, the lectionary readings help determine which is the most appropriate for each celebration of holy communion. In this great thanksgiving, the church praises

God for the continuing creation, for the gift of salvation through Jesus Christ, and for the presence of the Holy Spirit in this meal and throughout the world.

Other Possibilities

Some sets of lectionary readings suggest yet other ways to highlight the lectionary's readings throughout the service. For example, on a Sunday when the gospel narrative includes a suppliant asking Christ for mercy, there might be special attention to the assembly's singing of the Kyrie. On the Sunday that Isaiah 6 is proclaimed, there might be special attention to the assembly's singing of "Holy, holy, holy." The third Sunday in Easter, year C, when Revelation 5 is proclaimed is a good Sunday for the assembly to sing "This is the feast."

Augsburg Fortress publishes print and online resources to help enrich the Sunday service in Lutheran congregations as well as other churches that use the three-year lectionary. *Sunday and Seasons*, the annual guide to worship planning, provides considerable assistance in shaping the assembly's worship according to the lectionary. Though the contents may vary from time to time, they customarily include items such as helpful essays that can serve as discussion starters for a congregational worship committee; checklists to assist worship planners in seasonal and festival preparation; a descriptive paragraph that might be sent out to the members by email during the previous week or printed in the service folder; descriptors for each of the proper readings; suggested intercessions; suggestions for clip or projection art; images that might inspire the preaching; hymn suggestions; choir and instrumental suggestions; and biographical paragraphs introducing the faithful departed whose commemorations fall during the week. Attention to *Sunday and Seasons* makes the task of focus on the lectionary relatively easy for service planners. Consumers of materials distributed by other publishing houses need to be aware of whether those resources attend to the Revised Common Lectionary and, if so, which series of first readings is featured.

Art and Other Visuals

Some decisions about art and other visuals are determined by the liturgical season, but some visuals apply specifically to each set of lectionary readings. Lutherans are accustomed to the use of lectionary-based paraments and vestments. Those churches that print out a weekly worship folder can choose from one of the many clip-art liturgical resources an image for the Sunday that helps the assembly focus on the readings. At a midweek catechetical class, children might prepare for the Sunday readings, perhaps some of them making drawings that could be reproduced for Sunday morning. Some assemblies include talented artists who could engage in this ministry. Such coordination with the lectionary is a more creative use of any weekly printed material than no image at all or only a picture of the church building. Visuals that might be projected onto white walls or screens at the front of the nave can depict the biblical narratives that are proclaimed or display the images in the readings. Banners can be chosen to coordinate with the readings. Flower arrangements will not be identical each week, but will reflect the tone set by the day or season.

Congregational Activities

The liturgical year and the lectionary's readings for any Sunday guide the congregation as it schedules its various activities both within and outside the worship. Baptisms may be grouped and celebrated when the lectionary readings speak specifically about baptism, for example the Vigil of Easter or the Baptism of our Lord. Affirmations of baptism, such as confirmation, fit well on Pentecost. The menu at the coffee hour during Lent may be minimal. It would be exceedingly odd for a Christian wedding to take place during Holy Week.

Lectionary Study

Some congregations conduct regular adult classes to study the lectionary readings. Such study may take place either directly before the service on Sunday morning or in the middle of the previous week, when the conversation will assist the pastor in preparing the sermon. Denominational publishing houses have issued Sunday school curricula that follow the lectionary selections. Adult forums can schedule a focused study of specific books of the Bible that will be featured in upcoming lectionary readings.

The daily lectionary included in *Evangelical Lutheran Worship* (AE p. 1121–1153) is based on the Sunday lectionary. For each day it appoints two Bible readings and a psalm that correspond in some way to the Sunday readings. In this way, the days of the week flow to (Thursday–Saturday) and from (Monday–Wednesday) the selections of the lectionary. We prepare for the lectionary readings before, and we meditate on them after the Sunday assembly.

The Lectionary at Services Other than Holy Communion

When assemblies meet for worship services other than holy communion it remains the case that the lectionary focuses the worship and ties it to Christians around the world. For the Service of the Word provided in *Evangelical Lutheran Worship* (AE pp. 210–222), nearly all the suggestions offered here for holy communion apply. Were some other service order to use only one reading, and that service is on a Sunday, the gospel is the preferred reading. When a service order suggests the use of two readings, the gospel is always proclaimed, and the planners of the worship can choose from the two other readings one that complements the gospel. No matter what service order is used, the lectionary will govern choices about hymnody, selections among options, petitions in the intercessions, and uses of visuals. In keeping with Lutheran tradition, any preaching that takes place will ordinarily be based on the biblical readings that are proclaimed.

CHAPTER THREE

3 Sundays and Principal Festivals

In ancient times, the civilizations near the Mediterranean Sea established a seven-day week. With the naked eye, ancient peoples could see seven great heavenly bodies that moved differently than the stars: the sun, the moon, and the five planets Mars, Jupiter, Mercury, Venus, and Saturn. Because of the belief that these seven bodies had power over the earth, a seven-day week gave to each heavenly body jurisdiction over one-seventh of human affairs. The names on our calendar recall this archaic idea: Sunday governed by the sun, Monday by the moon, Saturday by Saturn. The names of the other days of our week have been changed from the Roman to the Norse deities Týr (or Tiw), Woden, Thor, and Freya. Conveniently, seven was also one-fourth of the twenty-eight-day cycle of the moon.

In the Bible is the Israelites' alternative explanation of the week. By creating the world in six working days, God established the pattern for human society, and by resting on the last day of the week, our Saturday, God established the Sabbath. As mentioned earlier, Exodus 20:11 says that the people's weekly rest mimics the rest of God, and Deuteronomy 5:15 connects this rest with the people's release from slavery. It is not clear when in history the day of rest became normative or when it came to include a synagogue service for the men. We know that some early Christians maintained the Jewish ritual of observing a Saturday Sabbath.

The gospels state that the first believers experienced the resurrection of Jesus on the first day of the week. It was on Sunday, after the Sabbath was over, that the women visited the empty tomb, the disciples ate with Jesus at Emmaus, Jesus appeared to all the disciples in the upper room, and Jesus appeared to Thomas. According to Revelation, it was on Sunday that John saw the risen Lord. These accounts indicate that in the formation of a Christian worldview, Sunday came to have precedence over Saturday. Paul writes about a collection taken on the first day of every week, probably because this day was already a day of

Christian meeting (1 Cor. 16:2). By the second half of the first century, in part to open up Christian practice to the Gentile world, Christians transferred their primary ritual from Saturday to Sunday, "the first day of the week." The destruction of the Jewish temple in 70 increased the tendency to distinguish Judaism from Christianity. By the year 150, Justin wrote, "We all hold this meeting together on the day of the sun since it is the first day, on which day God, having transformed darkness and matter, made the world. On the same day Jesus Christ our Savior rose from the dead."[1]

In 321, the Roman emperor Constantine, to demonstrate his preference for Christianity, made Sunday a day of rest for certain occupations, and throughout the fourth century church councils and theologians maintained that Christians were to keep Sunday as the Lord's day, rather than Saturday, as a day of rest. Whether one worked on Sunday depended on one's social status and occupation, but the Sunday gathering for word and sacrament could be scheduled before or after a day of work. After the Reformation, especially Calvinist Protestants sought to replicate sabbath on Sunday by forbidding social and commercial engagements of every kind on Sunday except for worship. This merging of sabbath rest and Sunday worship inspired many "blue laws" in some American colonies and early national practice.

In the second half of the twentieth century, cultural patterns in some Western countries, including the United States and Canada, led to considerable loosening of such restrictions on Sunday activity. In the twenty-first century, Christians are offered many socially approved options on Sunday morning, from sports activities to weekend visits at a second home. With Saturday filled with chores, some people see Sunday as their weekly day of relaxation and play, rather than as the day for religious assembly. Furthermore, contemporary spirituality has popularized the ideas that religion is a private matter and that one's connection with God need not include attendance at communal worship. Western individualism suggests that personal enrichment is the primary, if not the sole, purpose for such activities, and that if one feels that one is "getting nothing out of it," church attendance is unnecessary.

It has thus become newly important for the church to articulate the primacy of every Sunday as the day for all the baptized to gather in celebration of the resurrection and in devout prayer for the needs of the world. While many contemporary Christians yearn for a weekly day of sabbath rest, it is not for rest but for assembly for worship, that Christians keep Sunday. Sunday is the day of the resurrection of Jesus Christ, when we meet the risen Christ in and with one another. Christian faith claims that Christ's resurrection is the grounding of the life of the baptized, and so Christians assemble at the outset of each week to hear the word for their lives, exchange with one another God's peace, share in the meal of the risen Christ, and join together in the tasks of spreading God's mercy throughout the world. The ritual of gathering with the body of Christ at the beginning of each week renews our centering in the faith of the resurrection. So it is that calendars distributed by Christian publishing houses maintain the tradition of placing Sunday at the beginning of the week, rather than at its end, as only the second day of the weekend. A brief description of the annual round of Sundays is found in "Notes on the Services" (LE 10).

That every Sunday was viewed as the day of resurrection was demonstrated when church leaders were discussing the scheduling of an annual Easter Day. In the second century, some Christians kept an annual Pascha, along with their Jewish neighbors, on the first full moon after the spring equinox. Over the decades the emphasis of this celebration focused more on Jesus and less on the exodus. In the fourth century the decision was made that this annual festival, in line with every Christian celebration, had to occur on a Sunday. Thus Easter is set on the first Sunday after the first full moon after the spring equinox. The dates of Easter and related days through the year 2040 are listed in the leaders edition (LE 11). The fact that Christmas was not set on a Sunday indicates that when it became popular among Christians, it was not judged of primary Christian significance.

The biblical poem in Genesis 1 praises God for creating light on the first day of the week. Christians have used this opening chapter of the Bible to speak of Sunday worship as the vehicle through which the assembly is brought once again into the light of God. The Spirit hovers over the assembly on this first day of the week. Just as God gave light to the universe on this day, so Christ shines as our light on this day each week. Early Christians referred to baptism as enlightenment, and so Sunday is the weekly day to renew one's life in the light of new life.

Early Christians also had a strong sense that the resurrection of Christ inaugurated a new day. By referring to Sunday as "the eighth day," they expressed their faith that the baptized community was embarking on a new world in which sin and death had already been vanquished. The assembly gathers in the hope that the Spirit of God is present to transform human beings and recreate the world. When baptisms were moved away from a river bank to the interior of a church building, some fonts were designed as eight-sided in-ground pools. As the catechumens entered the water, they were drawn into the new eschatological reality of God's Spirit. The old world is past, and the believers live their days newly valued by the life of Christ.

Throughout the church's history, some Christians have used the Sunday designation found in Revelation 1:10, "the Lord's day." This day is the one made unique by the resurrection of Jesus Christ. By addressing Jesus with the Greek word for "Lord," *Kyrios*, early Christians not only designated Jesus as their Master but also were applying to him the title of authority that they gave to God. By the time of the writing of the Nicene Creed, the church referred also to the Spirit as "the Lord, the giver of life." Assembling on the Lord's day, we are drawn together into the life of the triune God.

Our lectionary recognizes the primacy of Sunday by assuming that many, if not most, Christians will attend worship services every Sunday. Thus there is continuity in the readings from one week to the next. This continuity is especially significant in the epistle readings, when over several weeks the semicontinuous selections develop a theological position or explain a Christian concept. The Protestant reformers found many of their key biblical truths in the epistles, and continuity is important for the sequential readings from the epistles to function as intended.

American consumer culture has popularized the idea that options must be provided so as to meet everyone's preferences. Thus some assemblies are questioning whether a weekly service on a day other than Sunday is an appropriate cultural adaptation of the liturgy. Among Roman Catholics, the hope that even persons who worked on Sunday morning would be able to worship on "the first day of the week" led to the practice of offering the first eucharist of Sunday on Saturday evening after sundown. Yet these churches have found it difficult to make of a Saturday evening mass a substantial communal celebration of the resurrection. If congregations decide that some other weekly service might be offered as an alternative to Sunday, care must be taken to give a theological reason for the scheduling. Sunday evening is a possibility. In some places in the primitive church, the Sunday gathering for worship was for the evening meal. Perhaps a Thursday service could build on a connection to Jesus' meal with his disciples before his death.

It is a good idea for congregations to reexamine the multiplication of services on a Sunday. Many churches with two or three Sunday services inaugurated this practice not to accommodate crowds but to provide options. Worship committees need to consider whether the desire for personal preference or the separation of one group of worshipers from another—families with children meeting apart from persons without children, youth segregated from adults—has not seriously harmed the unity of the congregation as one assembly gathered on the first day of the week around word and sacrament. One of the signs of the new day of the resurrection is the unity of diverse peoples in one body of faith. Perhaps the challenge to unify is a more appropriate Christian impetus than the proliferation of options. When the number of worshipers in a single congregation requires multiple services, it is best if the services on a Sunday are more identical than not, in order to resist the division of the congregation into separated groups. For example, choirs can sing at alternate services so as to keep one service from becoming in some way the preferred worship time.

The Green Sundays

For over half the calendar year Christians keep the discipline of a weekly assembly even though there are no regularly recurring festivals. A practical way to designate these standard Sundays is with the term "the green Sundays." The color for paraments and vestments is green, signifying the life of the church in the Spirit and recalling the tree of life that is Christ among us. Some churches use the terminology "ordinary time" for these Sundays (for example, Roman Catholic and Presbyterian churches). However, it is important that the label be understood, so as not diminish the extraordinary nature of each Sunday's celebration of word and sacrament. (In this usage, "ordinary" refers not to the quality of the Sunday but simply means that the Sundays are *ordered*—counted or numbered—rather than given specific or seasonal names.) Several of the thanksgivings at the table, I, VI, and IX, are especially appropriate for green Sundays, although any specific focus of the readings or the occasion may suggest other choices.

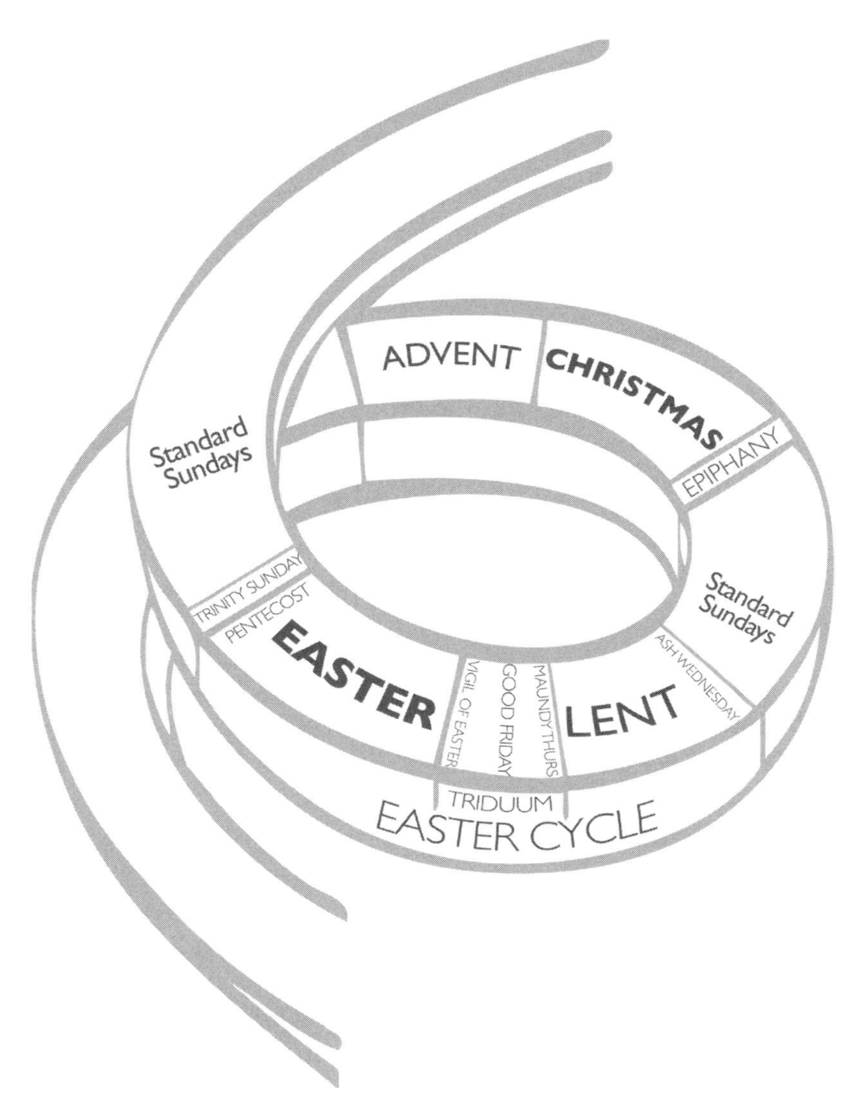

Fig. 1. *The church year can be seen as a continuing spiral, with the standard or green Sundays after Pentecost leading into the next Advent season.*

Two blocks of time in the liturgical year are marked by green Sundays. During the first block—the time after Epiphany—the Sundays between the Baptism of Our Lord and the Transfiguration of Our Lord are green Sundays. The time between Epiphany and Ash Wednesday was formerly called the season of Epiphany. It has never been a true season of the church year, but rather a time, like the time after Pentecost, to live with Christ and one another as the church.

People are sometimes confused by the varying lengths of these blocks of green Sundays. Easter is a variable feast, its scheduling computed cosmologically by the movements of the sun and moon. Because Easter is set on the first Sunday after the first full moon after the spring equinox, and this date varies from year to year, the number of Sundays between Epiphany and Ash Wednesday also varies, from three to eight. The number of Sundays that are dropped because of an early Lent are picked up after Pentecost. The Sunday directly before Ash Wednesday is the Transfiguration of our Lord, a Sunday adorned in white to celebrate the day when Jesus shone like the sun.

The second block of green Sundays occurs in the (approximately) six months that constitute the time after Pentecost. In *Evangelical Lutheran Worship*, green Sundays have been named in two ways. The calendar dates within which each Sunday will fall are stipulated, and the numerical ordering of each Sunday's place in the semicontinuous reading of the year's gospel is listed. Thus we have, for example, "Sunday, July 24–30, Time after Pentecost—Lectionary 17." That will be true in any year, no matter how early or late Easter falls. This naming convention provides a reliable, undated system as compared with "*N*th Sunday after Pentecost," since depending on the date of Easter, and therefore Pentecost, the Sunday that falls within the span of July 24–30, with its accompanying propers, could be the sixth or the eleventh Sunday after Pentecost—or anything in between.

Besides the calendar of Sundays and principal festivals (AE p. 14), *Evangelical Lutheran Worship* continues the use of a renewed listing of lesser festivals and commemorations (AE pp. 15–17). Although these are worthy of being observed on weekdays and as secondary focuses on Sundays, there is wisdom to not, in most cases, giving them preference over Sundays. Were the normal Sunday readings to be replaced with the readings for lesser festivals, commemorations, and occasions, the Sunday readings would be lost, and the focus on Sunday as the primary celebration of the resurrection might be obscured. For example, if a congregation uses the readings for Reformation Day and All Saints Day on the nearby Sundays every year, the readings for Sunday, October 23–29, Lectionary 30, and for Sunday, October 30–November 5, Lectionary 31, drop out, and in year C this includes the parable of the Pharisee and the tax collector and the story of Zacchaeus. For this reason, in most cases congregations are encouraged to consider observing such occasions in ways other than by replacing the lectionary selections that tie the green Sundays together. The focus of the lesser festival, commemoration, or occasion can be included in the green Sunday several ways: praying both prayers of the day; singing hymns appropriate to the festival; adding suitable petitions to the intercessions; including the names of those commemorated in the thanksgiving at the close of the intercessions; and displaying appropriate art in the worship space or on printed material.

Worship planners are encouraged to read the Notes on the calendar in the leaders edition (12–13), and determine how they are best applied in the local context. In some cases, it is recommended that the propers for a lesser festival falling on a green Sunday be used in place of that Sunday's propers—but that may not always be the best decision. For instance, on a Sunday, February 2, in year B, is it better for that particular assembly to observe the Presentation of Our Lord as proposed—hearing again the gospel of aged Simeon and Anna blessing Jesus that has been proclaimed just a few weeks earlier on the first Sunday of Christmas—or to hear the Sunday's gospel of the Beatitudes? Conversely, though the festival of St. Bartholomew is not one that is proposed to replace a Sunday's propers, a church named after that apostle may well want to lift up his witness by centering their celebrations on his commemoration.

Some churches in America have developed the practice of using Sundays for cultural observances, such as a national holiday or Mother's Day. Worship planners are urged to consider both how such observances may obscure the primary focus of Sunday as the proclamation of salvation in Christ and how any such narrow focus might alienate some members of the assembly, even as it intends to celebrate others. Such concerns are best dealt with in the intercessions and hymns, without interrupting the christocentric focus of the green Sundays. *Evangelical Lutheran Worship* provides hymns that attend to such observances: for national holidays, see especially "This Is My Song" (#887), and for Mother's Day, "Loving Spirit" (#397), or "Mothering God" (#735).

The green Sundays make clear that the liturgical year is not primarily a teaching technique for narrating the biography of Jesus. Rather, week in and week out, the church gathers to worship the triune God, sometimes to enact how a specific event in the life of Christ calls forth a festive celebration in the baptized community, but often to enact how word and sacrament inspire the assembly in its life of faith. The image of Christ as the tree of life on page 11 in the assembly edition depicts the Christ of the cosmos as the center of the full cycle of seasons. Every Sunday, winter, spring, summer, and autumn, we proclaim Christ, the wounds on his hands illumining our year like the stars in the sky.

The Christmas Cycle

Scholars argue over several competing theories as to the origins and development of the Christmas cycle. We do not know at what time of year Jesus was born. Early Christians did not observe Jesus' birth in any way. A celebration of Jesus' birth spread in the fourth century, to become nearly universal in the fifth. There were disparate worship patterns in Europe, the Middle East, and northern Africa, and several different calendars were used through these centuries. That the Nile flooded annually in early January and recalled to Egyptian Christians the new life of baptism is an example of the local realities that influenced the practice and meaning of this festive cycle. Since our data about the development of Christmas comes nearly entirely from some extant sermon texts, we have little access to what was in the minds and lives of most Christian believers.

One theory proposes that such a festival in late December has prehistoric roots in the peoples of the northern hemisphere observing the winter solstice. In the dark of the year, with vegetation dormant and food sources closely monitored, people celebrated with candles, evergreens, and feasting what must have seemed to them a magical restoration of the life of the universe: the return of the sun. According to this theory, even a Christian winter celebration is a natural phenomenon that requires little justification.

Many scholars propose that in the fourth century church leaders presented Christmas as an alternative to the Roman Saturnalia, with its excessive partying and consequent immorality. Sometimes this theory stresses Christmas as a Christian reaction against the culture. Other scholars see it as an insightful adaptation of the cultural practice, in which Christ was praised as the newborn sun. Other theories suggest that a cosmological calendar developed that tied the conception, birth, and death of both John the Baptist and Jesus to the four cardinal points of the sun, the equinoxes, and the solstices. According to this mindset, seminal events in Christian history coincide with the movement of the universe itself.[2]

There is evidence that some theologians of the fourth century resisted any celebration that relied on the New Testament's infancy narratives, because these stories seemed to conflict with the orthodox faith that the Son is equal with the Father. While the central date in the Western church was December 25, the preferred date in the Eastern church, January 6, focused not on Jesus' birth but rather on his baptism. That Christmas did not get transferred to a Sunday suggests its secondary status in the Christian worldview. Early theological focus of this festival was on the mystery of the incarnation, God present in our world. Liturgical and domestic attention to the baby Jesus seems not to have arisen until the twelfth century.

Similar confusion surrounds our understanding of the development of time before and after Christmas. In some places Advent was taught as an ascetic fast from rich food and sexual activity; in some places a forty-day unit replicated Lent; in some places the weeks functioned as catechumenal preparation for baptism at Epiphany; by 600, four Sundays became the usual length of a preparation for the celebration of Jesus' birth and baptism. Some places of the church came to observe twelve days of Christmas, culminating at Epiphany, January 6, and others forty days of Christmas, culminating at Candlemas, the Presentation of our Lord, February 2. Especially in the East, the focus on Jesus' baptism made Epiphany a primary occasion for baptisms.

The intensity of the Christmas celebration grew over the centuries. Several times through history, church leaders attempted to rein in the cultural excesses: in the colony of Massachusetts from 1659 to 1681, any celebration of Christmas was illegal. In the nineteenth century, gift-giving, especially to children, became commonplace, especially when St. Nicholas, commemorated on December 6, became associated with Christmas. In our time, Christmas partying extends throughout the month of December, usually concluding by December 26. (New Year is, in our culture, almost completely divorced from Christmas.) Much of the church has abandoned the observance of twelve or forty festive days following Christmas. In many Western cultural contexts, debates rage as to whether December celebrations, music, and decorations convey specifically Christian content, in which case they might be discouraged as being sectarian, or whether, like ancient solstice festivities, they are a natural human phenomenon in the northern hemisphere and should be granted nonreligious titles.

Evangelical Lutheran Worship invites us to see the Christmas cycle as a season beginning with the first of four Sundays in Advent, peaking in Christmas Eve and Christmas Day, and concluding twelve days later with the Epiphany of our Lord. Thanksgiving at the table III is especially appropriate for this entire season. In this prayer we bless God as the giver of life: the life in the universe, the life in human hopes and prophets' dreams, the life in Mary's story and in the Word made flesh. We acknowledge God's presence in the past, the present, and the future; we pray for the Spirit to come into us, for the word of God take flesh in us. The concluding doxology uses biblical language in calling God the Holy One of Israel, the Word of God incarnate, and the Power of the Most High. In this way we begin the liturgical year praising the triune God, who will effect in us now what was promised and experienced in the past.

Advent

The season. According to the Christian worldview, humans need God to bring us life and salvation, and Christmas celebrates this coming of God in the incarnation of Jesus Christ. Christians affirm that Christ comes not only in a past event but also in our present life and the world's unfolding future. So it is that Advent is not about Mary's pregnancy but about the church's continual prayer that God will come (the root meaning of "advent") to us, bringing life to a dying world. Advent in the northern hemisphere is a time to meditate on the darkness in the universe, the social order, the lives of many people, and our own hearts, and to pray for God's salvation and wholeness for all. The holy communion celebrated each Sunday of Advent brings to us the Christ who is ever present for us with mercy and joy.

The readings. The gospels for the first Sundays of Advent make clear that the season is not about waiting for baby Jesus to be born. We Christians gather to listen to his word coming to us today and tomorrow, and Jesus calls us to be ready whenever God arrives. The first readings include the promises in the Old Testament about how glorious that coming will be. The second readings encourage us in faith and call us to patience as we await the arrival of Christ. In all three years, the gospels for the second Sunday of Advent introduce us to John the Baptist, who begs us to prepare fully for the coming of Christ—in our understanding, and to live out our baptism into Christ. In the gospels for the third Sundays we listen to John as he calls us into hope and urges us to justice. Only on the fourth Sunday of Advent do we hear the narratives associated with the birth of Jesus and the parallels in the Old Testament about God's promised salvation.

The actions. Most churches use an Advent wreath. Select one sized proportionally to the space, and also use proportionality in the ceremony around the wreath. It is a beloved aid to prayer, but other aspects of the worship have far more importance. What can the Advent wreath communicate? As December progresses and the days grow darker, the increasing light signifies our prayer for the coming of the light of Christ into the world. The round circle of fire is an ancient human archetype, a symbol of the sun and the life it brings. The four candles need have no specific allegorical meaning. The old practice of two purple candles, one pink or rose, and the last purple arose in coordination with the readings and colors of older times. For our lectionary, the use of four white or blue candles is appropriate. The Advent wreath can be hung or placed on a stand in a prominent place, perhaps next to the font, and its candles can be lighted at the beginning of the service or before the prayer of the day. The Augsburg Fortress publication *Sundays and Seasons* provides prayers for use at the lighting of the candles.

Because our culture celebrates the turning of the year for the entire month of December, it is not easy to keep a prayerful Advent. It is appropriate to schedule all church-related Christmas parties during the twelve days of Christmas, rather than during the weeks of Advent. A children's pageant can be scheduled on Christmas Eve or the Sunday after Christmas. Such planning might be a welcome relief for harried families.

The propers. One of the liturgical treasures of Advent is the "stir up" prayers of the day. In *Evangelical Lutheran Worship*, on each of the four Sundays of Advent the prayer of the day begins with this medieval formula (the Latin word is *excita*). On the first and fourth Sundays, we ask Christ to bring us divine power, and on the second and third Sundays we ask God to renew our hearts and reform our wills. Traditionally it was said that these "stir up" prayers, interceding for the might of God's Spirit in us, accompanied the cooks as they stirred up their Christmas puddings.

The tone of a hopeful and prayerful time is reflected in such time-honored practices as singing the Kyrie but not the "Glory to God" nor any other canticle of praise. Hymn introductions and accompaniments may be kept modest. Advent options are provided among the prayers at the offering (AE p. 64) and the prayers after communion (p. 65). The great thanksgiving preface speaks counterculturally of the comfort and the judgment that the Redeemer brings. For the thanksgiving at the table, options III and XI are especially appropriate. During communion the singing of Taizé chants—#262, 472, 528, 751—can express our deep longing. The Advent section of *Evangelical Lutheran Worship* provides a rich collection of prayers and praises that beg God to come into the dark world with peace and joy. Some of these hymns are beloved standards of our tradition, such as "O Come, O Come, Emmanuel" (#257) and "Savior of the Nations, Come" (#263); some are new poetic prayers for wintertime, such as "Each Winter As the Year Grows Older" (#252) and "As the Dark Awaits the Dawn" (#261); some hymns come to us from other lands, such as "Come Now, O Prince of Peace" (#247) and "All Earth Is Hopeful" (#266). Singing Christmas hymns during Advent suggests that we have already arrived at the fullness of the season, and this practice diminishes the unique emphasis of Advent no less than would the singing of Easter hymns mar the observance of Lent. Perhaps the dismissal to "remember the poor" is an appropriate antidote to excessive holiday spending.

For the paraments and vestments, use the blue of our hope, the blue of our waiting. Hang long plain strips of blue fabric around the room. Wait until the fourth Sunday of Advent to put up Christmas decorations. If people want greens in the church before December 25, avoid the red bows or other additions that suggest the celebration is already here. As the days grow darker, use an increasing number of candles in the nave and sanctuary. Set the room's lights high enough for reading but low enough to keep company with the darkness outside.

Some Christians have suggested that the idea of Advent is dead, that the church cannot or ought not provide an alternative to the culture's month-long celebration, and thus that the church's Christmas season should begin in early December and last four weeks. *Evangelical Lutheran Worship* and the worship resources provided in its support reject this proposal. Rather, we are beckoned into a quiet and reflective Advent, a time to hope for God's salvation, Sunday and midweek services that feature sustained prayers for the world, a respite from the cultural hype of consumer happiness, a break from the commercial Christmas carols that blare in shopping malls. In Advent the church practices eschatological waiting, and in a culture that seeks instant gratification, this discipline in itself is good news from God.

Christmas Eve

The day. The church's celebration of the birth of Christ is now one of its primary festivals and ways of proclaiming the mystery of the incarnation. The most significant way that Christianity differs from its parent Judaism is in our belief that God became incarnate as a human being. Like Hinduism, Christianity believes that the transcendent deity took on flesh, entering into our experience as a human being, through whom the divine One effects the salvation of the world. Unlike Hinduism, Christians believe that there is only one such incarnation, who meets us weekly in word and sacrament and daily in our neighbors. To commemorate the incarnation, Christians keep December 25 as the feast of the Nativity of Our Lord. But, in keeping with an ancient practice that the celebration of a day begins on the prior evening, some Christians attend services only on December 24, Christmas Eve. Indeed, some Christian churches do not even schedule services on Christmas Day, although omitting worship on one of the primary festivals of the church is extremely questionable. Where that pattern is maintained, the challenge to plan an appropriate Christmas Eve service is even greater than when services on the two dates can share in the proclamation of the mystery of the incarnation.

The Revised Common Lectionary follows early medieval practice in that the Gospel of John is proclaimed at the church's primary festivals. Thus the lectionary appoints John 1 for Christmas Day and Luke 2 for Christmas Eve. Because many Christians attend church only on Christmas Eve, and to add the theological depth of John to the popularity of Luke, some assemblies are now designing their Christmas Eve service in the manner of Passion/Palm Sunday: the service begins with a procession to the crèche and the reading of Luke 2, and the service continues with the readings appropriate to John 1. This adaptation may be most appropriate for those churches that do not schedule a Christmas Day service.

Many congregations in North America schedule two different services on Christmas Eve. A common pattern is that the first, shortly after sundown, is geared to children and perhaps includes a pageant presented by the Sunday school. The second, scheduled late at night, evokes the allure of "midnight mass" and usually includes a candle-lighting ceremony. For both versions of Christmas Eve services, care must be taken to avoid the sentimentality with which our culture presents the story of Bethlehem. The challenge for worship planners is to provide a service satisfying to those people who attend services only at several festivals each year and yet be faithful to the Lukan text, which proclaims the surprising salvation of God that comes to the poor, living with injustice and sometimes under foreign domination.

The readings. The familiar Lukan narrative of the birth of Jesus is filled with details that pull us away from sentimentality. Luke situates this birth within the political world; the poor are manipulated by the governmental authorities; Jesus' journey to Bethlehem prepares us for his final journey to Jerusalem; his being a descendant of David sets up the paradoxical way that he was executed as king of the Jews; his rejection is suggested by there being no room in the inn; God comes to shepherds, who were underpaid and ritually unclean; and the angels, far from looking like sweet children, terrify the adults. Many Lutherans are less concerned than some other Christians with the historicity of these details, but we receive each as a symbol of the eventual death of Jesus and its meaning for the world. The first reading from Isaiah begins with light-dark imagery that recalls the winter solstice, and its praise of the newborn one corresponds with the social and political emphases of Luke. The call from Titus to live lives that are "self-controlled" is especially poignant at Christmastime. The readings have more resonance with the plight of migrant farm workers than they do with a visitor from the North Pole.

The actions. Some assemblies include a procession to the crèche at the beginning or during the service. The crèche can be set out in a prominent place, perhaps next to the font. The procession can include a crossbearer, candle-bearers, the assisting minister, and the presiding minister. The procession may include a young, old, or handicapped member who carries the image of baby Jesus and sets it in place. The figures of the crèche can be crafted by the children of the Sunday school or by a local artist. The procession may occur as part of the entrance rite, accompanied with a hymn about our journey to God in the manger, or the crèche might be the place from which the gospel is proclaimed.

If on the model of Passion Sunday both Luke and John are proclaimed, here is one possible order of service: an opening processional hymn; at the crèche, the proclamation of Luke 2, the prayer of the day for Christmas Eve, and the versicle "Let us go forth in peace, in the name of Christ. Amen." The procession resumes with the "Glory to God" and the prayer of the day for Christmas Day, followed by the readings for Christmas Day.

Many services include a ceremony of candle-lighting. The primary candle-lighting in Christian liturgies occurs at the Easter Vigil, where the candles, lit from the paschal candle, are signs of the light of the resurrected Christ that now illumines the entire assembly with the light of life. The meaning of the candle-lighting on Christmas Eve is less evident. Although many people find the ritual emotionally powerful, care must be taken that it be more than merely a sentimental moment. The flame can be passed throughout the room as the gospel procession is moving into place for the proclamation of the gospel, rather than during the singing of "Silent Night."

The service on Christmas Eve is one appropriate time to schedule the children's pageant.

If a Christmas tree is placed in the worship space for Christmas Eve and Day, it can be decorated in some distinctive way, such as the use of only stars. Setting up three undecorated evergreens leads Christmas toward Calvary, as does Luke 2.

The propers. The primary color for fabrics is white. For the canticle of praise, the "Glory to God" may be highlighted, since it repeats the song of the angels in Luke 2. The prayer of the day uses the imagery of light, especially significant for midnight services. Psalm 96, with its emphasis on the sovereignty of God that we see in Jesus Christ, might recall for us our Christmas trees by its reference to "all the trees of the wood" shouting for joy. Appropriate prayers for the time of the offering and after communion are provided (AE pp. 64, 65). The Christmas preface is a classic treasure, moving our hearts from the God we can see to the God we yet cannot. For the thanksgiving at the table, prayer III rehearses the meaning of the incarnation, moving from creation through the birth of Christ and into God's presence born among us.

Thanksgiving at the table XI, from the third or fourth century, expands on the meaning of the incarnation, while thanksgiving at the table IX is particularly festive. In *Evangelical Lutheran Worship*, beloved hymns and carols from Christian tradition have been joined by new compositions from around the world. We are dismissed, like the shepherds, to "share the good news."

Christmas Day

The day. In Christian tradition and according to the Revised Common Lectionary, Christmas Day is the primary celebration of the incarnation. Because Christmas Eve services in our culture tend to be oriented toward family, worship on Christmas Day is important especially for the many Christians who are not surrounded by family rituals during this holiday. Our culture's celebration of Christmas is largely founded only on warm emotions. Without needing to completely deny such an appeal, the church's ministry is founded on the gospel, and so it may well look for countercultural ways to celebrate the birth of Christ. The profound liturgy of Christmas Day is one such way.

The readings. Among the three sets of readings provided for the Nativity of Our Lord (which are not aligned to years A, B, and C), two are noted as being "particularly appropriate for Christmas Day." Set II, with its repeat of the Luke 2 gospel, was traditionally used for Christmas Dawn and might be a good choice for a midnight service if a full celebration of Christmas Day is offered on December 25. But the primary gospel for Christmas Day is John 1. In this magisterial poem, the Word of God speaks life and light into the world from the very beginning and has become flesh among us. Not only Jesus is a son of God, for through faith in this Word, we all become children of God. Christian theology has adopted this Johannine theology at the core of its Christology. In the rest of the third set of propers, Christians hear in the reading from Isaiah 52 a reference to the preexistent Word: "Your God reigns." The reading from Hebrews presents another New Testament explanation of the meaning of the birth of Christ: this Son is higher than angels and is the exact imprint of God's very being. Just as Luke 2 offers a stark contrast to consumerist gift-giving, so these readings present a strong theological corrective to cultural sentimentality over little baby Jesus.

The actions. Some worshipers, especially older adults, may not have been at Christmas Eve services. In this case a procession to the crèche with the reading of Luke 2 may be appropriate as the entry into the Christmas Day service. One suggestion for how this might be done is given under "Christmas Eve, the actions," above. Standing to receive the bread and wine is appropriate in light of the majesty of the readings: we are now seeing the return of God to Zion; we are purified by the Son of God; we have been given power to be children of God. A pre-service hymn sing with everyone joining in Christmas hymns and carols, some familiar, some new, may be as celebrative as a participating choir.

The propers. The primary color of fabrics is white. The propers of Christmas Day (the third set) present the incarnation in the broadest possible contexts. The prayer of the day asks that the gifts of the triune God come to us through Christ, the Redeemer. Psalm 98, another of the royal psalms, describes the victory of God within nature and the cosmos, and it lauds the arrival, not of an infant but of the judge of humankind. Appropriate prayers for the time of the offering and after communion are provided (AE pp. 64, 65). Particularly fitting for the thanksgiving at the table are III, which rehearses the themes of Advent and Christmas; VII, which is particularly celebrative; or XI, a meditation on the incarnation that comes to us from the third or fourth century. We are dismissed, Christ with us.

Sundays of Christmas

Despite what surrounds American consumers, Christian Christmas is not concluded by December 26. Each year will have one or two Sundays of Christmas. The gospels for the First Sunday of Christmas follow the child Jesus from his infancy through his childhood. Each of these gospels proclaims an aspect of the adult Christ: the infant Jesus already facing execution, Simeon foreseeing his death, and the child abiding not with his family but in the house of God. These Sunday readings pull us quickly away from any sentimentality that might have characterized our Christmas celebration. Some Christmas hymns in *Evangelical Lutheran Worship* that speak of both the manger and the cross are appropriate on these Sundays. Occasionally there is a Second Sunday of Christmas, which repeats John 1, a gospel with so much richness that it can serve the assembly twice in one year.

Some congregations will keep December 26 as the commemoration of Stephen, the first martyr; December 27, the commemoration of

John, apostle and evangelist; and December 28, the commemoration of the Holy Innocents, martyrs. Traditionally called "the companions of Christ," this group of martyrs and witnesses attests to the seriousness with which the Christmas season is to be celebrated. The baby Jesus, the Word become flesh, lived and died for the world, and Christian history commemorates those who lived and died because of Christ. Stephen sees Christ enthroned as he is slain; the gospel of John speaks of the death of Peter and the testimony of John; and the Holy Innocents recall to us the endless suffering and slaughter of innocent victims. Although it is no longer suggested that the propers for these lesser festivals replace those for the first Sunday of Christmas, some attention and reference to these days can serve to help worship planners shape Christmas festivities aware not only of happiness in families but also of a world filled with sorrow. January 1, the festival of the Name of Jesus, is a day, at the beginning of the secular New Year, to remember that at our baptism we were given the name of Christ and granted the blessing of the triune God.

Epiphany

The day. Like Easter, Christmas is a season, not merely a night and a day. Some churches have observed the season as lasting forty days, until February 2, Candlemas, but many others have kept Christmas for twelve days, concluding on January 6, Epiphany. Epiphany was anciently and is into the present a high festival in the Eastern churches. It was kept as a central baptismal day, especially where, early in the Eastern tradition, the baptism of Christ was seen as the proclamation of Christ's adoption as the Son of God. Already in the fourth century, Ambrose composed a hymn praising the epiphanies of Christ as divine, and the biblical references in Ambrose's hymn, such as the rising of the star and the changing of water into wine, have remained part of the extended proclamation of Epiphany in Christian churches. Over the centuries January 6, as Three Kings Day, became the primary domestic Christian celebration in the churches of southern Europe and then in the Caribbean, observed with processions, pageants, and gift-giving. That Epiphany usually falls on a weekday has led some contemporary churches to transfer the celebration to an adjacent Sunday. Although earlier worship resources referred to the Sundays between Epiphany and Ash Wednesday as the Epiphany season, this nomenclature has been changed to make more clear that the festival of Epiphany is the single date *concluding* the Christmas season, after which come a series of green Sundays and then the Transfiguration of Our Lord, constituting the time after Epiphany.

The readings. The gospel for Epiphany is the manifestation of Jesus Christ to the whole world as symbolized locally by King Herod, geographically by the visiting magi, and cosmically by the star. The gifts of gold, frankincense, and myrrh suggest not necessarily three visitors but the recognition of the infant as a king who, worshiped as divine, will be buried in a tomb. The first reading, from Isaiah 60, calls the people of God to rejoice at the light of God shattering the darkness of the world. According to the worldview of the poet, all people, even famous foreign kings, arrive to praise the light. It is an example of the influence of the Old Testament on the New that the kings of Isaiah 60:3 have in Christians' minds been superimposed upon the astrologers of whom Matthew writes. The reading from Ephesians is a magnificent passage that speaks of the mystery of the revelation of God in Christ. Epiphany calls us to join the magi as they see the surprising manifestation of the glory of God in the child Jesus.

The actions. Epiphany is an appropriate day for the children's Christmas pageant. Scheduling it at this time will assist the congregation in transferring things of Christmas from Advent to the twelve days of Christmas. Gifts of foodstuffs that are designated for a local food pantry can be added to the procession with bread and wine, to symbolize the gifts we now bring to the Christ child. In company with early centuries of the church, Epiphany is an appropriate time to schedule baptisms. As the magi brought their gifts to Christ, so we bring one another to a new life of baptism.

Some congregations schedule an evening event that includes the burning of the Christmas greens. Besides providing a festive occasion for the conclusion of the Christmas cycle and the end of Christmas decorations, the bonfire anticipates the fire at the Vigil of Easter.

The festival of Epiphany has become a traditional time for an annual house blessing. Gathering outside the house, Christians use chalk to mark the door frame of their home with the year and, often, the letters C, M, and B. The letters stand for Caspar, Melchior, and Balthasar, the names traditionally given to the magi, and also for the Latin phrase *Christe mansionem benedicat*, which translates "Christ, bless this house."

Throughout the year the markings will keep alive the prayer for God's blessing. Instructions for this home ritual, available in the Blessing for a Home in *Evangelical Lutheran Worship Pastoral Care,* can be distributed to worshipers beforehand.

The propers. The color for this day remains white. Three prayers of the day are offered: one likens our journey in faith to that of the magi, one uses the star and the treasures as metaphors for us, and one highlights the many nations for whom God's light shines. The use of Psalm 72 on Epiphany recognizes Jesus as the king to whom all the kings of the earth come in obeisance. King Jesus is praised as one who attends to the needs of the poor, an obvious contrast to many human kings. Similar to the praises of kings used in other parts of the ancient Near East, Psalm 72 expresses hopes that not only social justice but also natural fruitfulness will result from the reign of this monarch. The text of the great thanksgiving preface recalls several biblical stories that proclaim the manifestation of Jesus as the glory of God. Epiphany is the final service of the season for which the thanksgiving at the table III is appropriate.

Three hymns specifically focused on Epiphany are provided in *Evangelical Lutheran Worship*, and some in the Christmas section and several in the Time after Epiphany section are also appropriate. A beloved Epiphany hymn (also appropriate at many other times) is "O Morning Star, How Fair and Bright!" (#308), one of the two masterpieces for which Philipp Nicolai wrote both text and tune. Traditionally called the Queen of Chorales, *Wie schön leuchtet* praises the manifestation of God in Christ, also invoking the images of the morning star, King David, victory, a diamond, light, a flame, the body of Christ, the tree, heaven, food, treasure, warmth, fatherly love, ransom, the resurrected Christ, musical instruments, choirs, and Christ's presence with us on the journey of the coming year. For four hundred years, Christians have been enriched by this hymn.

Lent

Traditionally it was taught that Lent originated as an extension of several days of fasting in preparation for the Three Days of Maundy Thursday, Good Friday, and Easter. Scholars assumed that a short fast grew into a period of more or less forty days, in remembrance of Jesus' forty days of temptation. More recent scholarship suggests that Lent was actually an extension in the other direction, following Epiphany and the celebration of the baptism of Jesus. Early church documents indicate considerable variation in the development of the season. After the Council of Nicaea, a forty-day pre-paschal fast became nearly universal. Fourth-century sermons and pastoral catechesis describe Lent as a time to prepare catechumens for Easter baptism. Since it is through baptism that believers enter into the death and resurrection of Christ, the church saw the annual festival of the resurrection as the preeminent occasion for baptisms. In some locales the preparation for adult baptism was extensive. Lent was also the period of time that public sinners were excluded from the eucharist and assigned penance in the community, to be reconciled to the church and received back into communion on Maundy Thursday.

However, when both Easter and adult baptisms declined, and a medieval focus on personal sinfulness intensified, Lent became a forty-day period of penance for all Christians. Records suggest that in some places a rigorous fast in both food and sexual activity was preached. We have little knowledge to what degree Christians kept such a fast. The whole of Lent carried the biblical focus of the passion of Christ, which was seen as necessitated by personal sinfulness. This medieval pattern continues for some Christians to this day. Some midweek services focus on the details of Christ's passion, and individuals are urged to identify with his suffering or to demonstrate their penitence by "giving up" something for Lent.

However, in the twentieth century came a reevaluation of Lent. An emotional focus on the passion, proclaimed through a blending of the four gospels, did not correspond well with contemporary biblical exegesis, and for many people fasting had become so minimal that it had little meaning. Thus Lent according to the three-year lectionary resembles more the fourth century than the fourteenth. Easter is again seen as the optimal time for congregational baptisms. Lent is thus preparation for those baptisms as well as for the annual renewal in baptism for all Christians. Still, the medieval focus on amendment of life remains essential as the assembly prepares to renew its baptismal covenant, and each Sunday offers us the body of Christ given for the forgiveness of our sins.

Lent lasts forty days, as did the flood of Noah, Moses' visit with God on Sinai, Elijah's walk to the mountain of God, Jesus' temptation in the desert. According to one interpretation, the time from Ash

Wednesday until Holy Saturday results in forty days only by eliminating the Sundays, for Sunday is always a celebration of the resurrection. By that understanding, during Lent, Sundays are somewhat in Lent—for example, we do not say or sing "Alleluia"—and yet not fully subsumed under a medieval Lenten attitude of penitence.

There are three classic Lenten disciplines: giving of alms to the poor, praying, and fasting. Congregations may elect to focus their monetary gifts toward some specific need of those who are needy and suffering. Many congregations urge more regular prayer by providing daily devotional guides and by scheduling midweek services. Some contemporary Christians adopt a Lenten menu that limits the types of food eaten, for example, by refraining from foods high on the food chain, rather than one that imposes a severe restriction on the amount of food eaten. Some curtail the amount and expense of personal entertainment. Such attention to one's pattern of self-indulgence can have several different intents: to bond us with those who suffer; to allow for more money for alms; or to prepare our bodies and our minds for the fullness of the Easter celebration by practicing its contrast. It is important to stress that these or any other Lenten rituals are not necessary for gaining God's approval. Rather, they are behaviors that we choose to adopt to remind ourselves of the renewal of life that baptism calls forth.

The prayer after communion for Lent (AE p. 65) summarizes the meaning of the season. Our compassionate God gives us the bread of heaven. We join together, pilgrims through Lent on our way to Easter. Our fasting is a hunger for justice, our alms a making of peace, and our prayer the song of grateful hearts.

Ash Wednesday

The day. Because of the centrality of the paschal cycle in the life of the assembly, *Evangelical Lutheran Worship* has included the necessary parts of each liturgy in the pew edition. The Ash Wednesday service, which begins Lent, starts on page 251 of the assembly edition, and the Notes on the Services for Ash Wednesday are in the leaders edition, page 35. This service's ritual use of ashes reminds Christians of two central truths of the human condition. We are mortal. As Genesis 3 says, we are earth to earth, ashes to ashes, dust to dust. *Adam* comes from *adamah*, meaning soil, the human from humus. As well, we are sinners, and as Israelite tradition ritualized this, we repent in dust and ashes. As the depiction on page 251 suggests, we are encircled by the water of baptism, once again having the cross of Christ traced on our forehead.

An increasing number of Protestant churches are joining Roman Catholics by observing Ash Wednesday with the imposition of ashes. That so many even minimally observant Christians attend church to receive ashes indicates the human interest in symbolic ritual. Even without any biblical readings that speak of ashes, the ashes "say" the meaning of the day. We begin the Lenten forty days by acknowledging that we are mortal and will die, that we lament our sins, and that we need to be washed with baptismal waters.

The readings. The gospel is from Matthew's exacting Sermon on the Mount, from which comes the refrain "Be perfect." Matthew quotes Jesus as calling his followers to a life of generous and anonymous giving to those in need, an intense life of prayer, and a pattern of fasting that attracts no attention.

Two possible readings from the Old Testament are appointed. The first is from Joel 2, in which the prophet is urging the people to repent so that they will be saved from the plague that threatens. Everyone is called to the ritual of repentance, even nursing infants. When the text describes the coming of "a day of darkness and gloom," we need not imagine some specific threat; on this day of focus on human mortality, we know that the day of death is ahead of us all. The second option from Isaiah 58, a fierce call for social justice, uses the imagery of the fast and the ashes but calls the faithful to a life that embodies these rituals of repentance.

The epistle, from 2 Corinthians, emphasizes reconciliation with God. Paul understands that sin not only mars God's intent for humankind but alienates us from God. The reading includes the call of Lent: "Now is the day of salvation."

The actions. The entire liturgy for Ash Wednesday maintains a tone of solemn focus on sin and death. The people gather in silence, with no musical accompaniment. The opening song may be Psalm 51, the psalm traditionally associated with the penitent King David, or another such penitential psalm, Kyrie, litany, or hymn. Two options for the prayer of the day are offered: the first a classic prayer from Thomas Cranmer, the renowned liturgical author of the sixteenth-century Church of England, and the second a recent composition that incorporates the imagery of dust and ashes and makes reference to the Lenten disciplines. A substantial confession of sin follows the sermon. The litany makes clear that every individual sin affects the entire community and that we are all implicated by the sin of others. In the assembly we help one another by joining together to confess our joint sinfulness. So the prayer pleads in the plural voice for God to forgive a lengthy list of human failings. For this confession of sin, kneeling is appropriate.

During the twentieth century more and more Protestant churches adopted the symbolic ritual of the imposition of ashes. The ashes are made by burning the palms from last year's Palm Sunday, pushing the ashes through a sieve to achieve a fine powder, and then adding several drops of olive oil to the dust to render the ash easier to use. The number of people administering the ashes is dependent on the number of persons who will receive. The stations can be situated at the head of each aisle, at the usual place of communion, or by the font. Each minister holds in one hand a small glass bowl containing the ashes and with the thumb of the other hand marks the forehead of each participant with a clear cross. The ministers are also marked. The words spoken to each person during imposition, "Remember that you are dust, and to dust you shall return," make clear the meaning of the ritual: we turn to God, from whom comes life, because we know that we are creatures who face death. As the art on page 251 (AE) suggests, the hand that inscribes the cross is also a hand of blessing. At the conclusion of the imposition of ashes, the ministers need to wash their hands.

Evangelical Lutheran Worship offers one possible text as a call to repentance and an explanation of Lent. Depending on the content of the sermon, it may be helpful to read some such invitation to the imposition of ashes. Especially for those assemblies in which only some worshipers will receive ashes, thought must be given to what else, for example music, is offered during this time. If Psalm 51 has not yet been sung, here is the time. The ritual concludes with the prayer that we all be brought to the joy of Easter. Some of the assemblies who offer weekly communion emphasize the Lenten fast by omitting holy communion on Ash Wednesday. The idea is that on this solemn day we fast even from the food of the Lord's supper. Other Christians urge that especially on this day of penitence, our receiving the body and blood of

Christ is necessary. Each congregation's planning team should consider whether communion is included on this day.

The propers. If holy communion is included, thanksgivings at the table IV, VIII, and X are appropriate. The great thanksgiving preface for the day alerts us to the journey back to baptismal waters that is our Lent. The service concludes with a prayer written for *Evangelical Lutheran Worship* that rehearses all the elements of Lent: journey, forty days, renewal in baptism, alms, prayer, fasting, and the image of treasure with which the gospel reading concludes. The dismissal is a substantial reminder of all that Lent might become for those who "keep a good Lent."

Sundays in Lent

The days. The Sundays in Lent may be understood to be excluded from the forty-day count—note the preposition "in" rather than "of"—yet for many Christians these Sundays are in fact the sole way that Lent is observed. The color of fabric is purple, in remembrance of the royalty of Christ, who reigns from the cross. Some congregations, recalling the Israelite ritual of sorrow described in the Old Testament, use a fabric that resembles sackcloth. The tone of the season is restraint in all things. Although Christian baptism may be administered at any time in extraordinary circumstances, these Sundays of the year are the least appropriate times to celebrate the death and resurrection of Christ by scheduling baptisms.

The readings. The first Sunday of Lent in each cycle is the story of the temptation of Christ. In Matthew's gospel for year A, the narrative of Jesus' withstanding temptation is contrasted with the story in Genesis 2 and 3 about the woman and the man giving in to temptation. The readings call us all to see ourselves to be like the woman and the man, and thanks to our baptism, also like Christ, attended by angels. In year B, the brief Mark narrative of the temptation includes the account of Jesus' baptism and his stay for forty days with the wild beasts, and this reading is complemented by God's promise to Noah after the flood that the divine covenant of mercy shines like a rainbow in the skies. In year C, Luke's telling of the temptation is flanked by the creed in Deuteronomy 26. As we remember our baptism, we recite our creed, which like that of the Israelites rehearses the many ways that God has saved us, bringing us from death into life.

According to the three-year lectionary, Lent is a time for renewal of the life of the baptized. The readings for year A are especially designed for use in any year that a congregation is scheduling adult baptisms at the Easter Vigil. Sunday adult forums or midweek Lenten services may provide opportunities for studying the year A gospels from John, which since the fourth century have been used to prepare the catechumens for their baptism and to teach its meaning.

In year A, the first of the great Johannine Lenten narratives, appointed for the second Sunday, is John 3:1-17, in which Nicodemus seeks out Jesus at night, inquiring about the new birth that comes from God. The church uses the imagery of John 3 to liken baptism to the waters of the womb and the sacrament itself to a second birth, a birth "from above." On the third Sunday of Lent is the narrative from John 4 of the woman at the well. Here Christ himself is the water we need, the living water we drink so that we may live. On the fourth Sunday is the narrative of the man born blind. The early church called baptism "enlightenment" and used this story as a metaphor to describe baptism as the light that calls us out of darkness. Jesus instructs the blind man to wash away his blindness in the pool of Siloam, and this pool is another metaphor for the water of baptism. On the fifth Sunday of Lent, the narrative is the raising of Lazarus. As Augustine proclaimed when preaching on this text, we are all dead in our sins: some of us, he said, are already stinking! In baptism we, like Lazarus, are brought back to life. Perhaps in the tears of Jesus we see yet another metaphor for God's baptismal mercy. The hymn "Tree of Life and Awesome Mystery" (#334) is a new composition that provides one stanza for each Sunday of year A.

Year B features other passages from John: on the third Sunday, the cleansing of the temple; on the fourth Sunday the section from John 3 that likens Christ on the cross to the serpent in the wilderness, as well as the contrast between darkness and light; and on the fifth Sunday, Jesus' teaching about the grain dying so it may bear fruit. In year C come several familiar passages from Luke: the metaphor of the mother hen, the parable of the fig tree, and the parable of the runaway son. The fifth Sunday of year C is the Johannine story of Mary of Bethany anointing Jesus' feet, a story that, quite different from Luke's account of a nameless weeping sinner, focuses on the coming death of Christ. Each of these readings gives us imagery to describe the salvation given by Christ and the meaning of baptism in our lives.

The Old Testament readings include a remarkable collection of beloved passages: in year A, the call of Abram, the water from the rock, the anointing of the boy David, the valley of the dry bones; in year B, the promise to Sarah and Abraham, the ten commandments, the serpent in the wilderness, the promise of a new covenant; and in year C another account of God's promise to Abram, the invitation to "come to the waters," the first harvest in Canaan, and a promise of water in the desert. The epistle readings, especially from Romans, 1 Corinthians, Ephesians, and Philippians, are chosen to complement the particular emphases of the gospel. These lectionary choices provide treasures for the renewal of our lives as the baptized.

The actions. Congregations may choose to adapt their usual Sunday patterns in some way so as to distinguish Lent from the green Sundays. Perhaps there will be no flowers decorating the chancel, or only greens, or only purple blossoms. Flat pita bread or unleavened bread can be served at communion, with freshly baked leavened bread awaiting the Sundays of Easter. Communicants may kneel to receive the bread and wine, to contrast with the Sundays of Easter, when they will stand. After the service, the coffee time can refrain from serving sweets or fancy foods until the Sundays of Easter. Congregations may avoid scheduling parties and celebrative events. Restraint in all things is a sound Lenten practice.

The propers. The services of Lent begin with a rite of confession and forgiveness or thanksgiving for baptism. Either is best conducted from the font. A Kyrie is appropriately sung, but not an opening hymn of praise. Some assemblies use the Great Litany (#238) as an entrance hymn. The prayers of the day use language from the readings to pray for the renewal of our lives. The psalms are chosen not only to respond to the first reading but also to lead us toward the gospel reading. Before the gospel reading the Lenten acclamation replaces the Alleluia, since by long tradition "Alleluia" is not said or sung during Lent. It is good to keep this tradition in mind when choosing hymns and choir selections. The Lenten preface holds together the emphases of Lent: baptismal renewal, amendment of life, and the coming paschal celebration. For the thanksgiving at the table, especially IV, VII, and X are appropriate. A particularly fine prayer after communion is provided on page 65. During Lent, the dismissal call to "remember the poor" is especially apt.

Sunday of the Passion / Palm Sunday

The day. Christians keep the Sunday that begins Holy Week with a service that includes both action and story, both the celebration of the palms and the proclamation of the passion. The assembly should be prepared for a service that, marking the outset of the holiest week of the Christian calendar, will take longer than a usual Sunday service. Worship planners are urged not to omit a sermon but to encourage the preacher to deliver a short but intense homily on the meaning of the passion, since both the palm procession and the passion require interpretation for the faithful. *Evangelical Lutheran Worship* includes the necessary additions to the liturgy on pages 256–57 of the assembly edition, and suggestions for the service are given in Notes on the Services (LE 36). As the art on page 256 (AE) suggests, the day celebrates both the palm procession and the crucifixion of the one called King of the Jews.

The gathering on Palm Sunday. The liturgy begins with the much-beloved ritual of the palms. At least since the fourth century, and universally in the church since the eighth, Christians begin Holy Week with a palm procession in or around the church or at a pilgrimage site, so as to insert themselves into the narrative of the week and to recognize Christ coming into their midst in the present. We line the path to welcome Christ, we follow the cross into the church, just as in five days we will call for his crucifixion.

This ritual calls for careful preparation. For the palms, many congregations order palms sent from climates in which these trees grow. It may be instructive for everyone to learn something about the locales where the palms originate. Some congregations order enough so that each worshiper can carry a substantial frond, rather than a single spindle. The Web site of Lutheran World Relief has information about how to order ecologically friendly palms. Congregations may decide instead to gather branches from local trees or bushes. Some Eastern Europeans have substituted pussy willows for the palms that were historically unavailable to them. Children can be helped to construct a cross out of their palm frond during the service.

For the palm procession, worshipers assemble outside the church or, if the weather is uncooperative, in some space outside the nave. Ushers distribute both the worship books (or liturgy offprints) and the palms, assisting everyone to their places. After the opening call and response, the Palm Sunday narrative according to one of the four gospels is read. Following the reading, the palms are blessed. To "bless" the palms and those who carry them means to bless God for them and to ask, in the words of the Aaronic blessing beloved by Luther, that the Lord's face shine on us.

The assembly then processes into the church, waving its palms. Many assemblies sing the hymn "All Glory, Laud, and Honor" (#344), which legend says was written on this feast day in the year 821 by bishop Theodulph of Orleans. Imprisoned for suspected political machinations, he composed this text while the palm procession passed by his jail cell. Because this hymn is so traditionally associated with the palm procession, it is printed in place in the Passion Sunday liturgy (AE p. 257). Thought must be given to how to keep a moving crowd singing together. A brass instrument may be helpful, and percussion accompaniment can help keep the procession lively.

Of the three possible prayers of the day, the first, coming down to us from the eighth century, speaks of the passion and death of Christ; the second is a recent composition that focuses on the kingship of Christ; and the third holds together the two contrasting emphases of the day.

The readings. Walking into the church waving palms readies the assembly for its own experience of Jerusalem, which continues with the full reading of the passion account from Matthew, Mark, or Luke. Each year the gospel is prefaced with a first reading from Isaiah 50. Its description of the suffering one is heard by Christians as pointing to Christ, and its language is echoed in the passion narrative. The epistle each year from Philippians 2, probably one of the earliest Christian hymns, proclaims the humiliation of Christ, who chose death on the cross, whom on this Sunday we praise as Lord.

The lengthy reading of the passion ought not be shortened, but rather presented so expertly as to hold everyone's attention. Three lectors may divide up the reading; the assembly may be given short parts to speak; the choir may sing one of the available choral renditions; several soloists may use a medieval chant to proclaim the reading. Some assemblies may be gifted with an exceptionally talented lector whose proclamation of the two chapters is spellbinding. It is unlikely that a skit would serve to deepen the people's reception of the narrative. It is common for the assembly to remain seated until the reading arrives at the crucifixion itself: for example, at Matthew 27:32, Mark 15:21, and Luke 23:32. Some few assemblies, recalling that until the seventeenth century churches provided no seating, may decide to stand for the entire reading.

The propers. The procession with palms replaces an opening rite of confession or remembrance of baptism. Psalm 31, a lament of the suffering one, points Christians toward the passion. The great thanksgiving preface, by calling the cross a tree, is like the entire service, holding together the joy of the palms with the sorrow of the crucifixion. For this day, thanksgivings at the table IV, VII, or X are especially appropriate. Because of the length of the service, thanksgiving IX may be preferred. The assembly may be invited to wave their palm fronds once again as it sings the words, "Blessed is the one who comes in the name of the Lord. Hosanna in the highest." As befits the tone of solemnity, worshipers may kneel for communion. For the prayer after communion, the Lenten option (AE p. 65) once again prays for sustenance throughout the forty-day journey. The Christian tradition has collected many hymns that focus on the passion of Christ. Hymns #340–354 are particularly appropriate for this Sunday of the Passion.

The Three Days as the Center of the Year

In the ancient Mediterranean world, the spring equinox was celebrated as a central religious event. Winter and its threat of starvation were over; plants were coming back to life; night and day were equal. Most religions attest that there is no birth without pain, no meal without the death of animals and plants. So some nomadic peoples took the occasion of the hinge between winter and summer to offer to the deities a lamb from their flock. With this perennial gesture of a burnt offering, they expressed their joy at having survived another winter and their hopes for the life of the earth and their own flocks and herds. The Canaanites celebrated an agricultural springtime festival at the time of the barley harvest, the new crop of food symbolizing the fruitfulness of the new year.

The Bible describes Passover as the way the Israelites kept the spring equinox. On the first full moon after the spring equinox, each household was to slaughter a lamb and share a festival meal. By this domestic ritual they recalled that God had saved them, not from a winter of starvation but from slavery in Egypt. Memory has been layered on top of cosmology. As well, for a week in spring only, bread baked from the new barley was eaten, and no leaven left over from the previous year was used. All was new.

The Bible says that Jesus was executed at Passover and rose from the dead on the Sunday after the Passover. By the middle of the second century, some Christians had layered onto the Jewish Passover the primary celebration of their identity, which was rooted in the death and resurrection of Christ. Initially this annual solemn Christian Pascha stressed the death of Christ. The word *Pascha*, actually relating to the Hebrew *pesach,* meaning passover, was thought to connect with "passion." Jesus, the lamb sacrificed for the life of the world, replaced the paschal lamb described in Exodus 12. This Christian observance, observed on the Jewish Passover, might fall on any day of the week.

In the late second and third centuries, the festival evolved into an annual celebration of Christ's resurrection and the primary occasion for baptisms. The word *pascha* became connected with the idea of passage through the sea, for through Christ's resurrection all the baptized are brought through the waters into the new life of the Spirit. The narrative of the crossing the sea in Exodus 14–15 became central to the celebration. Since Sunday is always the day of the resurrection, Christian Pascha came to be scheduled on the first Sunday after the first full moon after the spring equinox. Because Christian ritual took place in the assembly rather than in the family, the domestic Passover meal had been replaced with a celebrative sharing of the bread and wine within the whole community of the baptized. Thus had the Jewish seder evolved into the Christian vigil of Easter.

By the fourth century this annual festival of the resurrection was spread out over the Three Days all through the Mediterranean world. In part, Christians are commemorating the events in the life of Jesus by meeting on the dates of his last supper and footwashing, his death, and his resurrection. However, since each of these separate events finds its meaning only by attending to the three together, the rituals of the Three Days were seen as one ritual, with only one dismissal, on Easter. Because baptism is believers' entry into Christ's resurrection, the Three Days were the culmination of the catechumens' preparation for baptism, and the baptisms were an essential part of the Easter Vigil. Augustine, whose writings became so important throughout Christian history and especially to Martin Luther, was baptized by Ambrose at the Easter Vigil in 387.

The Three Days—Lost and Found Again

The centuries brought many cultural and religious changes. The baptizing of infants throughout the year meant that baptism became disconnected from Christ's resurrection. Symbolically rich and biblically intense liturgical practice more and more moved from parish churches to monasteries and convents. For Christians whose lives were marked by considerable unrelieved pain, focus on the sufferings of Christ overtook the celebration of new life. Medieval attention to personal sin led to more private devotional practice and to less focus on the assembly's life together. At the time of the Reformation, its leaders worked to alter the medieval worship patterns but did not attempt a revival of the ancient practice of the Three Days.

During the centuries that the Three Days was no longer a vibrant congregational ritual, several alternate Holy Week rituals came to be used, also by Lutherans. Protestant Holy Week rites have tended to accentuate the role of the preacher in telling the story of Christ's passion. Services based on the Franciscan devotion of the Stations of the Cross trace the way that Jesus walked. The Devotion of the Three Hours, created in 1687 by a Jesuit priest in Peru, combines the four gospels and presents sermons based on "the seven last words" of Jesus. A Lenten devotion called Tenebrae developed out of the morning prayers of medieval monastic communities and includes psalms of lament, the reading of the passion, the extinguishing of candles, and a frightening crash. These rituals consider the death of Christ as an event separated from his resurrection. To balance these services of penitence and mourning at the cross, Easter Day came to focus attention on the moment of Christ's resurrection. Moravians developed the Easter sunrise service, and West Coast American Protestants popularized this ritual of celebrating the resurrection as they observed the sun rising. Many churches developed Easter Day into an extravagant celebration, with banks of flowers often obscuring the place for the meal and external musicians hired to provide extraordinary music for the largest worshiping assembly of the year.

The rites that deal separately with Christ's death and with his resurrection had led to Holy Week rituals that focused only on sorrow for personal guilt and to Easter services that celebrated the life of spring quite apart from the suffering and death of Christ. However, in the twentieth century, some Christian churches rediscovered the genius of the Three Days celebration and came to appreciate its pattern of holding in one theological understanding the passion, death, and resurrection of Christ. The current worship resources of the Evangelical Lutheran

Church in America and the Evangelical Lutheran Church in Canada, the Episcopal Church and the Anglican Church of Canada, the United Methodist Church, the Presbyterian Church, and the Roman Catholic Church all include similar versions of the restored ancient liturgies, and slowly these ancient rites are replacing less theologically profound patterns that had developed in their absence. The Ministers Edition of *Lutheran Book of Worship* did include the restored rites of the Three Days, but many pastors did not undertake to replace the parish's Holy Week observances with the Three Days pattern. *Evangelical Lutheran Worship* includes the service orders in the assembly edition, pages 258–270. There is no need for congregations to print out the texts of the service orders: a single sheet of paper listing hymn numbers and page references may be helpful. The full service orders are in the leaders edition, pages 628–653, with Notes on pages 36–42.

One method that any community uses when renewing its identity is to retell its story. Past events are kept in mind over the centuries because the story is repeatedly told. In the opening verses of Luke, the evangelist writes that the story of Jesus must be recorded and retold over the generations. So during the Three Days we hear the story of the passion, death, and resurrection of Christ as told in the Gospel of John. Through the centuries, John's gospel has been recognized as proclaiming most fully the divinity of Christ. So for these services that focus on his suffering and death it is theologically important to proclaim that this human is the incarnate God. The synoptic versions of this narrative are appointed for Passion/Palm Sunday and for Easter Day, Matthew in year A, Mark in year B, and Luke in year C. Thus each year worshipers hear two full accounts of the story of Christ's suffering, death, and resurrection.

The second method that communities use when renewing their identity is to enact the *meaning* of the story. An example of such enacted meaning is found in Genesis 1: Jews are to live out the meaning of God's ordered creation by keeping the day of sabbath. The ritual behavior brings into the bodies of the faithful the values they heard in the story. In the liturgies of the Three Days, communal symbolic actions invite the assembly into the meaning of the story that has been proclaimed.

One significant emphasis of the Three Days is its sense of time. Medieval patterns of Holy Week and Easter Day focused on the life of

Jesus, and so liturgical practice sought to return the minds of believers to the first century. However, a restored observance of the Three Days stresses instead that the church is the community born again by the resurrection of Christ, who annually renews its commitment to the baptized life. The mystery of the death and resurrection of Christ is not primarily a past event but is experienced in the present by the baptized community that is drawn by the Spirit into a future promised by God. On the paschal candle is inscribed the Alpha and Omega, symbolizing that Christ is the beginning and the end, and this year's date, reminding us that salvation is now. We need not dress up someone to represent Jesus: we together have been made into the body of Christ.

Some Lutheran congregations already use and honor these Three Days rites, while others are only beginning to replace their traditional practice with these service orders. Whether establishing new practices or moving more deeply each year into worship using these forms, congregations will be assisted in their Three Days celebration if there has been both sufficient education and broad involvement of every segment of the congregation. Those who are already accustomed to these rites find in *Evangelical Lutheran Worship* a slightly revised version of the familiar ritual pattern. Those for whom these services are new are welcomed into these old-new rites.

Ritual gains one layer of its personal and communal value in its repetition. Thus ritual must be learned, never judged on single usage. It becomes beloved over time. The restoration of the Three Days is an example of much reform of Christian worship, when congregations have been urged toward a pattern of worship that is not newly invented, not even dating from when our grandparents were young, but much older, a pattern used by Christians through the centuries. *Evangelical Lutheran Worship* and its attendant resources present these old-new rites with the confidence that they will effect for the entire assembly a more profound entry into the death and resurrection of Christ than did previous Holy Week services. The involvement of multiple leaders and participants will assist a congregation with a pattern of worship with which it might be unfamiliar.

Maundy Thursday

The day. Since ancient times, the sharing of a meal marked the establishment of a new relationship in the community. Food enlivens both one's own body and the body of the community, since the one table unites those at table into one assembly. The Bible tells many stories of Jesus' meal practice, but this last supper at the outset of his passion became paramount in the community's memory. On this last supper before his death, Matthew, Mark, Luke, and Paul all say that he established the meal of bread and wine as permanent signs of the covenant God made with us through Christ. The meal makes Christ present, and throughout the ages his followers could receive the benefits of his suffering, death, and resurrection in their sharing of the meal.

Matthew, Mark, and Luke report that this last supper was a Passover meal. It may be that the evangelists were making a theological point rather than a historical one. At Passover, the lamb signified God's covenant of life, and the unleavened bread recalled "the bread of affliction" of their sufferings during slavery. For the Christian community, the lamb is Christ himself. The bread of affliction is the body of Christ, and the blood on our doorposts the sign of God's salvation.

The Gospel of John also describes this last meal before Jesus' death, and as usual from the Fourth Evangelist, the account adds a layer of interpretation. In John 13, the gathered assembly receives both a shared meal and an enacted symbol. The new relationship established in the death and resurrection of Christ is to be a covenant of humble service, one to another. Jesus, the lord and master, performs the task of a household servant. If readers of Matthew, Mark, and Luke might imagine the phrase "the body of Christ" in an otherworldly or disembodied way, John places in our hands the actual feet of the next person at table. The title *Maundy* comes via Middle English from the Latin word for command, referring to Jesus' command that we are to love one another.

Thus according to Matthew, Mark, and Luke, we are to share the meal, and so become the body of Christ; and according to John we are to wash one another's feet, and so practice the new covenant of love for one another. In the Three Days, the service for Maundy Thursday (AE pp. 258–261) includes both the proclamation of Jesus' last supper and the symbolic enacting of the footwashing. The art on page 258 represents this pattern of worship: the tree of the cross is rooted in the service of footwashing and stands behind the eucharistic table. Because the Three Days is seen as one service, there is no concluding blessing at the close of the Maundy Thursday service.

The readings. The first story proclaimed on Maundy Thursday is the account of the Passover from Exodus 12. The angel of death will punish the oppressors, but the blood of the lamb will mark the door of the Israelites, and so God's chosen people will live. For Christians, the blood that saves us from death is the blood of Christ, shared in the meal at this service, held in mind in the devotion of Good Friday, and celebrated with story and song at the Easter Vigil. The blood smeared on the doorposts is like the cross traced on our forehead at baptism—a reminder of *whose* we are. The second reading, from 1 Corinthians, comes from Paul's reprimand to those first-century Christians at whose communal meals the poor were treated less well than were the rich. Paul narrates the account of the last supper, urging the Corinthians to establish ritual patterns that reflect the communal meaning of the Lord's death.

As we stand to hear the gospel, we know ourselves to be like the ancient Israelites, saved through the sacrifice of the lamb, and like the Corinthian community, called to become a truer proclamation of the death of our Lord. The gospel for Maundy Thursday is John's account of Jesus' last meal with his followers before he died. In John's chronology, set one day earlier than the synoptics, the slaughtering of the Passover lambs coincides with the crucifixion of Christ. John uses the memory of the last supper to emphasize that thanks to our incorporation into Christ, we are to love one another, serving one another in Christ's new covenant of love.

Thus we begin the Three Days by receiving Christ as the Passover lamb, the host at our meal, and the servant of all. Christians ought not conduct more-or-less Christianized seder meals, of which some contemporary Jews might approve and others would be offended, even outraged. On Maundy Thursday the assembly is eating the blessed meal with Christ, and the Easter Vigil celebrates the Christian way to escape from death and cross the sea into life. Congregations that wish to learn about the medieval and contemporary Jewish seder are urged to do so in educational settings, rather than by adapting the most sacred ritual of the Jewish people for their own use.

The actions. The first action unique to the liturgy of Maundy Thursday is an amplified order for confession and absolution. Worship planners will be assisted by attending to the Notes on the Services (LE 36–37). During medieval times, church members who were public sinners were excommunicated for the weeks of Lent, during which time they were to perform appropriate penance. These shunned members were received back into the church's fellowship on Maundy Thursday, in time to celebrate Easter, and hearing John 13, the community practiced Christ's command to love one another by forgiving them. Current practice has adapted and extended this ritual of forgiveness to include us all. During Lent we have considered the many ways that we do not live out our baptism and are all in need of forgiveness. The Maundy Thursday form for confession and forgiveness can include the laying on of hands, with an individual declaration of forgiveness, for any in the assembly who so desire it; many Christians find this ritual personally significant. If the number of participants is large, a continuous procedure is helpful.

After the sermon is the footwashing, which has been practiced on this day at least since the seventh century. There are a variety of ways to carry out this footwashing. In some churches the ordained minister washes the feet of twelve people, as if repeating the action of Christ. However, since all the baptized are the body of Christ, it is appropriate for members of the assembly to signify their service to one another by joining in the ceremony. As the rubric in *Evangelical Lutheran Worship* states, "The ministers and people may wash each other's feet."

Here is a simple yet solemn way to conduct the footwashing. Before the service, several stations are set up, depending on the anticipated number of participants. The stations can be at the places of communion or next to the font. At each station is a chair, a pitcher of warm water, a large stainless steel basin to catch the water, and a stack of small white towels. The first participants, perhaps the choir, come forward and sit in the chairs. The vested leaders of the liturgy kneel down in front of them. With one hand, the leader cradles each foot in turn by the ankle, and with the other hand the leader pours from the pitcher clean water over the foot, so that the water falls into the basin; then, after setting the pitcher down, the leader dries the feet with a towel. Each of the people whose feet have been washed then kneels before the next person to do the next washing. Thus everyone first is washed, and then does the washing. When all participants have had their feet washed, the vested leaders are the last to get their feet washed. Children can perform this ritual with intensity, and even toddlers can help their parents to dry the wet feet. Congregations do well to alert everyone in advance to wear footwear that can easily be removed.

The action to conclude the service is the stripping of the altar. Originally, this practice was the way that the altar linens were washed annually. During medieval times, each adornment of the sanctuary was assigned an allegorical meaning, so that each removal suggested the stripping of the body of Jesus before the crucifixion. For some contemporary Christians, the emptying of the sanctuary is a metaphor for both Christ and the church being emptied for death. As a lament psalm is sung, the assembly watches as the ministers assisted by several worshipers extinguish the candles and then carry into the sacristy the candles, the cross, the communion vessels, the books, any flowers, the paraments, the altar linens, any wall hangings, even any extra furniture. "You have laid me in the depths of the pit, . . . and darkness is my only companion," says Psalm 88. "Be not far from me, for trouble is near, and there is no one to help," says Psalm 22. Finally a bare altar-table stands naked in an empty chancel in a stripped church. Our eyes have prepared our minds for Good Friday. There is no dismissal. The assembly leaves in silence.

The propers. Psalm 116, appointed as the people's response to the first reading, uses the imagery of the Israelite Passover in speaking of the cup of salvation and the sacrifice of thanksgiving. The psalm identifies us as God's servant. Freed from our bonds, like the ancient Israelites, we are to serve. Like the entire liturgy, the psalm holds together the cup of salvation and the life of service. Depending on the setting chosen for singing the psalm, care may need to be taken that the concluding Hallelujah is omitted on this solemn day.

Two options for the prayer of the day are provided. The first, written for *Lutheran Book of Worship*, and the second, written for the 1993 Presbyterian *Book of Common Worship,* both build upon the Johannine gospel reading. The great thanksgiving preface to be used throughout Holy Week, like the Three Days itself, holds together the suffering and death of Christ with the life that God gives. Thanksgivings at the table IV, IX, or X are particularly appropriate for Maundy Thursday.

The hymn classically sung during the footwashing, more than a millennium old and often known by its Latin title "Ubi caritas et amor," is found in *Evangelical Lutheran Worship* in three forms: "Where Charity and Love Prevail" (#359), "Ubi caritas et amor," (#642), and "Where True Charity and Love Abide" (#653). Some assemblies sing the Ghanaian hymn "Jesu, Jesu, Fill Us with Your Love" (#708), during the footwashing. "Love Consecrates the Humblest Act" (#360) and the newer "Great God, Your Love Has Called Us" (#358) encapsulate the emphases of the day.

Good Friday

The day. Good Friday is a day of paradox. Even its name attempts to articulate a truth beyond words. One might assume that the commemoration of the leader's death would call forth unmitigated mourning among the followers. However, even on this second of the Three Days we assemble as people of the resurrection. Thus the restored Holy Week rites use paradox in keeping this Good day. We are not pretending that Christ is still dead, but rather in solemn devotion we acknowledge that the cross before us is God's gift of life.

Traditionally, this is the one day in the year that the church does not pray the great thanksgiving and celebrate holy communion, since the eucharist is always a celebration of Christ's resurrection. The service is a spare devotion at the foot of the cross. Some churches schedule the service around three in the afternoon, the hour of Jesus' death, but the ritual does not enact his death or burial. As the art on page 262 of the assembly edition suggests, surrounded by the passion story, we gather around the cross, from which flows the baptismal water through which the Spirit has brought us into his death. The assembly edition includes the service order (AE pp. 262–265), with Notes on the Service in the leaders edition (pp. 38–39).

The readings. The accounts of Jesus' passion and death in Matthew, Mark, and Luke focus on Jesus' suffering. These synoptic accounts are proclaimed on Passion/Palm Sunday, Matthew in year A, Mark in B, and Luke in C. Their description of the sufferings of Jesus provide a balance to that Sunday's joyous palm procession. Using the same technique of contrast, the gospel proclaimed on Good Friday is the passion according to John.

John's gospel narrates Christ's passion with magisterial details. Jesus' announcement of himself as the divine I AM brings the troop of soldiers to fall down before him. John calls the soldiers a cohort, which numbered about five hundred soldiers. Jesus answers boldly to the high priest, debates with Pilate, is robed in royal purple, arranges for the care of his family and followers, gives up his spirit, and is buried with a kingly amount of spices in a garden, a place associated with life.

Because John's narration proclaims that the death of Jesus is, paradoxically, the triumph of the divine Christ, many Christians have found it the most appropriate reading for Good Friday.

Just as on Passion Sunday, the passion can be proclaimed in a variety of ways. It can be presented by several readers. One option assigns the speeches of the crowd to the assembly itself. Many musical renditions are available, either sung by the choir in a choral rendition or chanted by three soloists using a medieval chant or contemporary style. If the passion account is read in sections interspersed with congregational hymn singing, care should be taken that the hymns express this same Johannine picture of the cross as Jesus' throne of glory, rather than as the source of his agony. Staging the passion as a play requires extraordinary care so that the narrative is not diminished by poor acting nor the gospel obscured by flashy stagecraft.

Recently some Christians have hesitated to read the passion from John because of its repeated negative references to "the Jews." Most biblical scholars agree that John's gospel was given its final form in about the year 100. Antagonism between the Jews who accepted Jesus as Messiah and those who did not had increased over the decades, and the evangelist John articulates this conflict by referring to those who opposed the Christian claim that Jesus is the Son of God as "the Jews." Since Jesus, many of his followers throughout the century, and the evangelist were Jews, it is clear that John's label is indeed an anachronistic term, and although it did not cause Christian anti-Semitism, over the centuries this terminology certainly enflamed it.

A congregational Lenten study of the John text will help illumine both the difficulties and the treasures of the Good Friday reading. Notes that describe these services, attend to these issues, and offer devotional suggestions can be distributed or e-mailed to everyone during Lent. For the proclamation itself, some assemblies render John's term "the Jews" as "the Jewish authorities," "the Judeans," or "the crowd" in sentences where one of those seems the clearest meaning. This issue is one of several demonstrating that Good Friday is an occasion when a sermon is essential. Assemblies need to hear how these complex readings speak to us the good news of God. Contemporary theologians are reexamining medieval theories of atonement and proposing new ones, and it is the preacher's responsibility to proclaim with gracious learning how Christ's death brings life to the baptized.

The preacher is assisted in explicating the death of Christ by relying on the images presented in the other biblical readings. Isaiah 52 and 53 describes the coming one as the suffering servant who carries our sorrows by bearing our sins; as a vulnerable young plant; as the lamb slaughtered in silence; and as the warrior dividing up the spoils of victory. A passage from Hebrews likens Christ to the Jewish high priest, who mediated between God and the people, pleading with God for divine mercy. In chanting Psalm 22 we join with Jesus' lament to God. This poem invites Christians to think of Christ as the one forsaken by God, a worm, surrounded by a pack of dogs, threatened by a hungry lion, yet the one before whom all the nations shall bow in homage. As Christians attend the cross on Good Friday, the biblical images assist our contemplation of the meaning of Christ's death. Christ is the suffering servant, the slain lamb, a small plant, a victorious warrior, a rejected worm, a helpless victim, our high priest, and the incarnate God. It is good that next year we will once more encounter this wealth of texts and meditate on their meaning for us all.

The actions. Although the synoptic gospels report that only some women watched the execution from a distance, John writes that Jesus' mother, several other women, and "the disciple whom he loved" stood near the cross. On Good Friday Christians join with those faithful few at the foot of the cross, and there we pray. Because this service is part of an ongoing three-day event, Good Friday begins simply, and proceeds to the readings, sermon, and the intercessions. From the third century on, a central feature of Good Friday worship has been a lengthy bidding prayer. During this prayer we experience how that circle of those brought to the foot of cross expands to widening circles of care. An assisting minister calls out the bids; a time a silence is provided for individual prayer; and the presiding minister concludes each unit by praying aloud the prayers found in the leaders edition (pp. 636–638).

Each single assembly widens itself already in the opening petition, as it prays for the church throughout the world. Subsequent petitions pray for the leaders of the churches and all the baptized; for those preparing for baptism; for the Jewish people; for religious people who are not Christian; for people who do not believe in God; for nature itself, even "all the worlds"; for public officials; and for everyone in need. Such substantial praying on Good Friday is the model for the intercessory prayer that is part of our Holy Communion service each Sunday.

A procession of the cross has been part of Good Friday devotions since at least the fourth century. In about the year 380, a woman named Egeria recorded her pilgrimage to the Holy Land during Holy Week. About eighty years prior, Emperor Constantine's mother, Queen Helena, had overseen the excavation at Golgotha of what she believed was Christ's true cross, and on Good Friday this cross was set up for veneration by the faithful. Egeria wrote:

> The bishop grips the ends of the sacred wood with his hands, while the deacons, who are standing about, keep watch over it. There is a reason why it is guarded in this manner. It is the practice here for all the people to come forth one by one, the faithful as well as the catechumens, to bow down before the table, kiss the holy wood, and then move on. It is said that someone (I do not know when) took a bite and stole a piece of the holy cross. Therefore, it is now guarded by the deacons standing around, lest there be anyone who would dare come and do that again.[3]

This procession to reverence the True Cross followed the reading of the passion narrative. In medieval times, many churches embedded what was believed to be a fragment of the True Cross in a gold or silver cross, and Christians continued the ancient pattern of processing up to the cross and kissing it in reverence.

Evangelical Lutheran Worship suggests that a cross be carried in procession up the center aisle, while the assembly repeats the classic dialogue, "Behold the life-giving cross, on which was hung the Savior of the whole world. Oh, come, let us worship him." In many churches, a rough-hewn six-foot cross is constructed, perhaps by a youth group, for use in this devotion. During the procession, the dialogue invites the assembly to see in the locally made cross an image of the cross on Calvary. The cross on Calvary then represents Christ himself, and we worship Christ, the Savior of the world. As befits Good Friday, the cross of death is praised as "life-giving." Although some Christians follow Egeria and visit Jerusalem, Christianity does not make pilgrimage mandatory. Rather, Christ is present every Sunday in the local assembly, and a cross nailed together by teenage members of the congregation can bring Golgotha to us.

This time of reverencing the cross can be kept in a variety of ways. Worshipers may remain seated in silent prayer; people may come forward to kneel around the cross; everyone may file by to reverence the cross, perhaps touching it, or tracing on their bodies the sign of the cross; taught by our Asian sisters and brothers, the assembly may stand and join in a profound bow; the choir may sing an appropriate anthem; instrumentalists may offer appropriate meditative music; the congregation may sing Good Friday hymns. A reader might declaim the eighth-century "Dream of the Rood," in which the cross itself speaks of the glorious Christ. Children may bring up dandelions they have picked and lay them at the foot of the cross. If the congregation includes a professional dancer, an interpretative dance of lament and transformation before the cross might be effective. Carefully selected video images of suffering and triumph can be projected, if this can be achieved with technical proficiency. A number of hymns in the Holy Week, Three Days section of *Evangelical Lutheran Worship* are appropriate for this time of meditation.

To accompany Friday's devotion at the cross, some churches use the litany "O my people, O my church." Called the Solemn Reproaches, this poetic prayer arose during the ninth century and imagines God's lament as the manner in which the church has treated Christ. Each stanza cites one of God's benevolent gifts and our ungrateful response. To the concluding phrase "and you have prepared a cross for your Savior," the people respond, using an ancient prayer (the Trisagion, or "thrice holy") in which God is addressed with three adjectives: "Holy God, holy and mighty, holy and immortal, have mercy on us." Several moving choral renditions are available.

It may be good for the congregation to consider the words of the Solemn Reproaches before Good Friday so that its meaning will be apparent. Just as when Christians refer to the Three Days as our Passover, so throughout the Three Days the church uses language from the Old Testament to describe our situation. Each stanza of this Good Friday litany cites what God has done for us: led us to freedom, fed us with manna, provided water from the rock. Yet by our sin we participate in preparing the cross of Christ, and God is reproaching us. Although in medieval times the Reproaches were worded in such a way that people construed them as condemning Jews, the most recent version of "O my people, O my church," provided in *Evangelical Lutheran Worship* and in the worship resources of several other Protestant churches, makes clear that the litany is the church's accusation of itself. We have been grafted into the tree of Israel, and yet we "made them scapegoats for your own guilt," says God. The last stanza, citing the Matthean parable of the last judgment—"I was hungry and you gave me no food"—suggests some of the ways we have helped to crucify our Savior. Through this powerful prayer for mercy we apply the Bible's stories of judgment and mercy to ourselves.

An alternate text to accompany the reverencing of the cross is "We Glory in Your Cross," which interleaves Psalm 67 with a refrain praising God for the cross and resurrection of Christ. The words encapsulate the paradox of Good Friday: "by your cross joy has come into the world." The text can be chanted by a cantor or sung by the choir.

For Good Friday, it is usual for the ministers to vest simply in an alb or a cassock.

The propers. Two options for the prayer of the day are provided. The first comes from the seventh century, the second from a twentieth-century collection of liturgical prayers. Psalm 22 is an important addition to the service. Many biblical scholars agree that its imagery, describing in poetic language the plight of the suffering one, served as one of the sources of the description in the New Testament of the crucified Christ. As befits the paradox of Good Friday, the psalm concludes with lively praise to God, before whom the whole world bows. The Good Friday service ends without a final prayer or closing benediction. The assembly leaves in silence, knowing that the liturgy continues on Saturday night with the Vigil. The service feels incomplete, as it ought to. The movement from Christ's suffering to death to resurrection is, finally, indivisible.

Some congregations plan their Good Friday service with no music whatsoever. Other congregations rely on the strong Lutheran hymn tradition to assist in the assembly's devotion. One suggestion is for the musician to assist the assembly's song by providing only the melody line.

The most famous hymn sung by Christians on Good Friday, called in Latin the "Pange lingua," celebrates the cross as the tree of life. Around the year 600, a woman named Radegund, the abbess of a convent in Poitiers, France, persuaded the accomplished Italian poet Venantius Fortunatus to live at her convent as its hymnwriter. Having secured for her convent a fragment of the True Cross, she asked Fortunatus to pen a Holy Week hymn in its honor. Each year Christians around the world sing his hymn, "Sing, My Tongue" (#355 and 356), to celebrate the paradoxical victory of the cross. The words of one stanza address the cross in this way:

> Faithful cross, true sign of triumph,
> be for all the noblest tree;
> none in foliage, none in blossom,
> none in fruit your equal be.
> symbol of the world's redemption,
> for your burden makes us free.

Contemporary hymnwriters have continued this tradition. A twentieth-century rendition of a sixteenth-century Hungarian hymn, "There in God's Garden" (#342), and the twentieth-century "Tree of Life and Awesome Mystery" (#334), both exemplify the way that Christians see in the wood of the cross a fruitful tree rather than an instrument of torture. If there are to be printed or projected images to enhance the worship, Passion/Palm Sunday is the day when images of unmitigated suffering are appropriate. Good Friday is the occasion for those more ambiguous images: the cross as the tree of life, Christ as the triumphant warrior, a king ascending his throne, the wounds of Christ pouring wine into our chalices.

Resurrection of Our Lord: Vigil of Easter

The night. The storytelling part of the Jewish seder begins with the youngest child asking, "Why is this night different from all other nights?" According to Jewish reckoning, one day is over and the next begins at sundown. Our culture maintains this pattern in its celebrations of Christmas Eve and New Year's Eve. The Three Days carries on this ancient tradition by celebrating the great Vigil of Easter on Saturday night. The Vigil of the Three Days is not a "prayer vigil" during which individuals pray throughout the night in a silent church, as if awaiting the resurrection. Rather, the Easter Vigil intends to be the most significant worship of the year, at which the whole church gathers for several hours to celebrate the resurrection *now.* On Easter morning, in the light of day, it is natural to celebrate the life of springtime. But when the assembly huddles together at night, we know ourselves to be in the tomb of night, and only with faith kindled by the power of the Holy Spirit can we sing of the resurrection. Just as on Good Friday we read a triumphant gospel, so for Easter we meet in the dark to praise the light of Christ.

It is only for momentous events that the community puts off sleeping for a nighttime meeting. An evening scheduling allows for the Vigil to take as long as it must. The night sky, perhaps filled with stars and a full moon, enlivens our consciousness with the cosmological signs of night and day. The ancient notion that the universe is constructed with the four elements of earth, air, fire, and water is played out in the elements of the Vigil. The very earthiness of the Vigil helps us to see ourselves as creatures of the earth to whom God gives life. The ashes of Ash Wednesday have turned into the fire of the resurrection.

The service order for the Vigil of Easter is in the assembly edition, pages 266–270; separate printing out of the service is unnecessary. The full service is in the leaders edition (643–653). The Vigil can be enacted in many ways. Some congregations situate everything in the nave and conduct the entire service with solemn formality. Other congregations begin the lighting of the fire outdoors, perhaps in the churchyard cemetery; they situate the service of readings in the parish hall, with the teenagers sitting on the floor or everyone more easily dancing in a conga line after the reading of the exodus; and they enter the sanctuary only for baptism and the meal. Worship planners are encouraged to consider all options and to choose the venues and style that best serve their congregation. Moving from one station to another helps to clarify the parts of the service and to make of the event a bodily communal journey into Christ's resurrection.

Some congregations, adapting the American Protestant pattern of Easter sunrise services, begin their Vigil about two hours before sunrise on Sunday, so that when the long liturgy is over, daylight has arrived. Some schedule the Vigil early on Saturday evening to more easily accommodate small children or elderly members. Some schedule the Vigil on Saturday night at 10:30, so that it will be past midnight, thus our Sunday, by the time of the sacramental meal. In making this decision, worship planners need not imagine that the service must be timed so as to get Jesus raised from the tomb. We gather as people of the resurrection; the service does not raise Jesus, but rather proclaims and celebrates his resurrection. Many congregations schedule the service Saturday night once it is dark, perhaps 8 or 8:30, since the lighting of the fire is more effective in the darkness, and yet worshipers can be home in bed by midnight. The third-century bishop Asterius preached this at the Vigil:

O Night brighter than day;
O Night brighter than the sun;
O Night whiter than snow;
O Night more brilliant than torches;
O Night more delightful than paradise;
O Night that knows not darkness;
O Night that has banished sleep;
O Night that has taught us to join vigil with angels;
O Night terror of demons;
O Night most desirable in the year;
O Night mother of the newly baptized;
O Night when the devil slept and was stripped;
O Night in which the beneficiaries received their inheritance without end.[4]

On this night of Christian Passover, the night different from all other nights, the church hears the stories of faith, sings the songs of the tradition, baptizes the newcomers, shares the bread and wine, and so is joined together with Christ, who is the light of the world.

Preparation for the Vigil. *Sundays and Seasons* provides lists that assist the congregation in preparation for the Vigil. Here are some examples of matters to consider. The sanctuary will be vested for Easter, in white or gold. Some assemblies prefer to complete the decorations, for example to set out flowers, only at the time of the meal. But, again, planners ought not imagine that the service is getting Christ raised from the grave: the service begins with the light of the resurrection. The bonfire has been set, preferably outside on the ground or in a brazier; the method of lighting the wood has been practiced; having doused the wood and kindling with lighter fluid will help the fire to burst up in a hearty fashion when the spark hits. A large paschal candle and candle stand are secured. Candles for each participant are available. If it is truly dark, the leaders may require a light source for reading. An evergreen bough is lying by the font. Attentive ushers are handing out worship books or service folders and suggesting where people may stand. A sudden rainstorm may require a change of plans. One result of the considerable planning required for the Vigil is that many people are involved in worship preparation, and this pattern can extend through the entire year, making it customary that members of the assembly assist in planning and leadership.

Gathering. The art provided on page 266 of the assembly edition illustrates the gathering rite of the Vigil. If possible, the community gathers out of doors, under the night sky, to watch the lighting of a substantial fire. Some anthropologists mark the origins of the creatures we call human with the discovery of the uses of fire: a communal center granting light, warmth, protection from predators, and a shared cooked meal. We contemporary Christians join with the many millennia of assemblies around fire, but for us the fire is "the light of Christ." The presiding minister invites the assembly "on this most holy night" to keep the Passover of Jesus Christ. The opening action of the Vigil, the lighting of the fire, symbolizes the light of Christ in the darkness of the world and the flame of the Spirit emerging from the tomb.

Still today, the Friday night sabbath meal of observant Jews begins with the woman of the household lighting the candles on the dinner table, bringing into the home the light of the first day of creation. Early Christians, lighting the lamps for evening prayer services, came to describe the evening light as a sign of Christ, illumining the whole world. One traditional tale suggests how indoor evening candles evolved into an outdoor bonfire. Christians settling in northern Europe encountered an annual pagan rite of the spring equinox, at which authorized priests, who were seen as controlling the power of light, struck a new fire to mark the returned sun. The people took home to their hearths coals to enliven their house fire for the next year. The story goes on that in the fifth century, encountering this ceremony, St. Patrick broke the law by himself striking a grand fire on Ireland's Hill of Slane, proclaiming that the true light of the spring sun and moon was Christ. Many Christians have enjoyed this annual bonfire ever since.

The fire is lighted. A flint or matches can be used. Take some moments to watch the fire blaze. Think of the fire of ashes, the fire of Pentecost. Remember God's appearance to Moses in the burning bush, the fire on Mount Sinai, God's pillar of fire leading the people to the promised land.

The presiding minister then inscribes the paschal candle, while calling out the praise to Christ as the beginning and the end. On Good Friday, the wooden cross represented Christ, and at the Vigil, it is the lighted candle that is an image of Christ among us. The candle is marked with a cross and inscribed with the Alpha (the beginning), the Omega (the ending), and the current year's date. Easter is not time-travel back to the year 33; rather, Christ's resurrection is now. Some presiding ministers trace with a finger a pre-marked candle, and others use a knife to cut the letters and the numbers into the candle. After the Vigil is completed, the paschal candle will be lighted for the liturgies of the fifty days of Easter, at the font for baptisms, and at the coffin or urn for funerals.

The presiding minister then lights a small candle or taper, or perhaps a long fireplace match, from the bonfire, being careful not to set alight any vestments. With this flame the presiding minister lights the paschal candle. At this time, or as part of the procession, assistants light several other candles from the paschal candle, and then the assistants pass the fire around so that everyone's candle is lit. Individual candles can be distributed at this time or before the service began. The spreading of the fire may be outdoors or in the place of the readings. Easter is the original occasion for a Christian candlelight ceremony. Through baptism, we shine as lights in the world, and at Easter we carry the illumination of the resurrection out into the world. The assembly then processes into the place of the service of readings, following the paschal candle and the ministers and chanting, "The light of Christ. Thanks be to God." Some congregations encourage everyone to keep the candles lit in the darkened room throughout the service of readings, for even contemporary people respond to the primal power of flame. The assembly can be reminded to be careful not to set anything or anyone on fire.

Once everyone is in place and the paschal candle is set into its stand, a cantor sings the Easter Proclamation. Coming to us from the fourth century, this prayer of thanksgiving for the Christian Passover sings repeatedly that "This is the night." Like most prayers of thanksgiving, the Easter Proclamation praises God for the creation of the world and for the salvation given us in Christ, and then prays for the power of God to transform us. This prayer of thanksgiving uses all the church's beloved metaphors to acclaim the resurrection. Tonight Christ is risen, all creation sings, earth rejoices, darkness is vanquished, we are redeemed from bondage, the true Lamb is slain, the Israelites escape through the sea, sin is purged away, the chains of death are broken, the night is as clear as the day, hate is cast out, heaven and earth are joined, and Christ the Morning Star sheds light on the whole human race.

There are longer and shorter versions of this proclamation, called in Latin the *Exsultet*, from its first word, "Rejoice." Medieval and contemporary musical settings are available. The translation in *Evangelical Lutheran Worship* includes the congregational response "This is the night." In one particularly poetic sentence, God is praised for the bees without which we would have no wax for the candle! Even in the fourth century, church leaders debated about these bees, Jerome arguing that bees had no place in the Easter Proclamation, but preachers like Ambrose and Augustine delighting in embellished poetic praise. So the bees can still buzz through the Easter Proclamation, reminding us that God gives to humankind life through the things of the earth and that we will now taste the sweet honey of the word of God.

Some manuscripts of the Easter Proclamation that have survived from medieval times are fully illustrated. The illustrations, which depict each of the images presented in the text, are drawn upside down, so that as the scroll was unrolled, its pictures could be seen by worshipers who were sitting close by. Perhaps a video display is our version of an illustrated Exsultet scroll.

Two options for the prayer of the day are provided. The first is a twentieth-century revision of the ancient Latin collect, and the second was composed for *Evangelical Lutheran Worship*. Each prayer uses the imagery of light and so sums up the Vigil's gathering around fire.

Word. The method and location of the four to twelve readings may follow the congregation's usual Sunday practice, or the service of readings may be conducted in another site and with several readers each. People may be seated in their pews or sprawled about in the church lounge. Practice for the readers can take place earlier in the week or on the previous Saturday morning. The pattern for each reading is as follows: The scripture is proclaimed. After the reading is an optional musical response of a psalm or a hymn, sung by cantor, choir, or the full assembly. Local worship planners may determine whether these responses can be the appointed psalms (page 269); or, using the model of a congregational hymn sing, beloved hymns; or some other combination of appropriate musical responses. If the space where the readings take place is kept dark, assembly musical responses that do not require reading light are particularly useful. After the response at least a full minute of silence is kept. It is helpful to keep this space of silence constant throughout the service of readings, so that the assembly knows what to expect. Finally, a prayer using the imagery of the reading concludes the unit. The assembly may be seated for the entire unit or may be asked to stand for each concluding prayer. Planners will decide how many of the twelve readings to include, beyond the primary four marked with an asterisk, and how many of the readings will have musical responses.

The Vigil readings begin with creation. Anthropologists report that on their most important annual festival, many ancient peoples declaimed their story of the creation of the world, as if the celebration returned the people to the perfection of the original earth. Similarly, at the preeminent Christian festival, we tell the story of the creation of the world. Of the several creation stories in the Bible, the Vigil reading is Genesis 1, the account that is entirely marked by grace. God created order and beauty out of chaos; the universe is constructed as a good place for its human inhabitants; males and females are created in the divine image; no evil, no sin, no death are yet imagined; and one day in seven is rest.

By this reading we are not pretending that Genesis 1 is scientifically accurate. Rather, God's creation of life presents us a picture of the resurrection. In Genesis 1, God begins creation with divine light. Through the resurrection of Christ, that divine light shines throughout time, and through baptism we bear that illumination in ourselves. For those churches that stress the baptismal character of the Vigil, Genesis 1 says that God hovered over primeval waters to create life, and similarly the church too is birthed from baptismal waters. For Christians searching for descriptors of the divine, Genesis 1 describes God as the benevolent mastermind of the cosmos, the provider who is praised for the evolving earth.

Possible responses for Genesis 1 are Psalm 136 or a hymn praising God's continuing creation, such as the Dakota hymn "Many and Great, O God, Are Your Works" (#837), accompanied with a drum, the Taiwanese hymn "God Created Heaven and Earth" (#738), or the hymn based on the writings of the medieval mystic Julian, "Mothering God, You Gave Me Birth," (#735).

The second required reading is the story from Exodus 14 and 15 of the deliverance at the Red Sea. With the enemy behind them and the sea in front of them, the people are surrounded by death. In the liturgy, we are those people. Yet by opening the door of the tomb, God saves us from death. The sea is a metaphor for baptism, for we have all gone through the waters, passing over to the safe side of the sea. In Exodus,

God is the liberator of the oppressed, bringing the people from deathly conditions to a land flowing with milk and honey.

The reading from Exodus 14–15 exemplifies how straightforward or how celebratory the Vigil's options are. A simple response to the reading is singing the canticle from Exodus 15, the people's joyful response to their salvation. For a congregational hymn, one suggestion is the eighth-century hymn by John of Damascus, "Come, You Faithful, Raise the Strain" (#363), which speaks of the resurrection using the imagery of the exodus. A choir might sing the African American spiritual "O Mary, Don't You Weep," in which Mary Magdalene is called to rejoice because "Pharaoh's army got drownded." For a more convivial Vigil, this is the year's most appropriate occasion for dance in the liturgy. Some congregations include talented dancers who, like a choir, can do for the assembly what it cannot do by itself. In some congregations, everyone is invited to join in a folk dance or a conga line, while the elderly members beat Miriam's tambourines.

The third required reading is the poem from Isaiah 55, in which salvation is freely offered to all. In this reading, we refer to the resurrection as a joyous banquet and an everlasting covenant. The waters of baptism are like rain making the ground fruitful. God, the Holy One, is like the host of the meal, our partner in covenant, the one above the clouds, sending down both mercy and rain.

Possibilities for assembly response include the lovely canticle from Isaiah 12; a hymn based in part on Isaiah 55, "As the Deer Runs to the River" (#331); or the African American spiritual "I've Just Come from the Fountain," which could be repeated later as a baptismal response.

However many readings are appointed, the final one is the narrative from Daniel 3 of the deliverance from the fiery furnace. In this rhetorically magnificent narrative, God saves the three faithful believers, just as God has saved Jesus from death, and in the end even the wicked king gives honor to God. As Shadrach, Meshach, and Abednego walk about in the flames accompanied by a mysterious Other, so in our baptism we receive the companionship of the Spirit of God. Along with Nebuchadnezzar, we praise the God who has walked with us in the flames.

The traditional response to the reading from Daniel 3 is the Song of the Three, the praise of the entire creation to God, sometimes called by its Latin name *Benedicite omnia opera*. Recorded in the apocryphal addition to the Book of Daniel (alternately titled as "The Prayer of Azariah and the Song of the Three Jews"), the song can be sung between a cantor or choir and the congregation.[5] An alternate is the Litany of the Saints, (#237), in which we praise God for the salvation of Christ and the multitude of the faithful departed who share with us the hope of the resurrection.

Evangelical Lutheran Worship offers eight more readings, for a possible total of twelve. The first is the tale in Genesis 7–9 of Noah's flood. As if in a second story of creation, God remakes the earth, bringing a new earth to birth from the waters of chaos. This story has provided for Christians one of our most beloved images of baptism. God is our rainbow, our ark, our dove. The children can bring their stuffed animals to the Vigil and with their beloved animals gather around the reading desk.

One of the most enigmatic narratives in scripture is the testing of Abraham in Genesis 22. In this story about moral ambiguity and religious surprise, God saves Isaac from death. We pray for the faith of ancient Abraham, and we discover that Christ is our ram.

Both the reading from Proverbs and its alternative from Baruch are poems in which God's wisdom is personified as a woman who beckons us to walk on her path of justice and who calls us to share her meal of life. This biblical passage uses female rather than male imagery to speak of the divine, and many contemporary Christians are glad to include this reading in the Vigil.

In the reading from Ezekiel 36, God promises to sprinkle us with clean water and to give us a new heart and a new spirit. Christians have recognized in this passage a description of baptism and the resurrection.

In the narrative from Ezekiel 37 of the valley of the dry bones, Christians see God calling back into life what is dead: the bones of Jesus, the bones of our human nature, our bones at the end of time, perhaps also the bones of the Egyptian army. The Spirit of the LORD has already come to us with the power of our baptism.

In the poem from Zephaniah 3, God promises us a homeland. God will gather all the people together and restore all things to wholeness. We recall the perfect world of Genesis 1 and see in the resurrection of Christ a beginning of this restoration. We praise God as our victory, our city, our beloved, our healing, our festival.

Already in Matthew 12:40, Christians were seeing in the legend of Jonah a picture of the death and resurrection of Christ. The Christian catacombs include drawings of the Jonah story, and some early theologians understood the three immersions of water in baptism to recall not the three persons of the Trinity but the three days of Jesus in the tomb. The reading of Jonah 1 places us with Jonah in the sea and, like him, saved by the mercy of God, and the suggested response is the song of Jonah. An acronym formed by the first letters of the Greek words for "Jesus Christ, God's Son, Savior" spells the Greek word *ichthus*, "fish," and Christian iconography has depicted Christ as the fish that rescued Jonah from death.

A final option is from Isaiah 61, a poem in which God promises to clothe us with the garments of salvation. The suggested biblical response is from Deuteronomy 32, in which Moses calls the people into faithfulness to God's covenant of life.

These readings offer us pictures of God's power of resurrection, metaphors for baptism, and images for God. We step into each reading. With the first humans we are created in the divine image, with the Israelites we are saved through the sea, with the animals we are in the ark, with Abraham we are attempting to obey God, and with Isaac we are saved from sacrifice. We are instructed by Woman Wisdom; we are the dry bones enlivened by the breath of God. Finally at our death we are indeed in the furnace of blazing fire, but we have faith in the one who "with the appearance of a god" is with us. All the readings are too good to miss. Congregations that cannot read them all may appoint the missed ones at next year's Vigil. Proclaimed superbly, the readings and responses make for perhaps an hour of the beloved stories of the faith.

In the reading from Romans, we are called through our baptism into the death and resurrection of Christ. We too have died, we too are raised from death, for we are the body of Christ.

Continuing the pattern that the gospel proclaimed during the Three Days from John, we stand to hear John 20. John presents the most beloved and detailed story of all the evangelists, beginning "while it was still dark": Peter and John find the tomb empty, and Mary Magdalene encounters her risen Lord in the garden. Like Mary of Magdala, we often do not recognize Christ when he stands before us, but he calls us to faith in the power of the resurrection.

Preachers need to resist the temptation to omit the sermon. At least in proclaiming the resurrection no one can say that the Vigil has not provided enough scripture to work with.

Baptism. Medieval Christians thought of baptism as the way an infant got saved from hell, and this led to baptism being administered privately a few days after birth. However, the church of our time, more like the early church, sees baptism in a far broader way: baptism inaugurates us into the kingdom of God, enrolls us into the family of believers, forms us into the body of Christ, pours into us the Holy Spirit, and joins us to the death and resurrection of Christ. Understood in these ways, baptism celebrated at Easter is particularly rich with connections. In the waters we are buried with Christ, to rise with his Spirit to new life.

If there are candidates for baptism, the Vigil continues with the order of Holy Baptism. The assembly follows the paschal candle and the ministers and moves to the font. The entire assembly joins with the candidates, their sponsors, and family to renounce the forces of evil and to recite the creed. As the art on page 227 of the assembly edition suggests, next to the burning paschal candle, the waters of baptism surround the baptized, who dons the white robe of the saved and stands before the cross of Christ. For the thanksgiving at the font, prayer V (LE 589) is especially appropriate for the Vigil. This celebratory thanksgiving praises God for all the waters of creation and for the stories of God's saving washings, and it prays for the outpouring of the Holy Spirit on us all.

As much water as possible is used. The practice of using only three drops arose in the Middle Ages as an answer to the inquiry of what was the minimal amount required. If the font is small or shallow, a large bowl can be set into the font. A cup or large shell can be used so that more water than a handful is poured three times over the candidate. An outdoors baptism will allow for the use of considerable water without concern about a wet floor. The fewer clothes that the candidates wear, the smaller will be any problem about getting clothing wet. Infants can be baptized naked or wearing only a diaper.

If there are no candidates for baptism, the Vigil continues with the Affirmation of Baptism. As the art on page 234 of the assembly edition suggests, each of the baptized resides in the waters of baptism. Over the head of each hovers the Holy Spirit. When using this rite, the assembly renounces the power of evil, recites the creed, and is commissioned to live another year in the new life of Christ. Martin Luther wrote that for the Christian each day is a return to the font, and at Easter the meaning of that return is celebrated to the fullest. Perhaps during the creed the presiding minister uses an evergreen branch to scatter water from the font onto the assembly; perhaps each person comes forward to the font and signs the forehead of another with water, as if to wash away the ash cross of Lent.

Because we are baptized, we pray to God for all the needs of the world, and so the prayers of intercession follow. The intercessions include petitions for the whole church, for the well-being of creation, for peace and justice in the world, for all in governmental authority, for all who are in need and for the sick and suffering, and the prayers conclude with thanksgiving for the lives of all those who have died in the faith and who await the resurrection. Especially appropriate at the Vigil is a plea that God care for the waters of the earth, the seas, the rivers, the lakes, the reservoirs, the wells.

Meal. Finally the assembly enacts the meaning of baptism and the power of Christ's death and resurrection by sharing in Holy Communion. Everyone, processing once again following the paschal candle, moves from the font to their places for the communion. As the famous sermon preached by John Chrysostom in the fourth century says it,

> Rich and poor together, hold high festival.
> Diligent and heedless, honor this day.
> Both you who have fasted, and you who did not fast,
> rejoice together today.
> The table is full: all of you, feast sumptuously.
> The calf is fatted; let no one go away hungry.
> Enjoy the feast of faith; receive the riches of God's mercy.[6]

Use freshly baked bread and good tasting wine. For the thanksgiving at the table, prayers IV, VII, or IX are especially appropriate. "Come to the banquet," the presiding minister may say, recalling the reading from Isaiah 55. With the words "Go in peace. Share the good news" we are sent with Mary Magdalene to spread the gospel. The Vigil has lasted two to three hours, but it has been so laden with the words and signs of salvation that we will be glad to return next year and immerse ourselves once again in the Three Days.

Resurrection of Our Lord: Easter Day

The day. Because it is hoped that an increasing number of worshipers will have celebrated at the Vigil of Easter, and because the Easter season lasts fifty days, and because for Christians each Sunday is a celebration of Christ's resurrection, the morning service on Easter Day is not the church's single celebration of the resurrection. Medieval regulations sought to require of Christians "their Easter duty," and it is still the case that some people attend church only on Easter Day. While exuberant music and festive flowers are appropriate, worship planners will want to reflect on how the Christian faith is perceived by those persons who hear the resurrection without the cross, those who might associate the worship of God with rented musicians. Perhaps the day of the Resurrection of our Lord is best thought of as a superb regular Sunday service. Since the Christian faith is an eschatological hope for the fulfillment of God's promises, the splendor of the Easter liturgy ought not suggest that we have already arrived at the fullness of God.

In many languages, Christians call this festival some variant of the word *Pascha*. This ancient nomenclature makes clear that the resurrection of Christ is our Passover from death to life. The word *Easter* derives, according to Bede, an eighth-century historian, from the goddess of springtime revered in the British Isles during paganism. English-speaking Christians may consider alternating the word *Easter* with the term *Pascha* to help reestablish the resurrection as our feast of Passover.

The readings. For the Easter gospel on Sunday morning, the lectionary in *Evangelical Lutheran Worship* (in one rare instance where it varies from the Revised Common Lectionary) returns to the synoptic gospel of the year: Matthew in year A, Mark in year B, and Luke in year C, with John as an alternate, particularly for congregations who have not yet adopted the Vigil. Continuing the pattern of Holy Week, both the synoptic and the Johannine accounts are proclaimed, the synoptic on Sunday and the Johannine at the Three Days. Those worshipers who attend both the Vigil and Easter morning will notice the difference in the New Testament accounts of the resurrection. In year A, the gospel from Matthew speaks of an earthquake and an angel rolling away the stone, as if all of heaven and earth participates in the resurrection. The contrast is most stark in year B, when next to John's beloved narration of the encounter between Mary Magdalene and the risen Christ in the garden is this closing sentence from Mark: that the women "went out and fled from the tomb, for terror and amazement had seized them; and they said nothing to anyone, for they were afraid."

Some worshipers may be familiar with the longer ending of Mark, which portrays the risen Christ making post-resurrection appearances; however, most biblical scholars are convinced that this is a later, inauthentic addition. In year C, Luke, who is especially interested in the emerging church, lists the largest number of followers, four by name, besides "the other women."

To complement the gospel, the first reading is from Acts, an Easter sermon ascribed to Peter. The final verses of Peter's address speak of God's judgment and God's forgiveness. Once again we encounter the two sides of the biblical message: both justice and mercy characterize our God. Alternate first readings from the Old Testament are suggested, especially useful for those congregations that did not celebrate the Vigil. In year A, the second reading from Colossians speaks the baptismal language that we have died and been raised with Christ. In year B, the second reading from 1 Corinthians is Paul's testimony to the resurrection and his confidence that we all will rise, as Christ did. In year C, Paul's discussion in 1 Corinthians continues with his eschatological hope for the final destruction of the enemy that is death.

The actions. Every Sunday, but especially on Easter Sunday, the assembly enacts the message of salvation by joining to Christ and one another in Holy Communion. The body of Christ has risen from the dead, and enlivened by the Spirit of the risen Christ, we share in that body and so become that body. On Easter we give thanks: we recall early-church Greek when we call the thanksgiving "eucharist." The paschal candle will be lighted before the assembly enters the worship space and the stand placed in a prominent place near the table or the font.

Thought can be given to the use of flowers on Easter Day. Many congregations use the donation of flowers as a way for members to give thanks for the lives of the faithful dead, and after the service these flowers are then brought to shut-ins. In some places, however, the number of potted flowers is so great that the table of the meal is obscured and the movements of ministers and people obstructed. Flowers are to adorn, but not displace, the central things of worship.

If a congregation sponsors an egg hunt, after church on Easter Day is the appropriate time. Eggs are archetypal symbols of new life, and Christians have seen in the life inside the shell a picture of Christ in the tomb. The deep red coloring used by Ukrainian Christians for their intricately painted eggs is said to remind us of the blood of Christ that poured down from the cross onto our basket of eggs.

The propers. The psalm response to the first reading recalls the reading at the Vigil about Israel crossing the Red Sea, for now we are the people rejoicing at God's victory over evil. "This is the day" on which the LORD has acted, we sing. We build upon the once-rejected stone, and so we think of the stone rolled away from the empty tomb. The "Alleluia" returns, as celebrative as possible. Appropriate prayers at the offering and after communion are provided (AE pp. 64–65). For the thanksgiving at the table, prayers IV, VII, or IX are most appropriate. For all the services of Easter, from the Vigil through Pentecost, it is appropriate to stand to receive communion, as if signifying the joy of the resurrection. The service may include the sending of ministers of communion who will take not only the sacrament, but also a flowering plant, to the homebound. "Go in peace. Share the good news." Along with the women running from the tomb, we are sent to proclaim the resurrection by living as the risen body of Christ.

Here are some suggestions for worship planners: The color of paraments and vestments is white or gold. White or gold fabric can be hung around the worship space. Of the many hymns that are sung, each one can come from a different century of believers, so that we join with Christians of many centuries, from around the world, in new words and tunes as well as with the familiar, to laud the resurrection. Before the service begins, the assembly can join in an Easter hymn sing, in this way engaging the whole assembly in a way different from their listening to choir anthems. Care must be taken that presented music not displace the primary instrument of worship, which is the voice of the assembly. Where Easter Sunday has come to replicate a concert, some changes may be called for. The prayers of intercession need to attend to the needs of the world so that our celebration is not distant from countless sufferers whose Easter is marked by pain and privation rather than celebration and plenty. The contributions from the gathering of the gifts can be dedicated to a local charity rather than to congregational maintenance, so that monetarily the assembly can be the witnesses that Peter's sermon describes.

Fifty Days of Easter

Our culture tends to complete a celebration the minute the party is over. But the Christian celebration of Pascha is not over on Easter Day. Easter

Day is at once the culmination of the Three Days and the beginning of fifty days of celebration. Easter lasts for seven weeks, through the Day of Pentecost, the fiftieth day. The white paraments and vestments remain in place until the red of the Pentecost celebration. The paschal candle is lighted throughout each service and is prominently displayed.

The readings. Although the liturgical year heeds the chronology presented in Luke–Acts, the seven weeks of Easter afford us the year's most sustained exposure to the high Christology found in the Johannine discourses. According to John's gospel, Christ's resurrection, his ascension, and the gift of his presence in the Spirit are not discrete events separated over time but rather are a single mystery experienced sacramentally within the community. Throughout the fifty days of Easter, passages from John 10, 13, 14, 15, 17, 20, and 21 are proclaimed. Particularly beloved by many Christians is the Fourth Sunday of Easter, when John 10 is divided up over the three years. On the Seventh Sunday of Easter, the High Priestly Prayer of John 17 is divided up over the three years, and although in John's gospel this chapter is situated on Maundy Thursday, its proclamation around the time of the Ascension gives a double meaning to Jesus' words about his going away and the community that remains in the world.

At the Easter Vigil, assemblies heard as many as twelve Old Testament readings that present stories and poems that complement the narrative of the resurrection of Christ. Thus during the weeks of Easter the first readings each Sunday come instead from Acts. By listening to the Acts of the Apostles, the church understands that the resurrection continues in the life of the church, with the power of the Spirit seen now in the followers of the risen Christ. The selections from Acts include apostolic sermons proclaiming the death and resurrection of Christ, descriptions of the primitive church, and narratives involving leaders in the church: Peter, Stephen, Paul, Mary, Philip, Matthias, Ananias, Tabitha, Lydia, Silas. For the second readings, year A presents passages from 1 Peter and year B from 1 John, both of which offer encouragement to the community as it lives out the baptized life. During year C, the second readings are the jubilant songs from Revelation: it is as if during the season of Easter we are already in heaven, singing with saints and angels around the throne and eating from the tree of life.

The propers. Worship planning teams can consider ways to maintain an Easter celebration throughout the season. These Sundays afford enough time to sing all the thirty hymns in the Easter section of *Evangelical Lutheran Worship*. It is not only Easter Day but throughout the season that we can sing "Christ the Lord Is Risen Today." Celebrative banners or strips of white fabric can continue to be hung around the sanctuary. Perhaps the offering of flowers can be spread out throughout the Sundays of Easter. Eastertime prayers at the offering and after communion are provided (AE pp. 64–65). The Easter preface calls Christ our Paschal Lamb, who has destroyed death and already brings us to eternal life. For the thanksgiving at the table, prayers IV, VII, and IX are particularly appropriate. We are dismissed in the confidence that Christ is with us.

Ascension of Our Lord

The day. The evangelist Luke was a talented storyteller, and his narrative presentations of the life of Jesus have become normative in the Christian church. An example is the chronology that Luke, and only Luke, gives to the resurrected Christ. Forty days, the unit that repeatedly in the Bible signifies sacred time, marks the period that Christ was seen by his followers after the resurrection. This forty-day unit has led much of the church since the fourth century to celebrate the Ascension of our Lord on a Thursday, the fortieth day after Easter. Some churches in the past and present have transferred the observance to a near Sunday. The worship planners of each congregation need to consider how and when to observe this festival.

Many churches, especially in the nineteenth and early twentieth centuries, highlighted the narrative of the Ascension by permanently displaying a picture of Acts 1 over the altar. Often this painting was quite literalistic, with only Jesus' feet still showing at the top of the picture. One wonders what was the received message of this image, particularly in a congregation that observed holy communion only several times a year.

A living theology will not use the observance of Ascension to proclaim that Jesus has left the scene and is no longer with us. Rather, in the mystery of the resurrection, humanity is brought alive to God. Pope Leo in the fifth century preached that Christ ascended into the eucharist. Some theologians, imagining heaven as similar to a medieval court, described the Ascension as Christ pleading our case before the divine majesty. Martin Luther, teaching the ubiquity of the resurrected Christ, understood the Ascension as Christ ascending into the cosmos.

Ecological theologians suggest that on Ascension we think of Christ as now in the earth itself. Jesus of Nazareth is not in a literal manner in our Sunday assembly and walking on our streets, but the Easter faith affirms that the risen Lord is indeed at our table and in our world. Our observance of the Ascension must be such that Christ is praised as greater and more immanent than we had thought, rather than lesser and more distant.

The readings. All three years appoint the same readings. The gospel reading is the account in Luke's gospel of Jesus' last words to his disciples. Luke says Jesus preached from all the Hebrew scriptures his own suffering, death, and resurrection. The reading includes two particularly Lukan emphases, the forgiveness of sins and the proclamation of the gospel throughout the world. The first reading is the second account of the Ascension written by Luke in Acts. This account serves as the introduction to Acts by stressing that the movement of the church spreads from Jerusalem throughout the world. In the account in Acts, Luke adds the detail of the two men in white robes, echoing the two men in dazzling clothes who appeared to the women at the tomb. Thus the resurrection and the ascension are tied together. The second reading, from Ephesians, is even more Johannine in understanding the resurrection and the ascension as the same thing. God brings Christ from the dead to the throne of heaven, thus filling all in all.

The actions. Because of the theological importance of affirming the continuing presence of Christ and the power of his reign, it is not helpful to extinguish the paschal candle during this service, as some liturgical manuals previously taught. The fifty days of Easter continue through Pentecost.

The propers. Ascension Day is another way to celebrate Easter. Thus the tone of paschal celebration is appropriate. The color remains white. Celebratory hymns are sung. The Easter hymns 392–394 are particularly appropriate for Ascension time. The Topical Index in the assembly edition (pp. 1178–1188) suggests other appropriate hymns from throughout the collection. Two options for the prayer of the day are offered. The first comes to us from the seventh century and emphasizes the intercession of Christ on our behalf. The second is a twentieth-century composition that emphasizes the idea from Ephesians that Christ fills all things. The psalm is 47 or 93, both ancient royal psalms that praise the grandeur and beneficence of the king. On Ascension

Day, we praise Christ as this king, now reigning over the universe. Prayers at the offering and after communion are the prayers for Easter. The thanksgiving preface refers to the ascended Lord as our great high priest, thus the one who stands before God pleading for us. We are dismissed in the faith that Christ is with us.

Pentecost

The day. The celebration of Easter concludes with the Eighth Sunday of Easter, the Day of Pentecost. Just as Sunday is the eighth day, the new day for the Christian life, so Pentecost is the eighth Easter, Christ's giving over of his Spirit to the church. Once again, the lectionary superimposes the theology of John onto the narrative of Luke.

The celebration is set on the fiftieth day, in observance of the chronology from Luke. The Jewish festival of Pentecost is the observance of the giving of the law on Mount Sinai. By fixing the descent of the Holy Spirit on Pentecost, Luke layers the assembly of the believers onto the people of Israel, the tongues of fire on their heads onto the fire on Mount Sinai, the Holy Spirit onto God's giving of the law. For Jews encountering this narrative, the Christian message would be clear: God is doing a new thing with the pattern of the old sacred story.

Christians since the second century have kept this fiftieth day as a celebration. Over the centuries, the day took on the unique emphasis of the descent of the Holy Spirit, and the day became disjointed from Easter as a festival, and even a season, of its own. The three-year lectionary reconnects Pentecost with Easter and appoints gospel readings from John. According to John's gospel, the resurrection of Christ and the outpouring of the Holy Spirit are not separated events: the meaning of one is the meaning of the other. Pentecost proclaims the death and resurrection of Christ by celebrating the outpouring of the Spirit of the risen Lord on the community of believers.

The readings. The lectionary provides the option of reading Acts 2 as either the first or the second reading. The narrative includes many biblical images of the coming of God: wind from heaven, flames of fire, miraculous speech, the last days, prophecies, visions, and cosmological catastrophes. Luke means to indicate that the entire populated world responds to the coming of the Spirit. The gospel readings come from John: Jesus breathing his Spirit into the disciples on the evening of Easter Day; or Jesus calling all to come to drink of his Spirit; or Jesus preaching about the coming of the Spirit of truth; or Jesus telling Philip and us that the Spirit of truth abides with and in us. According to John, the mystery of the death of Christ is realized in his resurrection, his continuing presence in the assembly of believers, and the gift of his Spirit within us.

The lectionary suggests for each year a narrative from the Old Testament that complements the story of Pentecost: in year A, the nearly comic tale of those Israelites who complained that the spirit of Moses was alighting on several outsiders; in year B, Ezekiel's vision of the valley of the dry bones; and in year C, the tale of the Tower of Babel. Each story provides some of the background to the New Testament's presentation of the gift of the Holy Spirit enlivening the earth and filling us with the language of faith. Alternatively, if an assembly reads Acts 2 as the first reading, the second reading is a supreme passage from 1 Corinthians or Romans in which Paul teaches about the Spirit of the resurrection Christ in the Christian community.

The actions. For many congregations, Pentecost is the preferred time to schedule baptisms or the affirmation of baptism. Contemporary scholarship has demonstrated that what was traditionally called confirmation developed because the rite of baptism got divided in half, with the local presbyter performing the water rite, but with the laying on of hands and the prayer for the sevenfold gift of the Holy Spirit reserved for the visiting bishop. In the Western medieval church, confirmation was elevated to sacramental status. Among Lutherans it is not a sacrament but came to function as a puberty rite, marking the passage from childhood to adulthood. In Western societies, it no longer marks puberty. Many Christian communions are now reexamining the meaning of the rite and its role in an individual's religious development. See *The Christian Life* (Using *Evangelical Lutheran Worship,* vol. 2) for a more thorough discussion of this topic.

The most theologically sound practice is to return the prayer for the Holy Spirit to its rightful place in baptism, as is provided for in *Evangelical Lutheran Worship* Holy Baptism (AE p. 231), and to explore various ways to celebrate the gift of the Holy Spirit in the affirmation of baptism. If Pentecost is the occasion for such a rite, congregations are urged to consider how to make this affirmation a meaningful event, especially if it is expected that young teenagers will participate.

A full rite of the reaffirmation of baptism can include a welcome of new members into the congregation, a formal return to participation of Christians who have been long absent from the assembly, or the reaffirmation of faith by persons who have experienced a life change or endured a life crisis. The rite of Affirmation of Baptism is provided in the assembly edition, pages 234–237, with Notes on the Services in the leaders edition (31–32).

Some congregations have celebrated Pentecost as "the birthday of the church." Such a celebration is best reserved for the coffee hour after services, when the primary focus will be on those whose baptism has been affirmed. Some congregations urge everyone to wear red clothing. Worship planners can use their judgment whether this will be a helpful ritual addition to the morning. Pentecost is the last Sunday of the celebrative cycle when the paschal candle is lighted and prominently displayed. Henceforth, until next Easter Vigil, it will stand near the font and next to the coffin or urn at funerals.

The propers. As is usual throughout the year, festivals associated with the Holy Spirit and the power of the Spirit in the lives of the saints are adorned in red. The paraments and vestments are red. Strips of red fabric may hang around the room or red banners be added to the procession. Perhaps the candles in the room are red rather than white. Some of the profusion of flowers associated with Easter may adorn the worship space, to announce that this day too is Easter.

It is wholly appropriate that somewhere in the service there be a thanksgiving for baptism, either as part of the gathering or after the sermon prior to the creed. If there is a baptism, a celebratory thanksgiving at the font (III, IV, or V) is appropriate. Three options for the prayer of the day are provided. The first, from the seventh century, and the second and third, recent compositions, each highlight language and imagery from the gospel for the year. The psalm for each of the three years includes the sentence that the Spirit of God continually creates the world. In a time when disputes in church and society about divine creation are common, this psalm reminds us that creation is a continuous action of the divine Spirit. This is the last Sunday for the prayers at the offering and after communion to be the Easter selections, thus rendering unity to the fifty days of Easter.

The great thanksgiving preface is unique for this one day and is not intended to be used in the Sundays that follow Pentecost. The preface combines all the emphases of Pentecost: the day completes Easter, pours down the fire of the Spirit, unites the people, stands us alongside all the witnesses to the resurrection, and joins us to the praise of God that arises from all the creatures of earth and the angels in heaven. It might be useful for congregational preparation for Pentecost for an adult forum or printed instructional material to teach the contents of this comprehensive preface. A particularly celebratory thanksgiving at the table is appropriate.

The hymns in the Pentecost section of *Evangelical Lutheran Worship* present a wide variety of images of the Spirit we celebrate. The Spirit is the fount of our being (#394), light and fire (#395), a gentle breath and restless wind (#396), a father, a mother, a friend, a lover (#397), our king and guide (#398), the root of life and cleanser of all things (#399), the might of wild weather (#400), gracious teacher (#401), the vision and strength we need (#402), the song of the dove (#403), our leader (#404), the power of the life of God (#405), and the wind of creation (#407). The classic hymn that invokes the Spirit on the assembly is from the ninth-century, "Veni Creator Spiritus" (#577/578). This wealth of Pentecost hymnody might suggest the scheduling of a hymn sing as preservice music.

Vigil of Pentecost. Since Pentecost is one of the three primary feast days in the church year, it makes sense that it would have a vigil associated with it, as do Christmas and Easter. And indeed, there is evidence of a vigil of Pentecost dating back at least to the fifth century. As with the vigil of Easter, the Pentecost vigil was one of the main times for baptisms to occur. The vigil orders that have been preserved in the Eastern church and adapted by some communities in the West combine aspects of evening prayer, a blessing of the font, a litany, and a celebration of the communion meal, not unlike the Easter vigil pattern.

Lutherans, beginning with *Lutheran Book of Worship,* have begun to reclaim this ancient service. Propers for it are presented in *Evangelical Lutheran Worship* (AE p. 36), though no liturgy is prescribed or suggested. Most likely, work will continue on the crafting of such a service; in the meantime, worship planners have freedom to work with the propers provided, shaping an order that might include the elements listed above and would meet the needs of the worshiping community for this time at the end of the Easter season.

A Final Lutheran Word

This chapter of instructions and suggestions for the Sundays and festivals of the liturgical year hopes to provide inspiration and encouragement as assemblies renew the worship practices of their assembly. However, Martin Luther reminds us never to claim too much for the church's worship. Our faith is that not our efforts, but rather God, will save the world. Yet such a gift of salvation deserves our best attempts at praise and proclamation. As we pray in *Evangelical Lutheran Worship* thanksgiving at the table I, "We give thanks to you, O Lord God Almighty, not as we ought but as we are able." In gratitude, we worship more deeply and widely and fully each year.

CHAPTER FOUR

4 Observing Lesser Festivals and Commemorations

Sundays and the principal festivals, as we have seen, are central to the church's worship. Every Sunday is a festival of the resurrection of Jesus Christ. Principal festivals are those that celebrate some aspect of God, most of them relating to God made known to us in Christ. What then is the character, and what is the role, of the lesser festivals and commemorations? The brief description in *Evangelical Lutheran Worship* portrays them like this:

> *Lesser festivals* are additional days when we celebrate the life of Christ, the witness of those who accompanied and testified to him, and the gifts of God in the church.
>
> *Commemorations* illuminate various aspects of the church's life and mission through the lives of women and men who have followed Christ in succeeding generations. [AE p. 13]

From its very beginning, the church has pointed to exemplary women and men, living and dead, as a way to encourage one another in our life of faith. For instance, the writer of 2 Timothy offers these words to the disciple: "I am reminded of your sincere faith, a faith that lived first in your grandmother Lois and your mother Eunice and now, I am sure, lives in you" (2 Tim. 1:5). The death of Stephen was recorded in Acts 6–7 not only as a point of history but to lift up his witness as he faced his death. As the church continued to grow, more such exemplars were added and publicized. The twelve apostles (Matthias replacing Judas) were prominent among them, most of them having met their death as martyrs. And indeed, martyrs were the category of witnesses most honored by the church, especially in its early centuries. The reason is not hard to guess: these were the Christians who had taken their trust in the triune God to its ultimate test. Because there were all too many martyrs, the list began to grow: Ignatius; Perpetua and Felicity; Polycarp; Agnes.

Over time, other stalwart believers besides those who gave their lives were recognized as being worthy of the church's remembrance and emulation. Great teachers were added to the list, as were hermits who had "died to this world," influential leaders, and missionaries. Each of these people was assigned a day (usually, when known, the day of their death) and, as worship became more formalized, propers such as readings and prayers were assigned to the celebrations. Gradually the priority of Sundays and principal festivals was hidden or overshadowed by a proliferation of saints' days and local observances. Sixteenth-century reformers sought to trim back this overgrowth that obscured the gospel proclamation in the celebration of Sunday and the principal festivals. That same rationale lies behind the rubrical notes about how to honor this priority, as detailed in *Evangelical Lutheran Worship* (LE 10). The witness of the saints is no less worthy of our attention—indeed, more recent lives continue to be lifted up—but the central focus on Christ's life, death, and resurrection must always be paramount.

Saints and Saints' Days in the Rhythm of the Church Year

Most people enjoy singing "Oh, when the saints come marching in, O Lord, I want to be in that number." Yet should someone call us a saint, we probably demur and deny that identification. Children of the Reformation may resist even the idea of recognizing saints. Behind much of this ambiguity is a confusion created by differing definitions of what a saint is. Too often we think of saints as people of perfection beyond our own limits. Some strands of church tradition tend to support the view that these relatively few saints are models that many of us will never become, saying that after death some people may officially be designated saints.

However, the biblical model stresses another description of saints. It is because of God's grace in creation and in Christ that people are called saints. It is because of grace, not because of works. We don't need to wait until we die before we are labeled saints. Paul in his letters addresses ordinary members of his congregations as saints. All of this reminds us that Christians are both saints and sinners. True, we do lack perfection or personal achievement or awarded merit badges or a certain level of sanctification. We may be much more aware of our sinfulness than of our saintliness. But the nature of our baptism into Christ is that by God's grace our sins are washed away, and we are gifted with the title "saints."

In the Large Catechism, Martin Luther rhapsodizes about the promise of the word of God in relation to our being called saints:

> God's Word is the treasure that makes everything holy. By it, all the saints have themselves been made holy. At whatever time God's Word is taught, preached, heard, read, or pondered, there the person, the day, and the work is hallowed, not on account of the external work but on account of the Word that makes us all saints.[1]

For further reinforcement we need only look to the biblical figures we call saints. Saint Peter denied Jesus three times in a crucial time of witness. Saints James and John sought positions of power from Jesus that contradicted a giving away of power. Saint Matthew had been a hated collaborator with a foreign power. Rather than achievement or holiness based on works, their sainthood appears to be given, a holiness from without, from the Holy Spirit.

A former enemy of the church who supported oppression of individual Christians and the church, Saint Paul begins letters to the churches he has founded or visited by calling them saints: "To all God's beloved in Rome, who are called to be saints" (Rom. 1:7). In his letter to the gifted but problem-plagued church at Corinth, Paul reminds them of their gift of holiness in Christ Jesus: "To the church of God that is in Corinth, to those who are sanctified in Christ Jesus, called to be saints, together with all those who in every place call on the name of our Lord Jesus Christ" (1 Cor. 1:2). Even the offering of the Corinthian church, which, "sharing in this ministry to the saints," reflected care for others who may not have deserved it (2 Cor. 8:4). Concerning this diaconal offering that "supplies the needs of the saints" (2 Cor. 9:12), Paul suggests that it is a gift given out of love for others. As regards the basis of sainthood, the argument of the letter to the Galatians is that we receive such holiness by grace as a gift. We are heirs of a gift we have not earned or deserved.

Jesus himself was accused of not meeting the religious standards of sainthood. Gossip spread that "the Son of Man came eating and drinking, and they say, 'Look, a glutton and a drunkard, a friend of tax collectors and sinners!'" (Matt. 11:19). Questions were raised about Jesus' breaking religious laws when he compassionately healed people on the sabbath. When Jesus offered the five-times-married Samaritan woman, a foreign woman labeled unholy, "living water . . . a spring of water gushing up to eternal life" (John 4:10, 14), she knew this was a radical breaking down of barriers. Jesus' disciples also silently had quizzical looks about this radical, gracious gift to one who had no claims on holiness. But Jesus' scandalous acceptance, even of us, is the gospel!

Within all of this, there is a radical new view of holiness and sainthood. It is a gift of grace given by God in Christ for the sake of all people and the whole world. Sainthood breaks old molds and witnesses to surprising, shocking grace.

So the celebration of saints' days, such as Peter and Paul or the other disciples or apostles, point to what it means to be in the company of Jesus and the working out of the Creator's plan for the world. Instead of limiting sainthood to a relatively small number, these persons witness to what we are all called to be in the mission of God. Jesus himself said, "As the Father has sent me"—and we know what God's love for the world did in Jesus—"so I send you" (John 20:21). In effect, Jesus now turns to the world and says, "World, I am sending these ordinary people, these saints, to you as the Father sent me into the world."

Thus Lutherans, looking to the Bible, find help in determining how to understand and treat what the church commonly calls saints. Because they are ordinary, sinful people (however extraordinarily gifted), we do not invoke the saints for aid or pray to them; rather, we remember and honor them for their witness to Christ. As both saints and sinners, they remind us of their need and our need of God's grace.

The Augsburg Confession, one of the Lutheran confessional documents, gives us guidance about the place of saints:

> Concerning the cult of the saints our people teach that the saints are to be remembered so that we may strengthen our faith when we see how they experienced grace and how they were helped by faith. Moreover, it is taught that each person, according to his or her calling, should take the saints' good works as an example. . . . However, it cannot be demonstrated from Scripture that a person should call upon the saints or seek help from them.[2]

Commemorations: Extraordinary Grace in Ordinary People

As we consider the people in the list of commemorations in *Evangelical Lutheran Worship*, we are apt to recall other people—those whose lives, words, deeds, service, challenges, and encouragement have been important to us. A diversity of persons and voices will likely come to mind: a teacher, a parent, a friend, an influential leader, a pastor, a Christian mentor, a camp counselor.

Likewise the church has put together a list of persons who have been witnesses to Christ in church, community, and society. The list of commemorations in the assembly edition (pp. 15–17) provides a range of people from nearly every century and from different parts of the world. Older typical lists of saints tended to be dominated by males from the mainstream who were lay religious or clergy. The list in *Evangelical Lutheran Worship* is not intended to be comprehensive. Although those named are considered worthy of commemoration, it is hoped that those names will also suggest others to be remembered and emulated, opening up consideration of the contributions of many people in varied situations.

Again, this reflects biblical practice. The Bible didn't limit itself to the "stars," the safe and well known, when suggesting those who might be commemorated. We have seen how otherwise unknown women—Lois and Eunice—were made examples. The genealogies of Matthew (1:1-17) and Luke (3:23-38) trace how God worked through a diverse and fallible group of people leading up to Jesus. The book of Hebrews recalls, commemorates, and gives thanks for people of faith like Abraham, Moses, Barak, David (the adulterer), and the prophets who served God's gracious purpose. Even Rahab, a prostitute, is pointed to as a heroically faithful saint. None of the people in that lineage were saintly through the whole course of their lives. There is realism in the scriptures about how God works through the lives and work of fallen human beings. They were all sinners, but God's grace called them saints in that they were part of God's working out God's purposes in the world. The extraordinary purpose and plan of God is accomplished through fallible, sinful people called to be saints. Sainthood relies on God's grace, not our merit badges.

Hebrews goes on to say that these people throughout the centuries are mentioned to encourage us in our own discipleship as we live out Christ's purpose for us in the world. The writer looks at the list that was compiled and says to future generations: "Therefore, since we are surrounded by so great a cloud of witnesses, let us also lay aside every weight and the sin that clings so closely, and let us run with perseverance the race that is set before us, looking to Jesus the pioneer and perfecter of our faith" (Heb. 12:1-2). This image is a main theme in the prayer of the day for the commemoration of saints:

> Lord God, you have surrounded us with so great a cloud of witnesses. Grant that we *[encouraged by the example of your servant/s name/s]* may persevere in the course that is set before us and, at the last, share in your eternal joy with all the saints in light, through Jesus Christ, our Savior and Lord, who lives and reigns with you and the Holy Spirit, one God, now and forever. [AE p. 59]

The preface within the great thanksgiving (see LE 180) includes the phrase "with the church on earth and the hosts of heaven, we praise your name and join their unending hymn." We are invited to reflect on and give thanks for the people commemorated in *Evangelical Lutheran Worship* and for those saints who have blessed our lives. They are among that great cloud of witnesses. By God's grace, we too are invited into this great community of communal memory. The commemorations name only a few of that great host of faithful people (call them saints if you will), and in so doing, point to the great community that surrounds us both on earth and amid the hosts of heaven.

Geddes MacGregor passes along an anecdote that illustrates this accompaniment we enjoy. "An Anglican priest in England was asked: 'How many people were at the early celebration of the Eucharist last Wednesday morning?' Perhaps the questioner was a skeptic who knew that not many would have been there, and possibly he was rubbing it in. The priest replied with this wonderful vision: 'There were three old ladies, the janitor, several thousand archangels, a large number of seraphim, and several million of the triumphant saints of God.' "[3] What a cloud of witnesses!

The names on the *Evangelical Lutheran Worship* list remind us to think broadly about saints. Included are a number of anonymous witnesses (such as Perpetua's companions and the martyrs of Japan and Uganda), individual martyrs, encouragers, challengers, advocates of justice, peacemakers, healers, renewers of the church and society, artists and scientists, and agents of loving service—all part of the great cloud of witnesses who uphold us and inspire us as people called to live out our baptismal callings. Some persons are like Elizabeth of Hungary and Martín de Porres, who provide a counter voice to the "prosperity gospel" all too prevalent today. The list of martyrs, like Stephen, Lucy, Dietrich Bonhoeffer, and Martin Luther King, remind us of the cost of discipleship. There is affirmation of people who have worked for the common good of the world. We give thanks for them. Brief biographies and notes on the various commemorations in *Evangelical Lutheran Worship* can be found in Appendix A of this volume, page 197.

All of these names suggest that individuals and each community will add their own names of people who have blessed them with their own faith stories. Thus the list of commemorations is fluid. Vinje Lutheran Church in Willmar, Minnesota, inscribed the names of many of these saints around their worship room. However, they also left a space open to remind us that new witnesses and servants of the gospel are constantly being added.

All saints are meant to be a blessing to others. This description can be applied to all of us as it was applied to Abraham. God said, "I will bless you . . . so that you will be a blessing . . . and in you all the families of the earth shall be blessed" (Gen. 12:2–3). It is in this sense that the people commemorated in the *Evangelical Lutheran Worship* list of commemorations are to be viewed. Down through the centuries we remember them because of the blessing their lives have been for others and for the world God loves.

We are reminded that we are also saints meant for blessing others in our families, our communities, our congregations, and our world. Through the commemorations we remember Christ's saving and blessing mission to the world and that God continues to work through and bless the world through ordinary people like us. We do well to stand in awe as we hear Jesus say to us, "As the Father has sent me, so I send you." Yes, the world needs saints who go marching out to bless the world. Yes, each of us is called to be one of that number.

Finally, commemorations are about baptism. Jesus said to his followers, "Let your light shine before others, so that they may see your good works and give glory to your Father in heaven" (Matt. 5:16). We often remember that phrase from its frequent use in the order for baptism (AE p. 231). Indeed, leaders in the early church at times referred to baptism as illumination. When we, and these saints of times past, were baptized, we became illuminated by the Spirit. The light is not about us, not about perfect lives, but about the Christ, the light of the world, who shines in us and through us to the glory of God.

Commemorations in Congregational Life

These commemorations can be incorporated into the life of the congregation in various ways. They can be used as sermon illustrations.

These persons can be named in the prayers. To remind members of this great cloud of witnesses, the list for that month could be included in the congregational newsletter or posted regularly on the church Web site. Persons responsible for devotions at committee meetings or other gatherings could use the "faith story" and witness of one of these persons. Confirmation classes and youth groups may be encouraged by these examples of how God's grace works in people's lives.

Excellent resources are available to help flesh out the lives of these people in the list of commemorations. Philip Pfatteicher's *New Book of Festivals and Commemorations* is an ecumenical resource that describes the life and work, and often includes the actual words, of these and other diverse voices who have served God's mission through the centuries.[4] *Bread for the Day,* a daily guide for individual or small-group Bible reading and prayer, published annually, lists the commemorations on their appropriate day and provides a brief description of each of the lesser festivals and commemorations.[5]

The propers for the commemorations (grouped according to category, AE pp. 59–61) provide biblical texts and a prayer for the commemoration around which a liturgy could be constructed on a weekday.

Imaginative Planning for Various Occasions

Sometimes people are confused by the church's use of the word *occasional.* In liturgical matters it usually doesn't carry its common meaning of "now and then." Rather, the term commonly refers to certain occasions that invite a community to worship and prayer. So there may be "occasional services" for occasions like installation of congregational officers. And there are other, less narrowly focused, occasions for which *Evangelical Lutheran Worship* (AE pp. 61–63) has provided propers.

Day of Thanksgiving. These propers will most often be used for an annual national Thanksgiving Day, which is why there are three sets of propers for years A, B, and C. However, other times will arise when the body of Christ will want corporately to offer thanks, and these readings and prayer may be of use then as well.

Christian Unity. Each year the Week of Prayer for Christian Unity commences on January 18, the Confession of Peter, and concludes on January 25, the Conversion of Paul. Begun by Franciscans in New

York in 1908, the week has been widely accepted. In such a divided and even warring world, peace talks and prayer among divided Christians is an important witness. When talking about Jesus' prayer that all his followers would be one and provide a witness to the world, the theologian Kent Knutson remarked that Christ only has one church, but because of our sin we do not know how to be one. Therefore, it is only in humility and repentance that we can approach one another. In local communities, prayer could be held in differing churches on each day or evening of the week, with members of other faith communities invited to join them in prayer. Another variation could be holding a community prayer liturgy on the first and last day of the Week of Prayer for Christian Unity, with suggestions for individual prayer on the other days of that week. Additional resources for the week are available at www.geii.org. Again, the propers available in *Evangelical Lutheran Worship* are also useful at other occasions in which Christian unity is prayed for and celebrated.

Dedication or Anniversary of a Church. A set of readings is provided for this use, as are two prayers. The first is more suited to a focus on the worship building, the second to occasions in which the worshiping community is at the center. Other resources for these occasions are provided in the occasional services book accompanying *Evangelical Lutheran Worship.*

Harvest. Though harvest festivals have become less common as life in the U.S.A. and Canada has become more urbanized, the tradition of pausing to give thanks to God for the harvest is still important. The harvest festival has roots deep in the Old Testament, in which it was called Sukkoth, or the Feast of Tabernacles (or Booths). Maintaining such a festival, even within city congregations, can be a step in keeping consumers aware of where their food comes from and of the people who labor to provide it, as well as the blessings of God, from whom it comes.

Day of Penitence. Whereas the services of corporate and, especially, individual confession and forgiveness (AE pp. 238–244) are recommended for use in the healing process of admitting our individual sinfulness and receiving God's forgiveness, there are times when the entire community needs to gather and express repentance. Examples might be a community crisis in which people have been wronged, or a moment when it seems appropriate to admit and seek forgiveness for sins of the nation of which we are part. Two prayers are provided; the first is broadly useful, the second concentrates on the guilt of the Christian community. Depending on the context, the order for Corporate Confession and Forgiveness might provide a framework for such a service. Hymns #599–609 may offer a starting point for song resources.

Day of Mourning. New to *Evangelical Lutheran Worship*, these propers are particularly appropriate at a time of tragedy that has widespread effect. They acknowledge those moments when we need to invoke God's presence in our grieving, an impulse familiar from the psalms of lament. Besides these propers and those many psalms, worship planners may find hymns #697–704 helpful.

National Holiday. Days that focus on important moments in the history and life of a nation are not primarily church days. In fact, it can be problematic to draw too close a connection between church and state at such times. Repeatedly throughout history, grief has been caused by nations claiming God's exclusive support. Nevertheless, with care, it is certainly appropriate to thank God for the blessings enjoyed by our nation and to intercede also for all nations and peoples. A particularly helpful hymn for such times is #887, "This Is My Song."

Peace. A broad term, *peace* encompasses everything from absence of open conflict to the wonderful, biblical concept of *shalom*—being whole through the gifts of God. The readings and prayer provided here are a starting point for worship that addresses this theme.

Stewardship of Creation. As the world becomes increasingly concerned over the fragile health of the planet God has given us for our home, it is appropriate that we recommit ourselves to our task as stewards of creation and intercede to God on behalf of all the facets of that creation: land, water in all its forms, air, plants, animals, minerals. Possible hymn resources include, but are not limited to, those in the Creation section of *Evangelical Lutheran Worship*, #730–740.

New Year's Eve. Oddly specific in this more general list, New Year's Eve is nevertheless a time when many people stop to take stock of their lives. This category provides propers for those communities or individuals who wish to mark this turning point in the secular calendar.

PART TWO

2

Daily Prayer

CHAPTER FIVE

5

Keeping Time for Daily Prayer

What is the place of daily prayer in Lutheran worshiping communities today? The Evangelical Lutheran Church in America and Evangelical Lutheran Church in Canada have issued statements encouraging a return to the service of holy communion, word and sacrament, as the primary form of worship. (See *The Sunday Assembly,* Using *Evangelical Lutheran Worship,* vol. 1, for a review of this reasoning, as well as the actual statements in the appendixes.) But there are other worship forms that enjoy a long and deep history within the church, particularly the services of daily prayer. What is to be the role of such services in light of the emphasis on holy communion?

It may be helpful to begin by examining briefly how daily prayer developed. Because there is paucity of detailed information about the actual biblical practices of communal prayer, scholars have posed various interpretations of the development of prayer patterns.[1] However, communal prayer, praise, and study of scripture are assumed. The synagogue gathering assumed that at least ten men would be present. Jesus said about communal agreement on prayer: "If two of you agree on earth about anything you ask, it will be done for you by my Father in heaven. For where two or three are gathered in my name, I am there among them" (Matt. 18:19–20). A Jewish parallel says: "Two that are sitting and occupied with the words of Torah, the Shekinah [presence of God] is among them."[2]

This tenacity in prayer is reflected in the idealized statement in the Mishnah that suggests nothing should interrupt our prayers:

> One stands up to say the Tefillah only in a serious mood. Zealous men used to wait an hour before they said the Tefillah, so that they might direct their hearts toward God. Even if the king greets a man during the Tefillah he may not return the greeting. Even if a snake was twisted around his heel, he may not interrupt it.[3]

While prayer was taken seriously, fluidity and creativity were present in old Jewish patterns as context was honored.

> The order of prayer was still relatively flexible, for while the general outline and the motifs of the prayers and blessings were well defined, their recital involved an element of improvisation and free composition. The latter was seen as a safeguard against mechanical prayer. Some *amoraim* (authorities) were singled out for praise because they recited a "new prayer" or a "new benediction" every day.[4]

This suggests that flexibility, fluidity, allowance for responding to the occasion, context, and creative improvisation can be considered along with a nurturing structure.

We don't know the details of Hebrew prayer practices, but we get hints about set times for prayer. Even though it was against the edict of the king in the country where the Jews were exiled, Daniel persisted in his individual prayer practice: "Although Daniel knew that the document had been signed, he continued to go to his house, which had windows in its upper room toward Jerusalem, and to get down on his knees three times a day to pray to his God and praise him, just as he had done previously" (Dan. 6:10). One of the psalms also alludes to this three-a-day pattern of prayer:

> "In the evening, in the morning, and at noonday,
> I will complain and lament,
> and God will hear my voice" (Ps. 55:17).

Some religious traditions, such as Islam, call for times of prayer at several times through the day. But even apart from such rituals, there is a natural rhythm of the day that invites prayer in the evening before retiring for the day, and in the morning upon rising. The psalms reflect that pattern.

> "It is good to give thanks to the Lord,
> to sing praises to your name, O Most High;
> to herald your love in the morning,
> and your faithfulness at night" (Ps. 92:1-2).
> "My God, I cry out by day, but you do not answer;
> by night, but I find no rest" (Ps. 22:2).

"You make the dawn and the dusk
to sing for joy" (Ps. 65:8).
"I arise early in the morning and I cry out to you,
I hope for your word.
My eyes are open in the night watches,
that I may meditate upon your promise" (Ps. 119:147-148).

Since the early Christian church grew out of Jewish traditions, it has been assumed that Christian prayer patterns were carried over from Jewish practice. However, recent scholarship has largely refuted this idea. In fact, after the destruction of the temple in Jerusalem, Jewish synagogue prayer may well have adapted practices of the early Christians, rather than the other way around.

Set times of prayer are implied in the *Didache,* one of the earliest noncanonical Christian writings. It appears that writer is suggesting that Christians substitute the Lord's Prayer in place of the Jewish practice of praying the *Shemoneh Esreh* (or the "Eighteen Blessings") as the center of the *Tefillah,* the daily prayers. After the writer instructs his readers to "pray . . . as the Lord directed in his gospel," he provides a text for the Lord's Prayer similar to that in the Gospel of Matthew. At its conclusion, he adds, "Pray this way thrice daily."[5] In other locations, however, we hear of prayer four, five, or some other number of times a day, so there seems not to have been any common pattern.

As in the psalms, morning and evening do, naturally enough, appear to be times for prayer. Cyprian (about 250) brings the new perspective of the resurrection of Jesus to these times of prayer.

> One must also pray in the morning, that the resurrection of the Lord may be celebrated by morning prayer. . . . Likewise at sunset and the passing of the day it is necessary to pray. For since Christ is the true sun and the true day, when we pray and ask, as the sun and the day of the world recede, that the light may come upon us again, we pray for the coming of Christ, which provides us with the grace of eternal light.[6]

Robert Taft, in his excellent book on the historical development of daily prayer, *The Liturgy of the Hours in East and West,* points to an eschatological theme present in the early church that called for a watchful, wide-awake state that reflects praying without ceasing. Taft says that morning and evening prayer, "like all liturgy, are simply moments expressive of the ceaseless hymn of praise that is Christian life." He illustrates this eschatological prayer stance by pointing to the *Canons of Hippolytus* from Egypt (about 336–340 C.E.). Using biblical material, the ancient author says:

> Let each one take care to pray with great vigilance in the middle of the night, for our fathers have said that at that hour all creation is assiduous in the service of praising God, all the angelic hosts and the souls of the just bless God. For the Lord testifies to this saying, "In the middle of the night there was a cry: Behold, the bridegroom has come, go out to meet him" (Matt. 25:6). At cockcrow, again, is a time when there are prayers in the churches, for the Lord says, "Watch, for you do not know at what time the Master will come, in the evening, or in the middle of the night, or at cockcrow, or in the morning" (Mark 13:35), which means we must praise God at every hour. And when a man sleeps on his bed, he must pray to God in his heart.[7]

This perspective reflects the psalmist's call for prayer without ceasing: "I will bless the LORD at all times; the praise of God shall ever be in my mouth" (Ps. 34:1).

Daily prayer within Christianity developed in at least two directions over the centuries. First, there is the so-called "cathedral" prayer pattern, which has also been called "the people's office or service of prayer."[8] This latter name for this first pattern, suggested by George Guiver, reflects the fact that not all gatherings were in a cathedral where priest and lay people gathered for daily prayer. Wherever they were held, the forms developed in this tradition required the participation of an active assembly and included hymns, psalmody, reading, and instruction. Cathedral-type prayers were more outwardly directed, both to God in praise and to other people in shared worship and in intercession. However, after the time of Constantine this form of daily prayer declined, and other forms became dominant.

A second direction grew out of monastic life, both desert monastic and urban monastic. The most influential of these was the desert pattern, developed primarily by hermits, where a more stringent pattern was developed to approximate "prayer without ceasing." In distinction to the cathedral offices, a major focus of these monastic offices was praying through the entire psalter. Paul Bradshaw helpfully points out that monastic prayer has as one of its goals spiritual education or formation.[9] Because of its origins, it can be performed with or without other people, and even in a group it does not require a strong leadership presence.

Gradually, as monastic communities became more established after the time of Benedict, patterns of prayer offices were developed at specified times of day and night. Seven hours was a common number, perhaps inspired by Psalm 119:164, "Seven times a day I praise you for your righteous ordinances," but there were many different arrangements. At its fullest, the times of prayer throughout a day could include:

- Vespers (at the end of the day)
- Compline (upon retiring)
- Vigils (sometime during the night)
- Matins/Lauds (at cock-crow, the end of the night)
- Prime (during the first hour of daylight)
- Terce (at the third hour, roughly 9:00 a.m.)
- Sext (at the sixth hour, roughly noon)
- None (at the ninth hour, roughly 3:00 p.m.)

At the time of the Reformation, Luther and other reformers restored Morning Prayer (Matins), Evening Prayer (Vespers), and Night Prayer (Compline) to worship in congregations, seminaries, and schools. However, the monastic pattern still influenced many of the orders. The services in *Evangelical Lutheran Worship,* with their core based on the ancient pattern of psalm (word) and prayer, invite active and imaginative participation by lay persons in this form of communal prayer. They also present opportunities for use in individual or household prayer.

Daily Prayer: A Relationship to God and the World

A biblical exhortation urges us to "pray without ceasing" (1 Thess. 5:17). The psalm writer says, "Every day I will bless you and praise your name forever and ever" (Ps. 145:2). Again and again the calls come to us: "I will praise the LORD as long as I live; I will sing praises to my God while I have my being" (Ps. 146:2); "My eyes are ever looking to you, O LORD" (Ps. 25:15); "Continually seek God's face" (Ps. 105:4); "From the rising of the sun to its going down, let the name of the LORD be praised" (Ps. 113:3).

Unfortunately, many contemporary Christians do not have any regular, daily prayer pattern. Still, God invites us into a daily relationship of gracious dialogue. Prayer is a gift of access for all the baptized and those seeking to live in a relationship with the God who has spoken, is speaking, and has promised to speak through Jesus, the living Word, and the Spirit, who helps us pray with sighs too deep for words as we ponder the scriptures, which still speak to us.

A daily pattern of prayer brings with it a sense of discipline similar to that an athlete or musician knows. When they do not have a discipline of practice, they usually lose the freedom to play the game or the music at the level to which they are accustomed. To change the metaphor, any relationship between individuals requires continued effort and communication by both parties in order to remain strong. Our relationship with God is nourished and deepened by the conversation of daily prayer. Daily prayer renews us. Prayer takes seriously the ongoing kinship established when we were baptized.

For Christians, prayer arises out of God's grace offered in Christ through word and sacrament. Baptism initiates us into the relationship from which prayer arises. As people say both that they *were* married and *are* married, so we say both that we *were* baptized and *are* baptized. We live in that relationship with all that it means and promises. The ELCA's *The Use of the Means of Grace: A Statement on the Practice of Word and Sacrament* asserts that "Baptism conforms us to the death and resurrection of Christ precisely so that we repent and receive forgiveness, love our neighbors, suffer for the sake of the Gospel, and witness to Christ" (UMG 14A). Daily prayer is one of the ways in which we claim that promised reality and renew and deepen our baptismal vocation for daily living this new life in Jesus Christ in the power of the Holy Spirit. Martin Luther pointed to Romans 6 when he spoke in the Small Catechism of the daily meaning of baptism as walking in newness of life (AE p. 1165).

Says the ELCA's statement: "There are many ways to encourage this daily dying to sin and being raised to live before God. They include confession and absolution, the reading of the Scriptures, preaching, the mutual consolation of the sisters and brothers, daily prayer and the sign of the cross, the remembrance of the catechism, and the profession of the creed" (UMG 17B). This is part of the lifelong learning and apprenticeship of all the baptized as we receive and live in the wonderful gifts given in baptism and the continuing gifts of grace in word and communion at the Sunday assembly. Daily prayer is one way in which we discover the importance of baptism for daily living and what it means to be caught up in God's gracious mission for the whole world.

When talking about "daily prayer," many people think primarily of their petitions to God. However, Christian prayer assumes a relationship that puts us in a dialogue in which we are called to listen as well as speak. Meditating on the word of God accompanies what we think of as *our* prayers. Heinrich Bornkamm summarizes Luther's view of this dialogue: "For one dare not forget that prayer has two component parts: talking and listening. How can we expect God to listen to us if we do not listen to [God]? In his typical rhetoric, Luther says, 'If we want our prayers to be heard, we must first hear God's Word; otherwise [God] will not hear us either, no matter if we weep and shout till we burst!' "[10]

Prayer takes its cue from the incarnation, that is, the Word become flesh. In prayer we do not escape the world in some spiritual way, but rather with Christ we enter fully into God's mission to and in the world that God created and loves. Prayer enters the world as truly as Jesus, the living Word, entered the world. Prayer engages the mission of God in the world in the name of Jesus in the power of the Holy Spirit.

Christian prayer believes and proclaims that the kingdom of God, God's royal rule, has come into the midst of the world in Jesus Christ. We begin the praise that will be on the lips of every creature at the culmination of history. It is God's kingdom we pray will come among us, where God's will is done on earth as well as in heaven.

Learning to Pray between the Lines

We often speak about reading between the lines. What is spoken may also, thanks to our knowledge of the person or situation, communicate much that is unspoken. When we use the rich texts of daily prayer, we enter this prayer most fruitfully when we pray between the lines. We bring our context, the present needs and situation, the world in which we live, our personal and communal concerns, and the mission of God for us so that they resonate between the lines of classic texts of scripture and prayers. In this way, they always speak a new grace and call us into a new dialogue of prayer. Those familiar texts are always speaking in new ways, because we face new challenges and changing situations.

Martin Luther demonstrated this praying between the lines in a pamphlet written in 1535. It was titled *A Simple Way to Pray for a Good Friend: How One Should Pray, for Peter, the Master Barber.* Luther takes his Small Catechism as the pattern for daily prayer. Each petition of the Lord's Prayer is prayed, but then Luther brings his own context and experiences to this memorized text and writes a half page on how this petition is working today in this place. Thus, a resonance is created between the well-known text and the world, the person's needs, the community's concerns, so that worshipers hear the Spirit speak to their situation. Therefore the Lord's Prayer, scripture, and traditional prayers speak in new ways with new grace.

Luther also cautions his friend Peter, the barber, not to merely repeat what he, Luther, has written, because that would not be praying between the lines.

> I do not want you to recite all these words in your prayer. That would make it nothing but idle chatter and prattle. . . . Rather do I want your heart to be stirred and guided concerning the thoughts which ought to be comprehended in the Lord's Prayer. These thoughts may be expressed, if your heart is rightly warmed and inclined toward prayer, in many different ways and with more words or fewer. I do not bind myself to such words or syllables, but say my prayers in one fashion today, in another tomorrow, depending on my mood and feeling.[11]

Again, then, it is like a human relationship. A husband may say to his wife, "I love you." The wife could respond, like some do about set forms of liturgy, "Can't you think of anything new to say?" However, if husband and wife have had a serious argument and there have been hurt feelings and hurtful words, then "I love you" may communicate an attempt to reconcile and share forgiving love. On the other hand, if they have had a great time together, and the husband says, "I love you," it reflects the positive energy of a nourishing relationship. In each situation, those same words can never be the same old thing. Life echoes in that timeworn phrase. In daily prayer, in hearing the scriptures, in any liturgy when we bring ourselves, our community, and world, this time can never be the same old thing. We have learned to pray between the lines just as the Holy Spirit constantly speaks between the lines.

Another illustration of this lively dialogue between the biblical and liturgical texts with the events and issues of daily life is a short piece written by Herbert Brokering. This pastor poet writes:

IF
    all the mental images and emotional picture of:
    major news networks
        sudden telephone calls,
        letters from family and friends,
        and the evening newspaper
        are the images on the minds
            of people gathered for worship,
            as they fold their hands
            and pray their supplications,
THEN
    could they also,
    while gathering their petitions for legislation,
    while advocating justice,
        and while seeing the six o'clock news,
        say intentionally and reverently,
        (even silently):
            "Hear us and help us, good Lord."
            Lord, have mercy![12]

These great texts then become a lens or way we view the world. The cry "Lord, have mercy" is a familiar dialogical response in the psalms and in our modern prayers. We cry "Have mercy" because we believe and trust that God is indeed merciful. When something bad happens, you may hear the exclamation, "Oh, mercy." A siren on an emergency vehicle can be heard as a Kyrie cry: "Lord, someone needs your mercy. Lord, have mercy." Seen this way, our service of daily prayer or our Sunday service of holy communion is not a thirty- or sixty-minute program but rather a way we view, live, and serve God's mission for the sake of the world.

God's Mission and Daily Prayer

As with most things, one can emphasize one aspect at the expense or diminution of another. One can so emphasize Christ's divinity that the human dimension of the Word-become-flesh is minimized. In daily prayer we can emphasize the praise of God and the extensive use of the psalms at the expense of intercessory prayer for the world. Paul Bradshaw argues that the cathedral or people's office was "the Church gathered for prayer, exercising its royal priesthood by offering a sacrifice of praise and thanksgiving on behalf of all creation and interceding for the salvation of the world." In contrast, he says that "the monastic office centered around silent meditation on the word of God and supplication for spiritual growth and personal salvation. Its ultimate aim was spiritual formation: the monk meditated on Christ in order to grow into his likeness, and prayed for the grace necessary for that."[13]

The prayers in *Evangelical Lutheran Worship*'s daily prayer liturgies (AE pp. 304, 316–318) do bring intercessory prayer for the world into balance with praise of the God who indeed so loved the world that God sent Jesus to this specific planet on which we live. Inward devotion needs outward expression.

Gordon Davies stressed that worship and mission are two sides of God's one activity for the sake of the world. About prayer, he says: "When the church prays, as when Christ prayed in Galilee, it is engaged in mission; it participates in the divine action for the world. . . . Thus, prayer, which places us on God's side, involves mission."[14] Therefore, as a community and its prayer leaders keep an eye on the world and intercede for its needs, our daily prayer liturgies will keep the missionary character of the gospel at the heart of communal and individual prayer.

Daily Prayer Flows out of and into Holy Communion

Daily prayer does not replace holy communion, but like the renewed daily lectionary it carries word and sacrament into the week and then carries our entire life and world back into this central engagement with the means of grace. As the common stuff of daily life (bread and wine) in holy communion assures us of the presence of Christ, so in daily prayer we claim that presence in all the common stuff of daily life. In the daily routine, we live as the body of Christ, the church, in the world and for the sake of the world.

"The Evangelical Lutheran Church in America is committed by its statement of purpose to 'worship God in proclamation of the Word and administration of the sacraments and through lives of prayer, praise, thanksgiving, witness, and service'" (UMG 3A). This statement reminds us that word and sacrament are not simply sixty-minute events, but that God's action through these means of grace is meant to flow out in daily prayer, witness, and praise. Further, as we live in daily communication with God during the week, we have much to bring back into the Sunday gathering around word and sacrament. There will be confession of failure, thanksgiving for God's grace during the week, laments growing out of our experience in this broken world. In other words, there is a dynamic relationship between Sunday and the days of the week, a relationship that is fostered through daily prayer.

To Preach or Not to Preach

At the time of the Reformation, the sermon was considered important for catechetical purposes and providing biblical material to people who may have been unable to read the Bible themselves. Therefore the sermon or biblical exposition was added to daily prayer liturgies. Today, especially when these prayer services are not the primary worship form for the community, it is worth taking a fresh look at the practice.

Context will play a large role. Is this truly *daily* prayer, in which a community (however small or large) gathers every day for this patterned prayer, shaped in significant ways by the surrounding Sundays or season? Then participants are likely to be practiced in apprehending the message carried by the psalms, the scripture, and a sermon may be unnecessary, even intrusive. These services were not originally conceived as being built around a sermon.

On the other hand, is this a midweek service, perhaps for Lent or Advent, and thus a significant-if-secondary worship service for the week? Is it understood by worshipers as a time when they want to be fed by the preached word? Then perhaps a way should be found to supply that need. If a full sermon is desired, that may mean finding a different form of worship better suited to a sermon, such as the Service of the Word (AE pp. 210–222), or it may call for appropriate adaptation of the daily prayer form. If a briefer form of proclamation will suffice, it is more easily accommodated within the daily prayer form. After all, the preached word remains an important focus for Lutheran worship.

The scriptures proclaimed in the readings communicate the living Word even as eating the bread and drinking from the cup in holy communion "proclaim the Lord's death until he comes" (1 Cor. 11:26).

Proclamation may take various forms, as suggested by the rubric on page 302 of the assembly edition:

> The reading of scripture is followed by silence for reflection. Other forms of reflection may also follow, such as brief commentary, teaching, or personal witness; non-biblical readings; interpretation through music or other art forms; or guided conversation among those present.

The local context, size of the worshiping community, the gifts of the community and the season of the church year all will help shape the way in which the proclamation is done. However, when the psalms and scripture readings are present without a full sermon, the word is still proclaimed and applied by hearers as they reflect in silence on what that word is saying to them.

If a full sermon is used, rather than a briefer form of reflection or response, an option is to move it outside of the prayer service in order to preserve the rhythm of that order. Thus, especially in the forms for Morning Prayer or Evening Prayer in *Evangelical Lutheran Worship*, the sermon could be preached following the prayers section of the service (AE p. 305, 318). *Lutheran Book of Worship* (pp. 137–138, 152–153) provides an outline of how this might be done. If a sermon or homily will accompany Night Prayer, it may best precede the service, so that the spirit of this form as the church's "bedtime prayer" might be preserved. Again, the particular circumstances will help shape the wisest course.

Expanding or Contracting the Order

It is clear from the options in *Evangelical Lutheran Worship* daily prayer liturgies and patterns that one can imaginatively add to the services to create a more festive and full service of prayer. It is also clear that one can use these patterns in a simpler way for individual or family prayer.

Reviewing Jewish and Christian practice of daily prayer reminds us that there has been flexibility of prayer and praise within an open structure or pattern that attended to local or area context. True, sometimes forms have become so rigid that even the Spirit may have trouble blowing freely. Yet we also recognize that traditional forms link us to the prayer of worshiping assemblies through the centuries and presently throughout the world. An evening hymn celebrates the fact that the orbiting earth means communal morning prayer and evening prayer are constantly being offered in the human realm, together with all the angels and saints in heaven.

> As to each continent and island
> the dawn leads on another day,
> the voice of prayer is never silent,
> nor dies the strain of praise away. [#569]

Congregations will do well to play creatively with the tradition but always remember that that rich tradition gives the community the "stuff" with which they can play. Too often the tradition is dismissed without doing the work to give the wisdom of the ages a contemporary voice and expression. Singing a new song does not mean abolishing all the old ones! That is why it is more advantageous to bring together the Bible and the present day, the wealth of the tradition and the creativity of the contemporary.

Subsequent chapters in this volume will propose ways in which specific prayer services can be simplified, elaborated upon, and varied.

Daily Prayer in Particular Seasons and Times

The seasons of Lent and Advent invite prayerful reflection on the gift and hope of our relationship with God in Jesus Christ. Most congregations hold midweek Lenten services and some provide midweek Advent services. These seasons provide excellent opportunities to use evening and/or morning prayer and put them deep into the memory bank of worshipers. With their emphasis on prayer, praise, and proclamation, these services offer solid grounding for a congregation's deepening of their life and mission. They also lend themselves well to the kind of contemplative mood that often seems appropriate during these seasons.

In addition to those seasons, though, other possibilities for use present themselves during the liturgical or church year. One rural pastor offers a prayer service once a week all year long with a catechetical exposition of the catechism. Another congregation sings and prays the service of Morning Prayer every Thursday morning, with opportunity following to drink coffee and discuss the texts for the upcoming Sunday.

To emphasize the time focusing on God's work in Jesus Christ during Holy Week, some congregations provide morning and evening prayer during the days prior to the Triduum (Three Days) of Maundy Thursday through Easter Sunday.

Evening prayer could be a way to approach the third major vigil of the year, the Vigil of Pentecost. This could be a counterpart to the Vigil of Christmas (Christmas Eve) and the Vigil of Easter. Propers are provided in *Evangelical Lutheran Worship*, and, as an alternative to a service of holy communion, which will likely be celebrated the next day, an evening prayer service shaped around Pentecost themes could be a welcomed approach.

Several congregations in an area may wish to schedule morning prayer and evening prayer every week, perhaps rotating among the congregations. This would provide a contemporary version of the cathedral office, where worshipers from parish churches would join together at the local cathedral.

Some congregations pray night prayer / compline after church council or committee meetings. The choir could sing the service of Night Prayer at the conclusion of rehearsals and thus be prepared to lead the congregation in praying with this form.

One predominantly white congregation in Iowa has a relationship with a predominantly black congregation in Chicago. When the Iowa congregation does evening prayer, they often emphasize that relationship by singing spirituals and songs reflective of their sister congregation.

Lesser festivals and commemorations that occur during the week also provide appropriate occasions to pray the daily prayer liturgies.

Pastors and musicians may find it helpful to talk with colleagues about possible ways to introduce and use more fully the rich tradition of daily prayer liturgies. For example, small groups can offer opportunity for conversation and community; they can also use daily prayer as a way to lift up a prayer ministry for the mission of the congregation and provide a sense of joining all the saints in praise and intercession.

Prayer in the Home

Martin Luther encouraged families and individuals to begin and end the day with prayer and provided simple forms for this in his Small Catechism (AE pp. 1166–1167). The ELCA's statement on *The Use of the Means of Grace* agrees with the importance of such prayer. "Morning and evening prayers and mealtime blessings in the household are also an extension of corporate worship" (UMG 13A). *Evangelical Lutheran Worship* offers resources to enrich such home prayer.

For worship forms, the services of morning, evening, and night prayer can be adapted for simplified use, as discussed in following chapters. Another possibility is the use of Responsive Prayer (Suffrages), on pages 328–331 of the assembly edition. Yet another option is Luther's forms for a morning blessing and evening blessing, mentioned above. Although these last options do not specifically provide for scripture, one or more readings can easily be added.

The Daily Lectionary (AE pp. 1121–1153) provides daily Bible readings that are important to the dialogue of prayer between God and God's people. It provides a helpful pattern for regular worship in the household, as well as a bridge from the past Sunday to the next Sunday so that individuals and households start making daily connections between Sunday and the rest of the week. This pattern enhances Sunday worship as well as daily life in home, work, community, and world.

A variety of resources are starting to appear based on the daily lectionary. *Bread for the Day,* an annual devotional resource from Augsburg Fortress, provides a very simple pattern of daily prayer for individuals and households. Included are the assigned daily scripture texts from the daily lectionary in *Evangelical Lutheran Worship*, an appropriate hymn, and a prayer. Simplified forms for Morning Prayer and Evening Prayer are included. Other devotional resources will likely be developed to assist individuals and households to use the rich resources provided in *Evangelical Lutheran Worship.*

To encourage fuller use of the church's commended worship book, each person in the home might have a personal copy of *Evangelical Lutheran Worship.* When immigrants came to this country with meager belongings, many brought their Bibles and hymnbooks as prized possessions. That is still a worthy consideration for every home and individual today.

Devotional guides based on the daily lectionary are simple ways to introduce people to daily attention to the word of God and prayer. Short pieces from the daily prayer liturgies can be suggested by leaders to introduce individuals to the communal liturgies of daily prayer.

The Daily Lectionary

The *Use of the Means of Grace* asserts that "the use of ELCA-approved lectionaries serves the unity of the Church, the hearing of the breadth of the Scriptures, and the evangelical meaning of the church year" (*UMG* 7A). The new daily lectionary in *Evangelical Lutheran Worship* expands on this statement and now helps worshipers more fully bring Sunday worship into relationship with daily prayer and reading scripture. Individuals who engage in the discipline of reading the daily lectionary will have common material for discussion with other Christians who follow this same pattern.

Various systems have been developed to assist Christians in their daily Bible reading. The system printed in *Lutheran Book of Worship* appointed the entire Bible to be read over a two-year period. The Moravian church publishes an annual guide in which the Old Testament passage is chosen in a non-systematic manner and then a New Testament passage selected to illumine it. In some systems, the books of the Bible are chosen to correspond in some way with the liturgical seasons. The ecumenical Daily Lectionary as printed in *Evangelical Lutheran Worship* (AE pp. 1121–1153) presents a pattern in which daily Bible readings are related to the Revised Common Lectionary for Sundays and festivals (AE pp. 18–53).

This daily lectionary had its origins in *Sundays and Seasons.* That publication provided a single reading each day, which corresponded with the Sunday readings and assumed the use of the complementary set of Old Testament readings each Sunday in the time after Pentecost. In 1997, a listing of all three years of daily readings was published under the title *Between Sundays.*[15] Voices from the ecumenical community sought to enlarge the single-reading list to incorporate an even broader range of scripture and make it more useful for corporate forms of daily prayer. In 2005 the ecumenical working group that had developed the Revised Common Lectionary, the Consultation on Common Texts, published a greatly augmented three-year cycle under the title *Revised Common Lectionary Daily Readings.*[16] The introduction to that volume provides detailed history and explanation of the project. This is the daily lectionary provided in *Evangelical Lutheran Worship.*

The daily lectionary centers one's daily devotions on the Sunday lectionary. The hope is that this coordination will enlarge the context and enrich the reception of the Sunday readings. From Thursday through Saturday each week, the selections prepare each participant for the coming Sunday readings, and from Monday through Wednesday the selections help worshipers to reflect on the readings they heard on Sunday. The selections connect in several different ways to the lectionary readings. Some include background material cited in or helpful for the Sunday readings; some provide parallel biblical passages; some elaborate on a theme or image central to the Sunday readings; some extend a semicontinuous reading with passages that are omitted on Sunday.

The schedule of reflecting on the past Sunday and preparing for the next Sunday is a wise and helpful aid in connecting daily prayer and Sunday worship. This plan brings word and sacrament into our daily prayer and daily living, and then we bring into the Sunday assembly all the experiences and events of the week at work, at home, in the community, and in the context of the world's events.

This daily lectionary includes a daily Old Testament text, a New Testament text, and a psalm. On Saturday and Wednesday, the New Testament text is from one of the four gospels, and on Thursday, Friday, Monday, and Tuesday from an epistle. To accommodate the semicontinuous option for the first reading, two possible sets of Old Testament readings are provided for the Sundays in the time after Pentecost. The psalm appointed for the Sunday is usually used on Thursday—Saturday, and another psalm is chosen for Monday—Wednesday.

Multiple options for use are possible. The two readings supply the needs of those keeping both morning and evening prayer. When a single reading is desired, the context may indicate which reading is preferred. When a midweek service of holy communion is scheduled, the Sunday gospel may be used, or perhaps one of the other gospel readings in the daily listings, together with one or two of the other listed readings.

This daily lectionary serves well for midweek worship, such as Advent and Lenten services, for academic institutions that maintain daily worship, and for church conventions, conferences, and retreats, which are then recognized as related to the primary Sunday worship of the church body. Preachers may find that meditation on the biblical selections will assist their sermon preparation.

For each of the three years A, B, and C, the daily lectionary listing is set up in this manner:

in bold type, the unit title
in regular type, the readings for Thursday through Saturday
in italics, the name of the Sunday or festival
in regular type, the readings for Monday through Wednesday

Exceptions are the days before and after Christmas, where the readings are listed by calendar dates, and the days of Holy Week, which have their own lectionary readings (pp. 30–31). In each of the three years, the readings that relate to the complementary set of Old Testament readings are printed first, followed by those that relate to the semicontinuous set.

Leadership of Daily Prayer

These services assume an acting, participating assembly. The daily prayer liturgies may be led entirely by lay persons. If there is a homily or sermon, that may be the only thing the pastor does in this service. It also becomes an opportunity for many people to undertake public leadership of prayer. It is a time for many lay people to ask as the disciples did to Jesus, "Lord, teach us to pray." These liturgies are an opportunity where musical gifts can be richly employed, as cantors lead us in the deeper resonance of the musical idiom of prayer. The hymn "When in Our Music God Is Glorified" reminds us of the power of music to serve the word: "How oft, in making music, we have found a new dimension in the world of sound, as worship moved us to a more profound Alleluia" (#850/851). Young people with the gift of song leadership are often willing and able to learn how their gifts can be matched with prayer in the worshiping assembly.

Two leaders can share roles. One may lead the spoken parts and the other chant or sing the musical parts. Others may read the scripture passage/s or provide brief comment or faith stories. When at home, a child may choose to be the leader in night prayer.

Common Themes and Patterns in Daily Prayer

When we examine the texts in *Evangelical Lutheran Worship* Morning Prayer, Evening Prayer, and Night Prayer, we soon discover that these liturgies are basically the Bible set to music, text, and action. The larger liturgical pieces are biblical passages set to music.

The main sections are opening, psalmody, word, and prayers. The following chart shows a similar pattern in the three liturgies for

Morning Prayer, Evening Prayer, and Night Prayer. Although the pattern is similar, variations make each service unique to the day and occasion.

Morning Prayer	*Evening Prayer*	*Night Prayer*
Opening		
Dialogue	Dialogue	Dialogue
Doxology	Hymn of Light	Night Hymn
	Thanksgiving for Light	Confession and Forgiveness
Psalmody		
Morning Psalm: 95:1–7a, 63:1–8, 67, 100, or other	Evening Psalm: 141, 121, or other	Night Psalm: 4, 33, 34, 91, 130, 134, or other
Additional psalms; optional psalm prayers	Additional psalms; optional psalm prayers	Additional psalms; optional psalm prayers
Song for day or season	Song for day or season	Song for day or season
Word		
Reading/s	Reading/s	Brief Reading
Reflection	Reflection	Reflection
Gospel Canticle: Song of Zechariah	Gospel Canticle: Song of Mary	Gospel Canticle: Song of Simeon
Prayers		
Prayers	Prayers	Prayers
Lord's Prayer	Lord's Prayer	Lord's Prayer
Blessing *or* Thanksgiving for Baptism	Blessing	Blessing
Peace	Peace	Peace

Silence. "For God alone I wait in silence; from God comes my salvation" (Ps. 62:1). People's busy lives, distractions from cell phones to portable music players, sounds assaulting from all directions—all of it leaves little room for silence. So unfamiliar is it that when silence is introduced into worship, worshipers often assume the leader has lost her or his place. However, when people become accustomed to and familiar with silence for reflection and prayer, they often find that far from a vacuum, silence can be a rich matrix for finding the presence of God and for prayer.

The traditional services of daily prayer are constructed on the outlines shown above, but they may also be understood as being founded on an underlying basis of silence. At their best, these services are not rushed. Though it may take time and instruction to introduce the way of silence to a worshiping community, it is worth the effort. Silence—being at peace—both aurally and visually can enrich many moments of the services, whether marked in rubrics or not. As the assembly becomes used to it, a minute or two at those places where silence is kept is not too much.

Psalmody. The psalms are at the heart of the daily prayer services, and appropriately so, since for thousands of years they have taught believers how to pray. Psalms are tutors in prayer whether it is praise and thanksgiving, confession and forgiveness, lament and argument, or petitions for blessing of all sorts of things. They are useful for communal gatherings and individual devotion.

Dietrich Bonhoeffer saw the psalms as a school of prayer. The robustness of the psalms in dealing with life's great ups and downs, its joys and angers, life and death, moved Bonhoeffer to cite Luther "to the effect that the Psalms, once taken to heart and incorporated into a daily program of prayer, make all other prayers seem so bloodless. 'Whoever has begun to pray the Psalter earnestly and regularly, will soon give leave to those other, easy, little prayers of their own' because they lack the 'power, passion, and fire' to be found in the Psalter."[17]

Bonhoeffer goes on to stress that churches or groups that sing or read the psalms weekly or even daily have a "priceless treasure." He emphasizes that the psalms give us hearty fare that contrasts with much lighter or shallow devotional material.

The psalms demonstrate for us that prayer is not a monologue. Christian prayer is a dialogue among God and the community and the individual. Within the psalms we find the judgments and promises of God spoken to us as well as a great diversity of concerns directed to God. That diversity, and the honesty with which those concerns are expressed, have surprised generations of believers. The psalms teach us that we should not "stuff it" but bring all of life before our God.

Because the library of psalms is so rich and varied, worship planners are encouraged to expand the use of them in daily prayer beyond the bare, one-psalm minimum. Consider using two or three, with time for reflection between them. They may be sung to the simple tones on pages 337–338 of the assembly edition, sung in an alternative form using resources that are widely available, or if necessary, spoken, though that tends to flatten the psalms, which were intended to be sung.

Psalm prayers. The custom of singing the Gloria Patri after psalms developed in the sixth century as a reaction against Arianism. Twentieth-century liturgical reforms moved toward substituting the still older tradition of following psalms in daily prayer with collects that referred to the psalm text but included Christian content. In *Evangelical Lutheran Worship,* that practice is continued, and the psalm prayers are printed after each psalm in the leaders edition. However, reflecting the view that the Hebrew scriptures are worthy of being used on their own terms, the psalms in daily prayer may also be sung without either psalm prayer or Gloria Patri.

Word. Historically, reading of scripture and sermons based on it have had a less prominent role in the daily prayer services than in services of holy communion. This trend is most clearly seen in the Night Prayer service, where traditionally the scripture reading is no more than a few verses. The choice of readings in Morning Prayer and Evening Prayer may depend on how, and how often, these services are used. If it is a weekly service, then use of the Sunday lectionary may be best. If it is truly a daily pattern, then the daily lectionary (AE p. 1121) might be most useful. There may be other uses in which alternative readings will serve well—for example, some congregations use readings from the Easter Vigil for midweek Lenten services.

For a discussion of preaching in the context of daily prayer, see above, page 153.

Following the Bible reading, the rubrics for the daily prayer services suggest a time of silence for reflection. Again, in keeping with the meditative character of daily prayer, this silence may be rather lengthy. Along with this silence (rather than in place of it), additional types of reflection may be used.

Prayers. Prayer is a central element in the daily prayer liturgies, though the suggested forms of the prayers vary throughout the day. The forms will be treated in more detail in the discussions of each service that follow. Although the suggested forms are more ordered in these services than in holy communion (in keeping with the generally patterned nature of daily prayer), there remain opportunities to offer petitions specific to the community in the present context.

The theologian Walter Bouman would often remark that the prayers in worship were the "business meeting of the church." Or as Martin Marty has said, "Intercession is loving your neighbor on your knees."[18] The liturgist Daniel Stevick puts it this way: "Intercession, which deals with large concerns, deals also with specific close-at-hand concerns. The intercession will be voiced in a particular congregation, with its own history, common experience, and present-day situation. The prayers of the people are this group's opportunity to articulate its own agenda for prayer."[19]

The scriptures encourage a confidence and hope in prayer. "In you, O LORD, have I fixed my hope; you will answer me, O Lord my God" (Ps. 38:15). A similar promise is given by Jesus: "Ask, and it will be given you. . . . For everyone who asks receives" (Matt. 7:7-8). Learning to pray in Jesus' name, knowing that the Spirit intercedes with sighs too deep for words, confident that God addresses us even as we address our heavenly Father—these constitute an important continuing aspect of the Christian life and mission.

Blessing. The blessing in daily prayer is often a simple close to the service. Because these services may be led by anyone, the form of the blessing is "bless *us*," rather than the "bless *you*" form traditionally reserved for ordained clergy. Two options for ending Morning Prayer are the thanksgiving for baptism (AE p. 307) or the thanksgiving for baptism/paschal blessing (p. 308). These will be discussed in chapter 6, Morning Prayer.

Again, what we do in communal worship is meant to relate to our families and others around us. We are blessed to be a blessing. Parents can bless their children before they leave for school. The blessing given to us is meant to be shared.

Peace. After the blessing, a rubric suggests that "the greeting of peace may be shared by all." Here, as with many actions and words in worship, the brevity may fool us into considering this element to have only one defined meaning: a simple wishing of peace, perhaps moving then into a common inquiry into others' well-being. However, viewing this seemingly benign action in its broader and deeper potential meanings points again to our need to learn to pray and worship more imaginatively *between the lines*.

This action at the end of the daily prayer liturgies is an abbreviated practice echoing the greeting, "The peace of Christ be with you always," which we share in the holy communion liturgy. (Here it is recommended that the greeting be shared immediately among those present, rather than being preceded by a greeting by the leader and a response by the assembly.) We greet each other not *in our name* but *in the name of Christ* and the peace that Christ gives us. It is the peace of God given in Christ Jesus that we share. Therefore, it is not just a "Hi! How are you?" It has a much more profound significance.

Like other traditional responses in worship, life and context echo between the lines and continue to speak new meaning and new grace. They are never the same old thing because of new people and a new context.

Indeed, it is a greeting that Jesus often used: "Peace be with you" (John 20:19, 21, 26). The apostle Paul started many of his letters with this greeting: "Grace to you and peace from God our Father and the Lord Jesus Christ." (See, for example, Rom. 1:7, 1 Cor. 1:3, 2 Cor. 1:2, Gal. 3:3.)

It was also an appropriate sending, much like this location in the daily prayer liturgies. After Jesus had healed a woman with a long-term illness, he said "Go in peace" (Mark 5:34). From the time of Aaron and Moses up through our own time, a form of benediction has declared: "The LORD bless you and keep you . . . and give you peace" (Num. 6:24-26).

This sign of peace speaks of reconciliation and unity given us in Christ but frequently poorly expressed in our life together. To the potentially divisive situation in the church at Ephesus, the writer reminds them that Christ "is our peace" (Eph. 2:13-18). Jesus reminds worshipers that if there is something separating us from one another, we should first seek reconciliation and make peace before we offer our gifts (Matt. 5:21-24).

Paul's comforting, confident words to the Philippian church fit the sharing of Christ's peace among worshipers: "The peace of God, which surpasses all understanding, will guard your hearts and your minds in Christ Jesus" (Phil. 4:7).

Further, Jesus calls his followers to be "peacemakers" (Matt. 5:9). In a world of conflicts and wars that destroy lives, where violence destroys relationships, peacemaking is an urgent sign of God's royal rule present in the world in Jesus Christ. Jesus further reminds us that world may not understand this peace we share: "Peace I leave with you; my peace

I give to you. I do not give to you as the world gives" (John 14:27; see also 16:33). It is an eschatological peace that is working like yeast but is also a foretaste of the peace to come. It is the future of God meeting us in the present.

One cannot take just one meaning to the exclusion of the others. This peace of Christ addresses all situations and gives what it signifies. The sharing of the peace is another action that invites us to "pray between the lines" as we bring the world and our situation to this simple, profound action.

Space and Clothing for the Daily Prayer Services

The focus of these services is not the altar-table. Because these services emphasize the scriptures, a reading desk that cradles the Bible or lectionary is an appropriate visual focus. If possible, the antiphonal nature of the psalms invites consideration of antiphonal seating where the two parts of the assembly face each other. At Evening Prayer, a simple large candle (but not the paschal candle, which has other connotations) may be set prominently as a symbol of Christ, the light of the world. Chairs for the leader/s may be arranged around the candle and reading

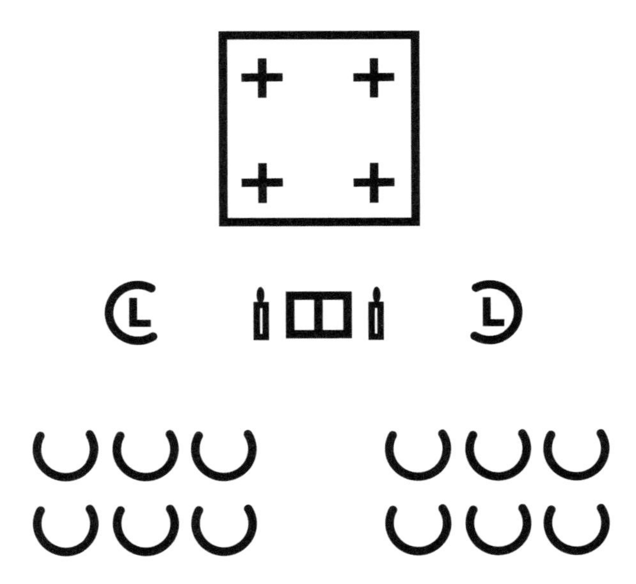

Fig. 2. *Various arrangements may lend themselves to daily prayer. Since the altar table is not used, it is best if it is not the visual focus.*

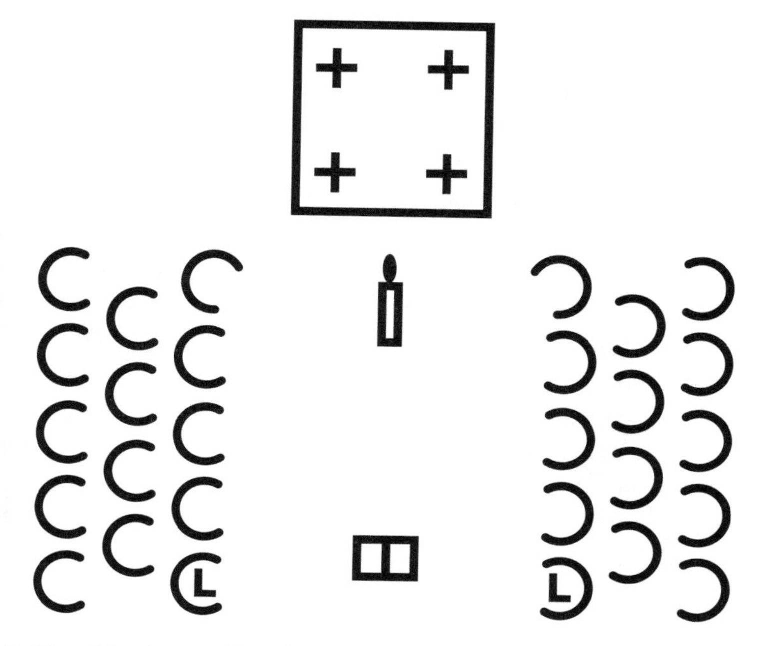

Fig. 3. *The antiphonal nature of the psalms invites consideration of antiphonal seating where the two parts of the assembly face each other.*

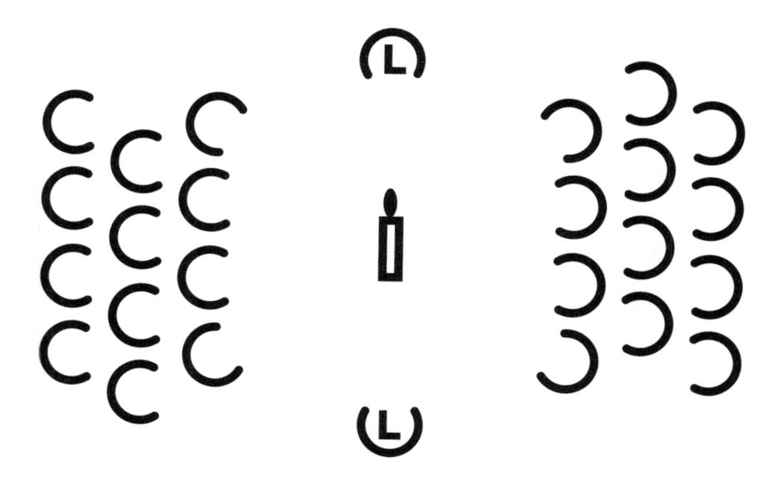

Fig. 4. *At Evening Prayer, a simple large candle may be set prominently as a symbol of Christ, the light of the world.*

desk. For Night Prayer, the arrangement may be informal, depending on the size of the group; its use as a "bedtime prayer" suggests that a dormitory or domestic setting is also appropriate.

When the daily prayer services take place in a congregation's normal worship space (sanctuary, chapel), each leader may wear the alb, a basic liturgical garment symbolizing that all Christians are clothed with Christ in baptism. A pastor who is preaching may wish to wear a stole over the alb, but otherwise the premise that leadership of these services is shared among all the baptized is better served when the leaders vest simply in albs, whether they are ordained or not. At a festive service of evening prayer, the principal leader/s may wish to add a cope (a cape-like garment, often with a hood, that fastens at the neck) over the alb. Some congregations continue an older tradition of using cassock and surplice for services of daily prayer, reserving the use of the alb (stole, chasuble) for services of holy communion. In more informal settings, liturgical vestments are often not used.[20]

CHAPTER SIX

Morning Prayer

Opening

What a way to begin the day! The Morning Prayer service begins, in one of the dialogue options, "O Lord, open my lips, and my mouth shall proclaim your praise" (Ps. 51:15). This has the sense of that joyous expectation of the psalmist: "This is the day that the LORD has made; let us rejoice and be glad in it" (Ps. 118:24). In fact, some religious communities that met regularly for morning prayer would not speak in the morning until they chanted or said together, "O Lord, open my lips, and my mouth shall proclaim your praise." These words could be suggested as the first words the individual speaks upon rising from sleep and looking toward the new day. If morning prayer is part of the individual's communal prayer experience, that single verse will suggest the larger liturgy of word, song, and action. The liturgy then becomes a way of viewing and approaching all of life.

When this option is used to begin Morning Prayer, it is most effective if the dialogue is not preceded by an opening hymn. Rather, when it is time for the service to begin, the assembly stands and simply begins the dialogue.

The morning prayer service has traditionally been chanted, and the tones provided are simple enough that virtually any community can learn them easily. A benefit of singing the service is that it tends to overcome peculiarities of individual voices. The simple melodies help to put everyone on the same level of dialogue. However, if necessary, the dialogue may be spoken. In this case, it is best if both leader and assembly parts are spoken, rather than one spoken and the other sung.

The psalms encourage us to begin the day with prayer and praise. "I will sing of your strength; I will celebrate your love in the morning" (Ps. 59:16); "I myself will waken the dawn. I will give thanks to you among the peoples, O Lord; I will sing praise to you among the nations" (Ps. 57:8-9). The praise of the people of God ultimately seeks to draw the whole world and all peoples into praise and prayer to God.

The "Glory to the Father" adds Christian praise to the holy Trinity. And except for the season of Lent, when the "Alleluia" is omitted, the Alleluia points to the Christian celebration of Christ's resurrection.

A second possibility for this brief opening dialogue has been added in *Evangelical Lutheran Worship*, again drawing on a psalm verse (Ps. 90:14) that is appropriate for morning and may be more fitting when this service is used later in the morning or when an opening hymn is desired, since it doesn't begin with "Open my lips." In a variation on the traditional Gloria Patri, the praise of the holy Trinity names life, salvation, and resurrection as gifts for every day.

Psalmody

At the beginning of this section, Psalm 95:1-7a (often called the Venite, for its opening word in Latin) is a text traditionally sung at morning prayer. The text, appropriately for assembly use in the context of sung prayer, is cast in direct address to God. In addition to the musical setting on pages 299–301, additional musical settings are at #224 and 225 in the assembly edition. To add desired variety and appropriateness to the community's prayer, the notes in the liturgy suggest other appropriate opening psalms that may be sung, including 63:1-8; 67; and 100.

As with the opening dialogue, the psalms in morning prayer are traditionally sung, rather than spoken, and this practice is encouraged in *Evangelical Lutheran Worship*.

The invitatory, "Give glory to God . . . ," invites people to praise and serves as an antiphon at the beginning and ending of Psalm 95 (the Venite). Additional seasonal invitatories that may be sung to the same tone and with the same response are provided on page 694 in the leaders edition.

After the first psalm, the assembly is seated, since the psalm section may get lengthy, especially with the times of reflection.

As has been noted earlier, the singing of psalms is at the very core of the daily prayer worship form. As such, it is usual for at least one additional psalm to be prayed, and frequently more. One additional psalm might be the one proposed for the day in the Sunday lectionary (AE p. 18) or the daily lectionary (AE p. 1121). Appendix F provides a listing of additional possible psalms for daily prayer, which may be especially useful in settings where a regular course of daily prayer takes place and a second or third psalm is typically included.

Silence follows each psalm. It serves as an active silence where each person reflects on the psalm and what it says to the person this day and for that person's mission in the world. For further thoughts on the place of silence, see the note on page 161. Because many worshiping communities are not given much time for silence, leaders may want to suggest ways for worshipers to enter fruitful times of silence. A minute or two of silence is not too much.

A leader may complete the silent reflection with a psalm prayer. They are found following each psalm in the leaders edition. Leaving a pause at the end of the prayer gives the congregation time to communally respond with their participatory "Amen." Instead of the older pattern of concluding each psalm with the Gloria Patri, the psalm prayers reflect the psalms' themes, often from Christian perspectives.

Various ways to sing or chant the psalms are available for musicians. As the hymnbook of the Bible, psalms are meant to be sung. The sixteen tones for singing the psalms (AE pp. 337–338) suggest that worship leaders explore more than one or two tones. Double psalm tones (tones 12–16) provide the possibility of singing two verses to the tone instead of only one verse. Worship leaders will find help in leading the worshiping community by reviewing the helpful material in the assembly edition, pages 335–336.

Sung praise may continue with other forms of song, such as a biblical canticle that is not from the book of Psalms. Especially suitable for inclusion is a hymn or song that fits the time of day or the season of the church year. This hymn is considered the primary hymn of morning prayer, somewhat parallel to the hymn of the day in the service of holy communion; thus standing is an appropriate posture for the assembly.

Word

If a morning prayer service is used in a pattern of weekday worship, then the daily lectionary (AE p. 1121), which draws out implications of the Sunday lectionary and expands on its themes, is a rich resource for the worshiping community. On the other hand, if this is an additional or occasional Sunday liturgy, then the Sunday and festival lectionary (AE p. 18) would customarily be used. Whatever the source of the readings, planners may use one or more readings, which may or may not include a reading from the gospels (unless the service is one of a congregation's regular Sunday options, in which case a gospel reading is advisable). Unlike holy communion, where the gospel is generally considered the primary reading of the service, daily prayer has no such preeminent reading. The gospel canticle serves as the gospel for the service.

After each reading a time of silence for reflection follows. As with the silence after psalms, this may well be a substantial pause in the service. While simple silence is usually best, on occasion guidance for a period of silence may be offered for worshipers to reflect on how this word speaks to the individual and the community.

The response to the scripture invites the imaginative and creative vision of the planners and leaders. Often a brief commentary on the reading appropriately draws out insights and application of the word. Personal witness or a faith story arising out of the text may be appropriate. Drama, music, dance, or visual images may accompany the reading or serve as insightful attentiveness to other forms of interacting with the scripture, beyond depending only on our ears. In some settings, an improvisatory conversation about the biblical text may stimulate worshipers' sense of call to active participation and application of the word in their own lives. The dialogical response to the scripture reading encourages the active participation of the worshipers with their thanksgiving for this word of life.

Whether or not such reflection beyond mere silence is employed, the time of reflection after the last reading may be concluded by singing one of the scriptural dialogues provided (AE p. 302). The first response reflects the affirmation of 1 Peter 1:23-25 about the "living and enduring word of God" that "is the good news that was announced to you." The second dialogue is from Hebrews 1:1-2. On some occasion the leader may want to expand on the biblical context of these two brief sung texts so that worshipers understand the larger message, which these short texts echo.

The gospel canticle (biblical song) traditionally sung at morning prayer is the song of Zechariah in Luke 1:68-79. The *Benedictus* (the Latin title literally means *blessed,* and again is simply the first word of the canticle in Latin) is rich in themes of the promises, peace, and salvation that have come to us in Jesus Christ. Besides the simple chant setting printed in the liturgy, other musical versions such as #226, 250, or 552 may be used. The hymn versions (#250 and 552) provide tunes that may be more accessible for some worshiping communities. If these liturgies are used on a regular pattern, these alternatives provide variety and add interest. Because this is a *gospel* canticle, the congregation is invited to stand in honor of the Christ who is praised.

"We praise you, O God" (*Te Deum*), another ancient canticle, may be used in place of the song of Zechariah. This hymn of praise uses creed-like language; some settings conclude with psalm-based versicles and responses based on the faith just confessed. Two musical settings are available, #227 and 228. A paraphrased text of the *Te Deum* is also available in a hymn version (#414).

Prayers

The prayer text suggests that silence follows each petition. The three dots (. . .) invite the worshipers to fill the brief silence with their specific thanksgivings and intercessions, so that the general petitions pick up the realities of the present-day context. Again, this becomes praying between the lines.

The first paragraph of the prayers consists of thanksgivings; similar phrases may be added or substituted that evoke, rather than define, kinds of blessings for which worshipers may be thankful. Similarly, the second section contains intercessions, and other categories may be added. Thanksgivings and intercessions arise out of the specific life and mission of this worshiping assembly in this particular context and in the concrete realities of local and world events. Prayer immerses the Christian assembly in Christ's care and mission for the world that God created and so loves.

The notes and rubrics remind us of the flexibility of this section: "another form of the prayers may be used" or "other appropriate prayers may be used." Among the possibilities are a standard intercessory prayer form such as is commonly used in holy communion, one or more collects, or responsive prayer—perhaps an adaptation of the Morning section of Responsive Prayer on page 329 of the assembly edition.

One or more of the provided classic prayers may follow. The first is a prayer that dates back to medieval times. The second is a twentieth-century collect from Eric Milner-White and George Wallace Briggs's *Daily Prayer.*[1] The third is Luther's morning prayer (AE p. 1166), cast in first-person plural.

At the conclusion of the prayers, the leader may chant or speak one of two invitations for worshipers to chant or speak the Lord's Prayer. (These invitations are found only in the leaders edition, page 700.) Though only the ecumenical form of the Lord's Prayer with chant notation is provided, users may, of course, substitute another form of the prayer, which may be sung or spoken.

If a thanksgiving for baptism is not included, the service concludes with a blessing, in the form of the Benedicamus ("Let us bless the Lord"), followed by a trinitarian blessing. A hymn may be sung; suggested morning hymns are #552–559. Greeting one another with the peace of Christ may follow.

Thanksgiving for Baptism

The option of closing morning prayer with a thanksgiving for baptism is especially appropriate on Sundays when we give thanks for baptism, through which we were joined to the death and resurrection of Jesus Christ.

A baptismal hymn or canticle can be sung while the worshipers move to the baptismal pool or font. Possibilities may be found in the section of baptism-related hymns (#442–459), as well as acclamations #209–214.

First form: Thanksgiving for Baptism (AE p. 307; LE 702–703). After the dialogue is chanted or spoken, the leader chants or speaks the prayer of thanksgiving for the gift of baptism. A chant setting is provided in the leaders edition. A minister pouring water into the font during the prayer can provide an attractive "voice" to this baptismal element.

As a reminder of baptism, the worshipers may be sprinkled with water or individuals may dip their fingers in the water and retrace the sign of the cross that was made over each of us in baptism. During this time, "We praise you, O God" (#227, 228, 414) may be sung if it was not used for the gospel canticle. Another hymn with baptismal themes may also be chosen.

The service is concluded with a baptismal blessing. Music for chanting the blessing is provided in the leaders edition, page 703.

Following the blessing, the worshipers may greet one another with the peace of Christ.

Second form: Thanksgiving for Baptism, Paschal Blessing (AE p. 308; LE 704–706). This form of the thanksgiving for baptism, brought over from *Lutheran Book of Worship,* makes a strong connection to Christ's resurrection and so is especially suited to use on Sunday, the church's weekly celebration of the resurrection. However, it could also be used separately, perhaps in a family's observance of a baptismal anniversary. The resurrection narrative as well as all the leader parts may be chanted using the music in the leaders edition.

After the resurrection narrative, "We praise you, O God" (#227, 228, 414) is sung. During the singing of this canticle the worshiping assembly may be sprinkled in remembrance of their baptism or they may move to the baptismal font or pool and dip their fingers in the water and retrace the sign of the cross as was done over their bodies at their own baptism.

The prayer reflects Luther's strong sense of living every day in the promise of our baptism. To use an analogy, a person could say, "I was married." To only say that might cause us to ask if the spouse had died or a divorce has occurred. Rather, we say, "I am married." Luther had a strong sense that not only were we once and for all time baptized but that we *are* baptized and living in that relationship with God and the community of the baptized.

Following the blessing, the worshipers may greet one another with the peace of Christ.

CHAPTER SEVEN

7

Evening Prayer

Opening

The service of light, or *Lucernarium*, is a visually dramatic entry into the liturgy of Evening Prayer (Vespers). A large, lighted candle gives visual focus to the pronouncement that "Jesus Christ is the light of the world." The paschal candle is not used for this service, because its symbolism points to Christ's resurrection; therefore, to preserve the paschal candle's symbolism, it is burned only during the fifty days of rejoicing during the Easter season, for baptisms when we are joined to Christ's resurrection with its newness of life, and for funerals when we claim the hope of eternal life promised us in Christ's resurrection.

If the large, lighted candle is carried into the assembly, it is quite effective to start the chanted dialogue from the entrance to the worship space. One may need to prompt regular worshipers to stand and turn at the appropriate time, or the leader may invite the worshipers to turn and face the candle. After the first line is chanted, the candle may be carried in silence to the middle of the assembly. Because the service invites ample periods of silence, this mode of entry signals and invites worshipers into the calm of active silence. Then the second line may be chanted by the leader from the midst of the assembly ("Stay with us, Lord, for it is evening"), with the worshipers responding ("and the day is almost over"). Then the candle may be carried in silence to its position of focus for the rest of the liturgy. The third line is chanted.

Seasonal dialogues are also provided and may be chosen to emphasize themes of the liturgical seasons. Where daily prayer is practiced on a regular basis, these alternatives provide variety as well as seasonal emphasis. However, the dialogue in place is appropriate at any time and in any season.

If a brief opening is desired, the service may continue directly with the Psalmody. However, for the fuller service of light, the ancient hymn of light "Joyous Light of Glory" (the *Phos hilaron*) or another hymn that speaks of Christ as the light is then sung. Other candles or votives may be lighted during the singing of this hymn. Visually this underlines the "pillar of fire by night" that led God's people to freedom and is celebrated in the thanksgiving for light. Several musical forms for the hymn of light are provided in *Evangelical Lutheran Worship* (#229–231, 560–563). Choirs may also present a choral setting of this third-century hymn text.

The thanksgiving for light is a chanted prayer giving thanks for God's gift of light and asking God to "enlighten our darkness by the light of your Christ." This prayer recalls for us how early church leaders spoke of baptism as our illumination. The leaders may stand behind the candle facing the congregation to underline the words about light with this visual focus.

When congregations use this opening service of light during Lent, it will resonate with worshipers when they celebrate the great Vigil of Easter with the procession of the new paschal candle and the singing of the extended Easter Proclamation (LE 645–647).

Psalmody

The traditional beginning of the psalmody for evening prayer is Psalm 141. Besides the musical setting within the printed liturgy, *Evangelical Lutheran Worship* provides two other options (#232, 233). Psalm 121 is proposed as an alternative psalm that stresses the protective help of our God who neither slumbers nor sleeps.

The original setting of Psalm 141 was presumably in the Jewish temple precincts where worshipers were watching the incense rising and were lifting up their hands in prayer at the evening sacrifice. A poet among them took this scene and gave us this devout prayer calling upon God for forgiveness and protection from evil.

The words of Psalm 141 also invite us to consider the ancient Hebrew practice of burning incense during the chanting of this psalm. One could use a thurible or a censer for the incense. Another way to burn the incense is to put a base of sand in a lovely bowl. On top of the sand one places the charcoal so that the bowl does not become too hot to handle. One can light the charcoal before the service starts, so it is hot enough to burn the incense at the singing of this psalm. The stand or table should be situated close to the large, white, lighted candle. Whether one uses a bowl of incense or a thurible, one may choose to use incense to honor the candle symbolizing Christ, the light of the world. The leaders, assembly, and the scriptures may also be honored in this way.

In the recent past some Protestants have rejected the idea of using incense as "too high church." It may be helpful to look at the biblical use of incense before introducing it in a congregation. In Exodus, Leviticus, Numbers, and Deuteronomy there is much attention to incense and its relation to temple worship. Yet one should note that the prophets also decried the use of incense when it was used to cover up social and personal injustice and sins.

In the New Testament, the priest Zechariah is taking his turn in the temple at the altar of incense when he receives the good news that he will have a son whom we know as John the Baptist (Luke 1:8-20). The child Jesus is brought a gift of incense by the magi from the East (Matt. 2:1-12). In the final book of the New Testament, there is an echo from temple worship that also speaks to the purpose of incense in evening prayer: the heavenly figures each holding "golden bowls full of incense, which are the prayers of the saints" (Rev. 5:8; see also 8:3-4). The sense of smell is a strong human faculty and can remind us that prayer involves the whole person. The rising smoke of incense also provides a visual reminder of our praise and petitions approaching our God. These other senses may remind us that worship and prayer involve the being of the whole person, not just the head or intellect.

Some people report having breathing problems when incense is used. While such reactions may at times be psychological, they still need to be taken seriously. At times, inferior incense or even the charcoal may be to blame. Some brands of incense are claimed to be nonallergenic. If use of incense is problematic, some research may be called for. And if it is a persistent problem, hospitality may suggest that incense be used only on special occasions.

Ample silence (perhaps one or two minutes) follows the opening psalm for prayerful reflection. A psalm prayer provided in the leaders edition after the psalm may conclude the communal silent meditation. All the psalm prayers may be sung. A model for chanting these prayers as well as other collects is provided in the music for the prayer in the leaders edition, page 705.

One or more psalms may follow. The above pattern would apply to each psalm, including silence and a psalm prayer. Sixteen tones for singing the psalms are provided in the assembly edition, pages 337–338.

While this provides variety, musicians may provide other settings and musical accompaniment for singing the psalms. Creative leadership by musicians will keep congregations from falling into monotony. On occasion a choir may sing one of the psalms alone, but as a rule, the assembly's voice should be primary in this section.

Additional song, such as a biblical canticle not from the psalms, may follow the sung psalms. Especially suitable for inclusion is a hymn or song that fits the time of day or the season of the church year. This hymn is considered the primary hymn of evening prayer, somewhat parallel to the hymn of the day in the service of holy communion; thus standing is an appropriate posture for the assembly. During seasonal worship such as Advent, Lent, or Easter, hymns that relate to the season are appropriate choices. Because many congregations do not have evening services, worshipers may be deprived of singing excellent hymns that reflect the rhythm of prayer at the end of the day. This may be a good reason to also include these hymns along with seasonal choices.

Word

One or more scripture readings are proclaimed. The daily lectionary (AE p. 1121) provides texts that point us back to last Sunday and forward to next Sunday. Using the daily lectionary is especially beneficial for communities that practice daily prayer together on a regular schedule.

Many congregations have midweek services during Advent and Lent. Evening prayer provides an excellent pattern for prayer and proclamation; its use during these times helps ensure that congregations do not lose their memories of these great traditions of prayer. Lenten or Advent themes may be suggested from the daily lectionary, and texts that relate to a chosen theme are also appropriate.

Again, the rubrics suggest that there be time for reflection following the scripture reading. During this time, everyone is given the opportunity to apply and appropriate what God is saying to each person as well as to the whole worshiping assembly. After this time of silence, additional forms of reflection may be employed. The notes (AE p. 313) suggest varied possibilities in addition to the usual sermon. Personal witness or faith stories that relate to the text could be shared by lay persons. Music, dance, drama, or projected visual effects can also effectively communicate and underscore the scripture's message. In some settings conversation about the reading/s could fit well with the dialogical nature of the whole liturgy.

A choice between two biblical dialogues appropriately concludes the reflection and leads into the gospel canticle. The first of these (John 8:12) reflects the time of day and also the service of light, where worshipers sang "Jesus Christ is the light of the world" at the beginning of Evening Prayer. The second dialogue (Hebrews 1:1-2) points to the Christ who is the living Word. The musicians may choose to prepare a classic responsory as an alternative to either of the biblical dialogues.

The gospel canticle associated with evening prayer is perhaps the most beloved biblical song, Mary's song (Luke 1:46-55), also known as the Magnificat. Because this song points to God's merciful care for the hungry and lowly plus a challenge to the proud, the mighty, and the rich, the song of Mary has been seen as socially and politically subversive. In some countries where this song is sung regularly and supports ministry to the poor and powerless, it has served much like the song "We Shall Overcome" for the civil rights movement in the United States. It may remind us that these texts indeed are part of the royal rule of God that has come in the person of Jesus Christ and that some people will accuse Christians of "turning the world upside down" (Acts 17:6).

Besides the musical setting of the gospel canticle included in the liturgy of Evening Prayer (AE pp. 314–315), several other settings and hymn versions are provided (#234, 235, 251, 573, 723, 882). For variety during a season where the service is prayed each week, one could use a different musical setting for each week. For some of the settings, it may be helpful to have a choir or a few persons who have practiced the new settings so they may give leadership to the worshipers if the music is unfamiliar. Another possibility is to have the choir or soloists sing other musical settings of Mary's song. However, if a congregation is not familiar with the liturgy, it may be wise to repeat a chosen melody so all is not new to worshipers.

Prayers

This prayer litany with its response inviting singing in harmony has lovingly been called "Byzantine barbershop." When chanted, the assembly begins its response as the leader gets to the word "Lord," so that they overlap on that word. The assembly may keep humming the last notes of their response while the leader sings the next petition. The continual humming seems to give worshipers a sense of joining with the petitions of the leader. Once the pattern is set, other petitions appropriate to this community may be added by the leader, or petitions can be adapted to the particular context and setting. In the ninth petition, where the words *name/s and* appear, the Christian names of the presiding/national bishop of the church body and the synod bishop may be inserted. This reminds worshipers of the community and mission that is shared with the church beyond their own congregation. The petition "Help, save, comfort . . ." is sung on a single pitch so that it leads naturally into silent reflection. At the blank in the last petition, the leader may insert names of those being commemorated on that day in the church calendar, or names of those in the congregation who have recently died, or skip over the option.

Again it is important to note that this prayer is a model and that other forms of prayer may used. A series of short prayers (collects) may serve the praying community, or more informal spontaneous petitions from the assembly may be appropriate. Responsive Prayer (AE pp. 328–331; LE 727–730) may also replace the prayers and blessing; when used in this way, the creed may be omitted. Local worship leaders and planners can explore the possibility of variety and flexibility in prayer style that fits their community.

One of the three prayers on pages 317–318 may follow the litany prayer. The first is a twentieth-century collect from Eric Milner-White and George Wallace Briggs's *Daily Prayer.*[1] The second is a beloved fifth-century prayer for peace. The third is a plural form of Luther's evening prayer for household use included in the *Small Catechism* (AE p. 1167) One may choose to chant the prayer using the pattern suggested above for the psalm prayer.

The Lord's Prayer typically concludes the prayers. It may be spoken or sung to the melody provided.

The blessing follows the short dialogue (Benedicamus) between leader and worshipers. Two forms are provided. The first blessing, from Philippians 4:7, echoes frequent use by pastors and caregivers when they minister to the sick or discouraged. The second blessing calls on the triune God to bless us and keep us in God's protection. When a pastor gives this blessing, the blessing may end with ". . . bless and preserve *you,*" and the pastor may make the sign of the cross over the worshiping assembly. A lay leader uses the plural *us* as printed in the liturgy and along with the congregation may make the sign of the cross over herself or himself.

After the blessing, a hymn may be sung. Several appropriate evening hymns are clustered in ELW (#560–573).

Following the blessing, the worshipers may greet one another with the peace of Christ.

CHAPTER EIGHT

Night Prayer

Night prayer (compline) is the centuries-old "bedtime prayer" of the Christian community. This brief pattern of prayer was the last thing religious communities or households would do before they blew out the candles or extinguished the lamps at bedtime. Before we turn out the lights today, it would be beneficial for individuals, households, or church groups to have in mind these classic prayers and commendation of our lives to God.

In spoken form, this short liturgy could be used to close meetings at church. The leader of the whole service can be a lay person. Families, households, or individuals could use this in their homes before going to bed. Children love to lead this short liturgy, especially when mom and dad make confession and then they declare God's forgiveness to them! Choirs could close their choir practices at least periodically by singing Night Prayer and thus be prepared to lead the congregation when Night Prayer is used. Individuals who memorize short portions will likely find these verses coming to mind as they lie in bed or wake up at night. Think of how individuals might find short verses peaceful, restful, calming, and an exercise of trust in God's watchful presence even while a person sleeps. Think of short texts from this service and how they might aid calmness and repose:

Almighty God grant us a quiet night and peace at the last (p. 320).

Now in peace I will lie down and sleep; you alone, O God, make me secure (p. 327).

Into your hands, O Lord, I commend my spirit (p. 323).

Guide us waking, O Lord, and guard us sleeping; that awake we may watch with Christ and asleep we may rest in peace (p. 324).

This last is a significant short prayer families (or an individual) could memorize and pray together before bedtime, even though they might not do the entire Night Prayer liturgy.

If this service were to be used for midweek Advent or Lenten services, planners might develop a simple service of the word and then use Night Prayer as the closing prayers. An order might consist of a gathering hymn, a simple greeting ("The Lord be with you. / **And also with you.**"), a prayer relating to the theme, scripture reading, proclamation in various forms suggested in Morning Prayer and Evening Prayer, silence for reflection, and then use Night Prayer for the congregation's "bedtime" prayer. Because many worshipers are not familiar with this service, this may be a way to introduce it.

Night Prayer in Detail

Prayer at the close of the day usually means our physical, emotional, and mental resources are depleted or at low ebb. Taking that into consideration, the service tends to be simple, restful, and without much ceremony. The Night Prayer service in *Evangelical Lutheran Worship* can be spoken or sung. The chant form is simple. The setting can be anywhere, but if sung it may be helpful to have the resource of a piano or other musical accompaniment.

If this service is done where there is flexible seating, one may arrange the seating in a circle if the group is small or in an antiphonal arrangement with the two sides facing each other. Perhaps a single candle could be in the middle of the assembly, with lights lowered just enough so people can see the words and music. The service may be led by a single leader; assisting ministers are not generally needed.

Opening

After the busy day, it is good to gather in silence for centering the individual and the community gathering for common prayer.

When the leader senses that the community is united in palpable silence, the leader may stand and motion for all to stand as they are able. The leader may open with a gentle voice that reflects the petition "Almighty God grant us a quiet night and peace at the last." One of two dialogues is then sung or spoken. Both reflect the rhythm of day and night, its beginning and its ending, and all that the day has brought. The first dialogue is from Psalm 92:1-2. The second is from Psalm 42:8.

A night hymn may be sung. "All Praise to Thee, My God, This Night" (#565) is a traditional hymn familiar to many, and the text is most appropriate for this service. Some may sing chosen stanzas in canon. Another night hymn may also be chosen.

Two options are offered for confession and forgiveness. Silence precedes the confession and is appropriate as worshipers reflect on the day's events, with its relationships, thoughts, words, and deeds. The reciprocal form in the right column traditionally has been used in this liturgy and provides a fresh perspective that suggests that all of us are called to live in communal confession and forgiveness. Dietrich Bonhoeffer stressed the need for communal confession for Christian community and pointed to the healing context in James 5:16 where the writer says, "Confess your sins to one another, and pray for one another." Bonhoeffer goes on to say:

> Those who remain alone with their evil are left utterly alone. It is possible that Christians may remain lonely in spite of daily worship together, prayer together, and all their community through service—that the final breakthrough to community does not occur precisely because they enjoy community with one another as pious believers, but not with one another as those lacking piety, as sinners. For the pious community permits no one to be a sinner. Hence all have to conceal their sins from themselves and from the community. We are not allowed to be sinners. Many Christians would be unimaginably horrified if a real sinner were suddenly to turn up among the pious. So we remain alone with our sin, trapped in lies and hypocrisy, for we are in fact sinners.[1]

The communal confession and forgiveness can be a step toward that reconciling grace that is present in the daily return to the baptismal structure of our lives where, in Luther's words, we "die through daily sorrow for sin and through repentance, and . . . daily a new person is to come forth and rise up to live before God in righteousness and purity forever" (AE p. 1165).

Psalmody

Several psalms with themes appropriate for the end of the day are suggested for use. Psalm 4 is an example of a text that could be memorized and recalled at those moments one cannot fall asleep. "In peace, I will lie down and sleep," the psalmist says. If one cannot fall asleep, perhaps there is something that is not at peace in us or in our day or in our relationships. Dealing with those issues, we might find that "you alone, O Lord, make me rest secure." One of the two blessings at the end of Night Prayer echoes this psalm verse. Other psalms are suggested as well. Psalm 136 might be sung antiphonally between the leader and worshipers by half verse, so that the assembly keeps repeating "for God's mercy endures forever" as a response to the leader's recounting of God's actions on behalf of God's people.

After each psalm, following ample silence for reflection, the leader may pray a psalm prayer. The psalm prayers are found in the leaders edition after each psalm.

A song or hymn appropriate to the end of the day may be sung. Several appropriate hymns are provided in the Evening section of *Evangelical Lutheran Worship* (#560–573). "To You, before the Close of Day" (#567) is a sixth-century compline office hymn. The chant form of the hymn fits the chant of the Night Prayer service. The text prays that God would save us from insomnia and nightmares that rob us of renewing rest. Even the simple chant tune feels a bit sleepy. Paul Gerhardt's hymn, "Now Rest beneath Night's Shadow" (#568), is another that resonates with the themes of night prayer. "Now the Day Is Over" (#570) is a familiar simple text and tune that reflects the movement of the whole service as well. "Now It Is Evening" (#572) is a provocative evening hymn that reaches out beyond our own selves to the lonely, hungry, neglected, and strangers. It leads our praise and prayer into mission.

Word

The Word section is brief in this liturgy. One or two verses are typically read as a "little chapter." Eight selections are provided in place. However, groups who use Night Prayer may want to explore other verses as well. For example, a verse stressed in the lectionary texts for the past Sunday may reinforce the community's memory of the Sunday's proclamation. Note the character of this verse, though: it is one of trust and peace, rather than the more energetic, outward-focused scripture that may be more appropriate at a different time. Alternate choices will do well to follow suit.

Extended silence is suggested so that people will have time to meditate on the implications of that verse for their individual lives, the household, or this particular worshiping community.

A dialogical responsory follows the silence. The psalmist first said these words: "Into your hands I commend my spirit, for you have redeemed me, O LORD, God of truth" (Ps. 31:5). Echoing Jesus' words from the cross (Luke 23:46) that entrusted his life and death to God, the praying community speaks or sings Christ's words to entrust our lives to God once again at the end of this day. As we go to sleep, this responsory exhibits radical trust in God that "if we live, we live to the Lord, and if we die, we die to the Lord; so then, whether we live or whether we die, we are the Lord's" (Rom. 14:8).

The gospel canticle is the song of Simeon from Luke 2:28-32. This *Nunc dimittis* is the traditional gospel canticle for compline. Faithful Simeon, who had looked forward to seeing God's Messiah, now can die or live in peace, because he has seen God's salvation. This is why this canticle has a similar message when it serves as the closing hymn of holy communion. In the word and meal, we have also seen the Lord's salvation, and so we can depart in peace to serve God's mission in the world or we can depart in peace to face all uncertainties. This canticle also is often used at funerals. In a sense, this canticle reminds us that whenever we have been singing this song in compline, we have been rehearsing for that final compline (the word comes from the Latin, meaning "ending") when all that our baptism signifies now comes to pass. These great texts warrant our deep reflection and deserve to be etched vividly in our memories. That usually happens only as we return to them again and again in prayer and reflection. Then they become our prayer as well as faithful, old Simeon's prayerful song.

The refrain sung both before and after Simeon's song merit memorization. Congregations may wish to have children memorize this prayer and encourage them to pray it in the evening as they go to sleep. It would be an excellent prayer for parents to pray together with their children before bedtime. There is a sense that this short prayer signals the larger memory of all of night prayer and how it places our lives in God's care and protection as we slip off to sleep.

Many other composers have set Simeon's text to music. In addition to the musical version in place, *Evangelical Lutheran Worship* provides (#200–203) a melody from the Detroit Folk Mass, a melody with Spanish and English words, and a plainsong version. A Finnish folk tune (#313) and a German melody (#440) give hymn text adaptations of Simeon's song. Some of these may be appropriate when the *Nunc dimittis* is sung at a funeral for the faithful departed.

As an alternative placement reflecting the practice of some forms of compline, the song of Simeon may follow the Lord's Prayer in this service.

Prayers

The prayers section begins with another biblical dialogue sung or spoken between the leader and the praying community. The verses come from Psalm 39:12, Psalm 17:8, and Psalm 17:15.

Several classic prayers follow. One or more of them may be prayed, although one is usually sufficient within this service's simple form. Appendix G in this volume provides the last five prayers set to the same chant tone as the first one. These prayers could be commended to confirmation students and their families as part of their faith and prayer formation.

The Lord's Prayer may be spoken or sung. The version in place is the ecumenical version set to a chant melody. Alternatively, either it or another version may be sung on a single note, or spoken by all.

Two blessings are provided. The blessing is a more traditional trinitarian blessing. The sign of the cross may be retraced over a person's body as a remembrance of baptism in the name of the Father, Son, and Holy Spirit. The second blessing echoes Psalm 4:8, one of the psalms suggested for Night Prayer.

Following the blessing, the worshipers may greet one another with the peace of Christ. This action recalls Simeon's joyful response after he had seen the Lord's salvation in the baby Jesus: "Now, Lord, you let your servant go in peace." The service of Night Prayer reflects the sturdy faith and trust that believes we also have seen the Lord's salvation.

CHAPTER NINE

Other Prayer Forms

Responsive Prayer (Suffrages)

This short prayer office provides a brief order for prayer. *Suffrages* is from the Latin, meaning prayers of intercession. As noted earlier, one could use this form and choose the prayer appropriate to the time of day for a retreat on prayer patterned after the tradition of the multiple times of prayer practiced in religious communities. The four brief prayer times of Responsive Prayer together with the three more extensive services of Morning Prayer, Evening Prayer, and Night Prayer could form the structure of a prayer retreat.

These forms can be used for household, individual, or small-group prayer. They also serve well as a pattern for devotions for church committees. A psalm or hymn may be added at the beginning, followed by a scripture reading, or these may be inserted after the dialogue on page 329. When used for daily prayer, the daily lectionary (AE p. 1121) is a good source of texts, because its readings draw out implications of the past Sunday and also help prepare for the following Sunday. The readings for Monday through Wednesday unfold themes from the previous Sunday's worship. The readings from Thursday through Saturday prepare for and point toward the next Sunday's lectionary texts.

After calling on the thrice holy God, the Lord's Prayer is prayed and the creed is confessed. This reflects the ancient Hebrew pattern of a set form centered in the prayer the Jews called the Tefillah, Amidah, or the Eighteen Benedictions. For Christians the Lord's Prayer became their daily prayer. The Shema (Deut. 6:4-9, 11:13-21; Num. 15:37-41) served as the Jews' creed. For Christians the baptismal creed was confessed in its place.

Following the creed, a dialogue composed of psalm verses is spoken between leader and group. For morning dialogues, the psalm verses are 88:13; 71:8; 145:2; 65:5; 103:1; 103:4; 102:1. For the dialogue "At other times" the psalm verses include 85:7; 51:12; 67:2; 9:18; 51:11;

102:1. Taking this pattern, a leader or planning group could create their own scriptural dialogue.

This short pause for prayer echoes the Morning Blessing and Evening Blessing from Luther's Small Catechism (AE pp. 1166–1167, LE 890–891). In fact, the prayer for morning and the prayer for evening are from the Small Catechism. The noon and afternoon prayers serve those specific hours of the day.

The prayer for daily work is a good reminder of the gift of work that carries out our baptismal vocation. The prayer "Before Travel" has become a standard prayer at retreats and conferences as people prepare for travel home. This prayer could also be easily adapted and used on Sundays when groups prepare to travel on mission trips or other activities or when members are preparing to leave the congregation for a new home.

Appropriately, this brief prayer service concludes with God's blessing.

Litany of the Saints and Great Litany

These final prayer forms are found not in the liturgical section of *Evangelical Lutheran Worship* but in the service music section (#237 and 238), simply because they are set to music.

While shorter responsive litanies (such as the Kyrie litany in holy communion) are often used in worship, these longer litanies are lesser-known gems. The Litany of the Saints is suggested for use in the Vigil of Easter, and some congregations have the custom of using the Great Litany on the First Sunday in Lent. Can the riches of these ancient forms of prayer still find a way into our worship? The following suggests some ways to renew us as we discover some possible ways to incorporate these expansive prayers in our contemporary settings.

The litany form can be traced back at least as far as Psalm 136, where the psalmist gives thanks for God's saving and providential care and then concludes each verse with the confession "for God's mercy endures forever." Twenty-six times that phrase is repeated! This sets up a rhythm of prayer that is, in some ways, more like Eastern mantras than our more accustomed Western prayers that require careful attention to the words being spoken. Words are still important in litanies, but so is the sense of constant motion in prayer, as though the prayer takes on a life of its own. The Great Litany has thirty-one antiphonal responses as we pray for God's mercy, deliverance, help, and peace for us and the whole world. After using the Great Litany in a congregation, a new member from another tradition said to her pastor, "That about covers everything!" Indeed! This intense prayer is meant to bring ourselves, the world, the gospel, and our many needs to God in prayer.

The Litany of the Saints was created in the early centuries of the church, and forms are in use in both the Eastern and Western churches. The version found in *Evangelical Lutheran Worship* (#237) is a recent Lutheran adaptation, replacing the original prayer for the saints to "pray for us" with a response that gives thanks for the named saints. It also gives thanks for the mighty acts of God and, building on that history, asks for God's continuing grace.

At the time of the Reformation, Luther revised the Litany of the Saints in a form that became well used and popular. The form of the Great Litany (#238) in *Evangelical Lutheran Worship* reflects Luther's revision. In common with some other revisions, however, in places it groups petitions with a common response. This shortens the time it takes to pray the litany, but it also loses the rhythmic pattern of the original. If desired, this earlier rhythm is easily reclaimed by the assembly's singing the response after each semicolon. (In such a case, the leader will, of course, need to terminate each phrase using the notes provided.)

Using the Litanies

Planners may choose to use the Great Litany during Lent, due to its focus on the various dimensions of Jesus' life, death, and resurrection, plus some penitential focus and a broad range of prayer petitions. Some might be intimidated by its length, but it could serve as almost the entire gathering section, replacing confession and forgiveness, a gathering hymn, as well as the Kyrie. During this season the canticle of praise is also typically not sung. The deletion of these three parts would allow ample time for the singing of the Great Litany.

If evening prayer is used for midweek services during Lent or Advent, the Great Litany could replace the litany form in vespers. It could also replace the prayers in morning prayer.

The Great Litany can also form the nucleus of a separate penitential service. Planners could preface the litany with a greeting, a hymn or a psalm, and a brief lesson and response. After the litany, planners may choose to conclude with a prayer of the day or another short prayer appropriate to the occasion, the Lord's Prayer, and a blessing. Because of the penitential nature, the sharing of the peace may be appropriate. There may be times of crisis when this litany would express the needs and concerns of worshipers.

The Litany of the Saints is suggested for use within the Vigil of Easter (see rubric, AE p. 269). Within the holy communion service it could be used on occasion as a gathering song or as a form for the prayers. (Its similarity to the creed might suggest that the creed be omitted on such an occasion.) The list of witnesses to the faith would recommend its use on All Saints or similar festivals. And like the Great Litany, it could form the core of a separate prayer service.

Because of the length of both litanies, an appropriate tempo is vital to sustaining the prayer. It is also important that the leader is able to sustain the chant in a way that draws the community into the prayer. The rhythm works best when there is little or no pause between petition, response, and the next petition. An alternate way of singing the litanies is to do them antiphonally between two groups of the assembly, perhaps with a choir divided between the two groups to assist them. Because these litanies may be unfamiliar to many, a small group may rehearse and give leadership to the larger worshiping community.

Appendixes

APPENDIX A

Evangelical Lutheran Worship Lesser Festivals and Commemorations

Brief Descriptions

January 1

NAME OF JESUS

The observance of the octave (eighth day) of Christmas has roots in the sixth century. Until the recent past, Lutheran calendars called this day "The Circumcision and Name of Jesus." The emphasis on circumcision is the older emphasis. Every Jewish boy was circumcised and formally named on the eighth day of his life. Already in his youth, Jesus bears the mark of a covenant that he makes new through the shedding of his blood on the cross. That covenant, like Jesus' name, is a gift that marks the children of God. Baptized into Christ, the church begins a new year in Jesus' name.

January 2

Johann Konrad Wilhelm Loehe, renewer of the church, 1872

Loehe (approximate pronunciation: LAY-uh) was a pastor in nineteenth-century Germany. From the small town of Neuendettelsau, he sent pastors to North America, Australia, New Guinea, Brazil, and the Ukraine. His work for a clear confessional basis within the Bavarian church sometimes led to conflict with the ecclesiastical bureaucracy. Loehe's chief concern was that a congregation find its life in the holy communion, and from that source evangelism and social ministries would flow. Many Lutheran congregations in Michigan, Ohio, and Iowa were either founded or influenced by missionaries sent by Loehe.

January 15

Martin Luther King Jr., renewer of society, martyr, 1968

Martin Luther King Jr. is remembered as an American prophet of justice among races and nations, a Christian whose faith undergirded his advocacy of vigorous yet nonviolent action for racial equality. A pastor of churches in Montgomery, Alabama, and Atlanta, Georgia, his witness was taken to the streets in such other places as Birmingham, Alabama, where he was arrested and jailed while protesting against segregation. He preached nonviolence and demanded that love be returned for hate. Awarded the Nobel Peace Prize in 1964, he was killed by an assassin on April 4, 1968. Though most commemorations are held on the date of the person's death, many churches hold commemorations near Dr. King's birth date of January 15, in conjunction with the American civil holiday honoring him. An alternate date for the commemoration would be his death date, April 4.

January 17

Antony of Egypt, renewer of the church, c. 356

Antony was born in Qemen-al-Arous, Upper Egypt, and was one of the earliest Egyptian desert fathers. Born to Christian parents from whom he inherited a large estate, he took personally Jesus' message to sell all that you have, give to the poor, and follow Christ. After making arrangements to provide for the care of his sister, he gave away his inheritance and became a hermit. Later, he became the head of a group of monks who lived in a cluster of huts and devoted themselves to communal prayer, worship, and manual labor under Antony's direction. The money they earned from their work was distributed as alms. Antony and his monks also preached and counseled those who sought them out. Antony and the desert fathers serve as a reminder that certain times and circumstances call Christians to stand apart from the surrounding culture and renounce the world in service to Christ.

January 17

Pachomius, renewer of the church, 346

Another of the desert fathers, Pachomius (puh-KOME-ee-us) was born in Egypt about 290. He became a Christian during his service as a soldier. In 320 he went to live as a hermit in Upper Egypt, where other hermits lived nearby. Pachomius organized them into a religious community in which the members prayed together and held their goods in common. His rule for monasteries influenced both Eastern and Western monasticism through the Rule of Basil and the Rule of Benedict, respectively.

January 18

Confession of Peter

Week of Prayer for Christian Unity begins

The Week of Prayer for Christian Unity is framed by two commemorations, the Confession of Peter (a relatively recent addition to the calendar) and the older Conversion of Paul. Both apostles are remembered together on June 29, but these two days give us an opportunity to focus on key events in each of their lives. Today we remember that Peter was led by God's grace to acknowledge Jesus as "the Christ, the Son of the living God" (Matt. 16:16). This confession is the common confession that unites us with Peter and with all Christians of every time and place.

January 19

Henry, Bishop of Uppsala, martyr, 1156

Henry, an Englishman, became bishop of Uppsala, Sweden, in 1152 and is regarded as the patron of Finland. He traveled to Finland with the king of Sweden on a mission trip and remained there to organize the church. He was murdered in Finland by a man he had rebuked and who was disciplined by the church. Henry's burial place became a center of pilgrimage. His popularity as a saint is strong in both Sweden and Finland.

January 21

Agnes, martyr, 304

Agnes was a girl of about thirteen living in Rome, who had chosen a life of service to Christ as a virgin, despite the Roman emperor Diocletian's ruling that had outlawed all Christian activity. The details of her martyrdom are not clear, but she gave witness to her faith and was put to death as a result, most likely by the sword. Since her death, the church has honored her as one of the chief martyrs of her time.

January 25

Conversion of Paul

Week of Prayer for Christian Unity ends

Today the Week of Prayer for Christian Unity comes to an end. The church remembers how a man of Tarsus named Saul, a former persecutor of the early Christian church, was turned around by God's grace to become one of its chief preachers. The risen Christ appeared to Paul on the road to Damascus and called him to proclaim the gospel. The narratives describing Paul's conversion in the Acts of the Apostles, Galatians, and 1 Corinthians inspire this commemoration, which was first celebrated among the Christians of Gaul.

January 26

Timothy, Titus, and Silas, missionaries

On the two days following the celebration of the Conversion of Paul, his companions are remembered. Timothy, Titus, and Silas were missionary coworkers with Paul. Timothy accompanied Paul on his second missionary journey and was commissioned by Paul to go to Ephesus, where he served as bishop and overseer of the church. Titus was a traveling companion of Paul, accompanied him on the trip to the council of Jerusalem, and became the first bishop of Crete. Silas traveled with Paul through Asia Minor and Greece and was imprisoned with him at Philippi, where they were delivered by an earthquake.

January 27

Lydia, Dorcas, and Phoebe, witnesses to the faith

On this day the church remembers three women who were companions in Paul's ministry. Lydia was Paul's first convert at Philippi in Macedonia. She was a merchant of purple-dyed goods, and because purple dye was extremely expensive, it is likely that Lydia was a woman of some wealth. Lydia and her household were baptized by Paul, and for a time her home was a base for Paul's missionary work. Dorcas is remembered for her charitable works, particularly making clothing for needy widows. Phoebe was a *diakonos*, a deaconess in the church at Cenchreae, near Corinth. Paul praises her as one who, through her service, looked after many people.

January 28

Thomas Aquinas, teacher, 1274

Thomas Aquinas (uh-KWY-nus) was a brilliant and creative theologian of the thirteenth century. He was first and foremost a student of the Bible and profoundly concerned with the theological formation of the church's ordained ministers. As a member of the Order of Preachers (Dominicans), he worked to correlate scripture with the philosophy of Aristotle, which was having a renaissance in Aquinas's day. Some students of Aristotle's philosophy found in it an alternative to Christianity. But Aquinas immersed himself in the thought of Aristotle and worked to explain Christian beliefs in the philosophical culture of the day.

February 2

Presentation of Our Lord

Forty days after the birth of Christ we mark the day Mary and Joseph presented him in the temple in accordance with Jewish law. There a prophetess named Anna began to speak of the redemption of Israel when she saw the young child. Simeon also greeted Mary and Joseph. He responded to the presence of the consolation of Israel in this child with the words of the Nunc dimittis. His song described Jesus as a "light for the nations."

Because of the link between Jesus as the light for the nations, and because an old reading for this festival contains a line from the prophet Zephaniah, "I will search Jerusalem with candles," the day is also known as Candlemas, a day when candles are blessed for the coming year.

February 3

Ansgar, Bishop of Hamburg, missionary to Denmark and Sweden, 865

Ansgar was a monk who led a mission to Denmark and later to Sweden, where he built the first church. His work ran into difficulties with the rulers of the day, and he was forced to withdraw into Germany, where he served as a bishop in Hamburg. Despite his difficulties in Sweden, he persisted in his mission work and later helped consecrate Gothbert as the first bishop of Sweden. Ansgar had a deep love for the poor. He would wash their feet and serve them food provided by the parish.

February 5

The Martyrs of Japan, 1597

In the sixteenth century, Jesuit missionaries, followed by Franciscans, introduced the Christian faith in Japan. But a promising beginning to those missions—perhaps as many as 300,000 Christians by the end of the sixteenth century—met complications from competition between the missionary groups, political difficulty between Spain and Portugal, and factions within the government of Japan. Christianity was suppressed. By 1630, Christianity was driven underground.

Today we commemorate the first martyrs of Japan, twenty-six missionaries and converts who were killed by crucifixion. Two hundred and fifty years later, when Christian missionaries returned to Japan, they found a community of Japanese Christians that had survived underground.

February 14

Cyril, monk, 869; Methodius, bishop, 885; missionaries to the Slavs

These two brothers from a noble family in Thessalonika in northeastern Greece were priests and missionaries. After some early initial missionary work by Cyril among the Arabs, the brothers retired to a monastery. They were later sent to work among the Slavs, the missionary work for which they are most known. Since Slavonic had no written form at the time, the brothers established a written language with the Greek alphabet as its basis. They translated the scriptures and the liturgy using this Cyrillic alphabet. The Czechs, Serbs, Croats, Slovaks, and Bulgars regard the brothers as the founders of Slavic literature. The brothers' work in preaching and worshiping in the language of the people are honored by Christians in both East and West.

February 18

Martin Luther, renewer of the church, 1546

On this day in 1546, Martin Luther died at the age of sixty-two. For a time, he was an Augustinian monk, but it is his work as a biblical scholar, translator of the Bible, public confessor of the faith, reformer of the liturgy, theologian, educator, and father of German vernacular literature that holds him in our remembrance. In Luther's own judgment, the greatest of all of his works was his catechism, written to instruct people in the basics of faith. And it was his baptism that sustained him in his trials as a reformer.

February 23

Polycarp, Bishop of Smyrna, martyr, 156

Polycarp was bishop of Smyrna (in present-day western Turkey) and a link between the apostolic age and the church at the end of the second century. He is said to have been known by John, the author of Revelation. In turn he was known by Iranaeus, bishop of Lyon in France, and Ignatius of Antioch. At the age of eighty-six he was martyred for his faith. When urged to save his life and renounce his faith, Polycarp replied, "Eighty-six years I have served him, and he never did me any wrong. How can I blaspheme my king who saved me?" The magistrate who made the offer was reluctant to kill a gentle old man, but he had no choice. Polycarp was burned at the stake, his death a testimony to the cost of renouncing temptation.

February 24

Evangelical Lutheran Worship moves the festival of St. Matthias to May 14 in agreement with other Western calendars.

February 25

Elizabeth Fedde, deaconess, 1921

Fedde was born in Norway and trained as a deaconess. In 1882, at the age of thirty-two, she was asked to come to New York to minister to the poor and to Norwegian seafarers. Her influence was wide-ranging, and she established the Deaconess House in Brooklyn and the Deaconess House and Hospital of the Lutheran Free Church in Minneapolis. She returned home to Norway in 1895 and died there.

March 1

George Herbert, hymnwriter, 1633

As a student at Trinity College, Cambridge, England, George Herbert excelled in languages and music. He went to college with the intention of becoming a priest, but his scholarship attracted the attention of King James I. Herbert served in parliament for two years. After the death of King James and at the urging of a friend, Herbert's interest in ordained ministry was renewed. He was ordained a priest in 1630 and served the little parish of St. Andrew Bremerton until his death. He was noted for unfailing care for his parishioners, bringing the sacraments to them when they were ill, and providing food and clothing for those in need. Herbert is best remembered, however, as a writer of poems and hymns such as "Come, My Way, My Truth, My Life" (ELW 816).

March 2

John Wesley, 1791; Charles Wesley, 1788; renewers of the church

The Wesleys were leaders of a revival in the Church of England. Their spiritual discipline (or method) of frequent communion, fasting, and advocacy for the poor earned them the name "Methodists." The Wesleys were missionaries in the American colony of Georgia for a time, but returned to England discouraged. Following a conversion experience while reading Luther's *Preface to the Epistle to the Romans*, John was perhaps the greatest force in eighteenth-century revival. The brothers' desire was that the Methodist Societies would be a movement for renewal in the Church of England, but after their deaths the societies developed a separate status.

Charles wrote more than six hundred hymns, including "Hark! The Herald Angels Sing" (ELW 270), "Christ, Whose Glory Fills the Skies" (ELW 553), and "Love Divine, All Loves Excelling" (ELW 631).

March 7

Perpetua and Felicity and companions, martyrs at Carthage, 202

In the year 202 the emperor Septimius Severus forbade conversions to Christianity. Perpetua, a noblewoman, Felicity, a slave, and other companions were all catechumens at Carthage in North Africa. They were imprisoned and sentenced to death. Perpetua's father, who was not a Christian, visited her in prison and begged her to lay aside her Christian convictions in order to spare her life and spare the family from scorn. Perpetua responded and told her father, "We know that we are not placed in our own power but in that of God."

March 10

Harriet Tubman, 1913; Sojourner Truth, 1883; renewers of society

Harriet Tubman was born into slavery in Maryland and remained a slave until about age thirty when, fearing she would be sold and moved farther south, she escaped with the help of the Underground Railroad. After that, she helped about three hundred others to escape until slavery was abolished. After the Civil War, her home in Auburn, New York, became a center for women's rights and served the aged and poor.

Sojourner Truth, too, was born a slave, in New York state. Her birth name was Isabella. After slavery was abolished in New York in 1827, she was freed and, while working as a housekeeper, became deeply involved in Christianity. A number of years later, she discerned a call to become a preacher. Taking the name Sojourner Truth, she set out on an evangelistic journey, where people found her testimony to be deeply moving. In later life, she also became a popular speaker against slavery and for women's rights.

March 12

Gregory the Great, Bishop of Rome, 604

Gregory was born into a politically influential family. At one time he held political office and at another time he lived as a monk, all before he was elected to the papacy. Gregory's work was extensive. He influenced public worship through the establishment of a lectionary and prayers to correlate with the readings. He established a school to train church musicians. Gregorian chant is named in his honor. He wrote a treatise underscoring what is required of a pastor serving a congregation. He sent missionaries to preach to the Anglo-Saxons who had invaded England. And at one time he organized distribution of grain during a shortage of food in Rome.

March 17

Patrick, bishop, missionary to Ireland, 461

At sixteen, Patrick was kidnapped by Irish pirates and sold into slavery in Ireland. He himself admitted that up to this point he cared little for God. He escaped after six years, returned to his family in southwest Britain, and began to prepare for ordained ministry. He later returned to Ireland, this time to serve as a bishop and missionary. He made his base in the north of Ireland and from there made many missionary journeys, with much success. In his autobiography he denounced the slave trade, perhaps from his own experience as a slave. Patrick's famous baptismal hymn to the Trinity, "I Bind unto Myself Today"

(ELW 450), can be used as a meditation on Lent's call to return to our baptism.

March 19

Joseph, Guardian of Jesus

The gospels are silent about much of Joseph's life. We know that he was a carpenter or builder by trade. The Gospel of Luke shows him acting in accordance with both civil and religious law by returning to Bethlehem for the census and by presenting the child Jesus in the temple on the fortieth day after his birth. The Gospel of Matthew tells of Joseph's trust in God, who led him through visionary dreams. Because Joseph is not mentioned after the story of a young Jesus teaching in the temple, it is assumed that he died before Jesus reached adulthood.

March 21

Thomas Cranmer, Bishop of Canterbury, martyr, 1556

Cranmer was serving as bishop of Taunton in England when he was chosen by King Henry VIII to become archbishop of Canterbury, largely because Cranmer would agree to the king's divorce from Catherine of Aragon. Cranmer's lasting achievement is contributing to and overseeing the creation of the Book of Common Prayer, which in revised form remains the worship book of the Anglican Communion. He was burned at the stake under Queen Mary for his support of the Protestant Reformation.

March 22

Jonathan Edwards, teacher, missionary to American Indians, 1758

Edwards was a minister in Connecticut and described as the greatest of the New England Puritan preachers. One of Edwards's most notable sermons found its way into contemporary anthologies of literature. In this sermon, "Sinners in the Hands of an Angry God," he spoke at length about hell. However, throughout the rest of his works and his preaching he had more to say about God's love than God's wrath. His personal experience of conversion came when he felt overwhelmed with a sense of God's majesty and grandeur, rather than a fear of hell. Edwards served a Puritan congregation, where he believed that only those who had been fully converted ought to receive communion;

his congregation thought otherwise. Edwards left that congregation and carried out mission work among the Housatonic Indians of Massachusetts. He became president of the College of New Jersey, later to be known as Princeton University.

March 24

Óscar Arnulfo Romero, Bishop of El Salvador, martyr, 1980

Romero is remembered for his advocacy on behalf of the poor in El Salvador, though it was not a characteristic of his early priesthood. After being appointed as archbishop of San Salvador, he preached against the political repression in his country. He and other priests and church workers were considered traitors for their bold stand for justice, especially defending the rights of the poor. After several years of threats to his life, Romero was assassinated while presiding at the eucharist. During the 1980s thousands died in El Salvador during political unrest.

March 25

Annunciation of Our Lord

Nine months before Christmas the church celebrates the annunciation. In Luke the angel Gabriel announces to Mary that she will give birth to the Son of God, and she responds, "Here am I, the servant of the Lord." Ancient scholars believed that March 25 was also the day on which creation began and was the date of Jesus' death on the cross. Thus, from the sixth to eighth centuries, March 25 was observed as New Year's Day in much of Christian Europe.

March 29

Hans Nielsen Hauge, renewer of the church, 1824

Hans Nielsen Hauge was a layperson who began preaching about "the living faith" in Norway and Denmark after a mystical experience that he believed called him to share the assurance of salvation with others. At the time, itinerant preaching and religious gatherings held without the supervision of a pastor were illegal, and Hauge was arrested several times. He also faced great personal suffering: his first wife died, and three of his four children died in infancy.

March 31

John Donne, poet, 1631

This priest of the Church of England is commemorated for his poetry and spiritual writing. Most of his poetry was written before his ordination and is sacred and secular, intellectual and sensuous. He saw in his wife, Anne, glimpses of the glory of God and a human revelation of divine love. In 1615 he was ordained and seven years later he was named dean of St. Paul's Cathedral in London. By that time his reputation as a preacher was firmly in place. In his poem "Good Friday, 1613. Riding westward," he speaks of Jesus' death on the cross: "Who sees God's face, that is self life, must die; What a death were it then to see God die?"

April 4

Benedict the African, confessor, 1589

Born a slave on the island of Sicily, Benedict first lived as a hermit and labored as a plowman after he was freed. When the bishop of Rome ordered all hermits to attach themselves to a religious community, Benedict joined the Franciscans, where he served as a cook. Although he was illiterate, his fame as a confessor brought many visitors to the humble and holy cook, and he was eventually named superior of the community. A patron saint of African Americans, Benedict is remembered for his patience and understanding when confronted with racial prejudice and taunts.

April 6

Albrecht Dürer, 1528; Matthias Grünewald, 1529; Lucas Cranach, 1553; artists

These great German artists revealed through their work the mystery of salvation and the wonder of creation. Dürer's work reflected the apocalyptic spirit of his time. Though he remained a Roman Catholic, he was sympathetic to Martin Luther's reforming work. Grünewald's paintings are known for their dramatic forms, vivid colors, and depiction of light. Cranach's work includes many fine religious examples and several portraits of Martin Luther. Cranach was also widely known for his woodcuts.

April 9

Dietrich Bonhoeffer, theologian, 1945

Bonhoeffer (BON-heh-fer) was a German theologian who, at the age of twenty-five, became a lecturer in systematic theology at the University of Berlin. In 1933, and with Hitler's rise to power, Bonhoeffer became a leading spokesman for the Confessing Church, a resistance movement against the Nazis. He was arrested in 1943. He was linked to a failed attempt on Hitler's life and sent to Buchenwald, then to Schönberg prison. After leading a worship service on April 8, 1945, at Schönberg prison, he was taken away to be hanged the next day. His last words as he left were, "This is the end, but for me the beginning of life." *Evangelical Lutheran Worship* includes a hymn (626) by Bonhoeffer, "By Gracious Powers."

April 10

Mikael Agricola, Bishop of Turku, 1557

Agricola was consecrated as the bishop of Turku in 1554, without papal approval. As a result, he began a reform of the Finnish church along Lutheran lines. He translated the New Testament, the prayerbook, hymns, and the mass into Finnish, and through this work set the rules of orthography that are the basis of modern Finnish spelling. His thoroughgoing work is particularly remarkable in that he accomplished it in only three years. He died suddenly on a return trip from negotiating a peace treaty with the Russians.

April 19

Olavus Petri, priest, 1552; Laurentius Petri, Bishop of Uppsala, 1573; renewers of the church

These two brothers are commemorated for their introduction of the Lutheran movement to the Church of Sweden after studying at the University of Wittenberg. They returned home and, through the support of King Gustavus Vasa, began their work. Olavus published a catechism, hymnal, and a Swedish version of the mass. He resisted attempts by the king to gain royal control of the church. Laurentius was a professor at the university in Uppsala. When the king wanted to abolish the ministry of bishops, Laurentius persuaded him otherwise. The historic episcopate continues in Sweden to this day. Together the brothers published a complete Bible in Swedish and a revised liturgy in 1541.

April 21

Anselm, Bishop of Canterbury, 1109

This eleventh- and twelfth-century Benedictine monk stands out as one of the greatest theologians between Augustine and Thomas Aquinas. He is counted among the medieval mystics who emphasized the maternal aspects of God. Of Jesus Anselm says, "In sickness you nurse us and with pure milk you feed us." Anselm is perhaps best known for his "satisfaction" theory of atonement. He argued that human rebellion against God demands a payment, but because humanity is fallen it is incapable of making that satisfaction. But God takes on human nature in Jesus Christ, Anselm proposed, in order to make the perfect payment for sin.

April 23

Toyohiko Kagawa, renewer of society, 1960

Toyohiko Kagawa (toy-oh-hee-koh ka-ga-wah) was born in 1888 in Kobe, Japan. Orphaned early, he was disowned by his remaining extended family when he became a Christian. Kagawa wrote, spoke, and worked at length on ways to employ Christian principles in the ordering of society. His vocation to help the poor led him to live among them. He established schools, hospitals, and churches. He also worked for peace and established the Anti-War League. He was arrested for his efforts to reconcile Japan and China after the Japanese attack of 1940.

April 25

Mark, Evangelist

Though Mark himself was not an apostle, it is likely that he was a member of one of the early Christian communities. It is possible that he is the John Mark of Acts 12 whose mother owned the house where the apostles gathered. The gospel attributed to him is brief and direct. It is considered by many to be the earliest gospel. Tradition has it that Mark went to preach in Alexandria, Egypt, became the first bishop there, and was martyred.

April 29

Catherine of Siena, theologian, 1380

Catherine of Siena was a member of the Order of Preachers (Dominicans), and among Roman Catholics she was the first woman to receive the title Doctor of the Church. She was a contemplative and is known for her mystical visions of Jesus. This gift of mysticism apparently extended back into her childhood, much to the dismay of her parents, who wanted her to be like other children. Catherine was a humanitarian who worked to alleviate the suffering of the poor and imprisoned. She was also a renewer of church and society and advised both popes and any persons who told her their problems. Catherine's contemplative life was linked to her concern for the poor and suffering. She is a reminder that prayer and activism belong together.

May 1

Philip and James, Apostles

Philip was one of the first disciples of Jesus, who after following Jesus invited Nathanael to "come and see." According to tradition, Philip preached in Asia Minor and died as a martyr in Phrygia. James, the son of Alphaeus, is called "the Less" (meaning "short" or "younger") to distinguish him from another apostle named James who is commemorated July 25. Philip and James are commemorated together because the remains of these two saints were placed in the Church of the Apostles in Rome on this day in 561.

May 2

Athanasius, Bishop of Alexandria, 373

Athanasius (ath-an-AY-shus) attended the Council of Nicaea in 325 as a deacon and secretary to the bishop of Alexandria. At the council, and when he himself served as bishop of Alexandria, he defended the full divinity of Christ against the Arian position held by emperors, magistrates, and theologians. Because of his defense of the divinity of Christ, he was considered a troublemaker and was banished from Alexandria on five occasions. As bishop, one of his paschal letters to surrounding bishops gives a list for books that should be considered canonical scripture. He lists the twenty-seven New Testament books that are recognized today.

May 4

Monica, mother of Augustine, 387

Monica was married to a pagan husband who was ill-tempered and unfaithful. She rejoiced greatly when both her husband and his mother became Christian. But it is because she is the mother of Augustine that she is best known. Monica had been a disciple of Ambrose, and eventually Augustine came under his influence. Almost everything we know about Monica comes from Augustine's *Confessions*, his autobiography. She died far from her home but said to her son, "Do not fret because I am buried far from our home in Africa. Nothing is far from God, and I have no fear that God will not know where to find me, when Christ comes to raise me to life at the end of the world." Her dying wish was that her son remember her at the altar of the Lord, wherever he was.

May 8

Julian of Norwich, renewer of the church, c. 1416

Julian (or Juliana) was most likely a Benedictine nun living in an isolated cell attached to the Carrow Priory in Norwich (NOR-rich), England. Definite facts about her life are sparse. However, when she was about thirty years old, she reported visions that she later compiled into a book, *Sixteen Revelations of Divine Love*, a classic of medieval mysticism. The visions declared that love was the meaning of religious experience, provided by Christ who is love, for the purpose of love. A prayer and a hymn attributed to Julian are included in *Evangelical Lutheran Worship* (p. 87, #735).

May 9

Nicolaus Ludwig von Zinzendorf, renewer of the church, hymnwriter, 1760

Count Zinzendorf was born into an aristocratic family and after the death of his father was raised by his Pietistic grandmother. This influence was a lasting one, and he moved away from what he felt was an overly intellectual Lutheranism. When he was twenty-two, a group of Moravians asked permission to live on his lands. He agreed, and they established a settlement they called Herrnhut, or "the Lord's watch." Eventually worldwide Moravian missions emanated from this community. Zinzendorf participated in these missions and is also remembered for writing hymns characteristic of his Pietistic faith, including "Jesus, Still Lead On" (ELW 624).

May 14

Matthias, Apostle

After Christ's ascension, the apostles met in Jerusalem to choose a replacement for Judas. Matthias was chosen over Joseph Justus by the casting of lots. Little is known about Matthias, and little is reported about him in the account of his election in Acts 1:15-26. Matthias traveled among the disciples from the beginning of Jesus' ministry until his ascension. His task, after he was enrolled among the eleven remaining disciples, was to bear witness to the resurrection.

Matthias was formerly commemorated on February 24, though the reason for that date is not known. More recently the Roman Catholic Church moved the celebration to May 14, so that it falls after the celebration of Jesus' resurrection, when Matthias was chosen as an apostle.

May 18

Erik, King of Sweden, martyr, 1160

Erik, long considered the patron saint of Sweden, ruled from 1150 to 1160. He is honored for efforts to bring peace to the nearby pagan kingdoms and for his crusades to spread the Christian faith in Nordic lands. He established a protected Christian mission in Finland that was led by Henry of Uppsala. As king, Erik was noted for his desire to establish fair laws and courts and for his concern for the poor and sick. Erik was killed by a Danish army that approached him at worship on the day after the Ascension. He is reported to have said, "Let us at least finish the sacrifice. The rest of the feast I shall keep elsewhere." As he left worship he was killed.

May 21

Helena, mother of Constantine, 330

Wife of the co-regent of the West, Helena (or Helen) was mother of Constantine, who later became Roman emperor. After he was converted to Christianity, he influenced her also to become Christian. From that point she lived an exemplary life of faith, particularly through acts of generosity toward the poor. She is also remembered for traveling through Palestine and building churches on the sites she believed to be where Jesus was born, where he was buried, and from which he ascended.

May 24

Nicolaus Copernicus, 1543; Leonhard Euler, 1783; scientists

Remembering scientists such as Copernicus and Euler offers an opportunity to ponder the mysteries of the universe and the grandeur of God's creation. Copernicus is an example of a renaissance person. He formally studied astronomy, mathematics, Greek, Plato, law, medicine, and canon law. He also had interests in theology, poetry, and the natural and social sciences. Copernicus is chiefly remembered for his work as an astronomer and his idea that the sun, not the earth, is the center of the solar system.

Euler (OY-ler) is regarded as one of the founders of the science of pure mathematics and made important contributions to mechanics, hydrodynamics, astronomy, optics, and acoustics.

May 27

John Calvin, renewer of the church, 1564

John Calvin began his studies in theology at the University of Paris when he was fourteen. In his mid-twenties he experienced a conversion that led him to embrace the views of the Reformation. His theological ideas are systematically laid out in his *Institutes of the Christian Religion*. He is also well known for his commentaries on scripture. He was a preacher in Geneva, was banished once, and then later returned to reform the city under a theocratic constitution.

May 29

Jiřī Tranovský, hymnwriter, 1637

Jiřī Tranovský (YEAR-zhee truh-NOF-skee) is considered the "Luther of the Slavs" and the father of Slovak hymnody. Trained at the University of Wittenberg in the early seventeenth century, Tranovský was ordained in 1616 and spent his life preaching and teaching in Prague, Silesia, and finally Slovakia. He produced a translation of the Augsburg Confession and published his hymn collection *Cithara Sanctorum* (Lyre of the Saints), the foundation of Slovak Lutheran hymnody.

May 31

VISIT OF MARY TO ELIZABETH

Sometime after the Annunciation, Mary visited her cousin Elizabeth. This occasion is sometimes referred to simply as "The Visitation." Elizabeth greeted Mary with the words "Blessed are you among women," and Mary responded with her famous song, the Magnificat. Luke's gospel tells that even John the Baptist rejoiced and leapt in his mother's womb when Elizabeth heard Mary's greeting. On this festival two women are seen: one, seemingly too old to have a child, bears the last prophet of the old covenant, and the other, quite young, bears the incarnate Word and the new covenant.

June 1

Justin, martyr at Rome, 165

Justin was born of pagan parents. At Ephesus he was moved by stories of early Christian martyrs and came under the influence of an elderly Christian man he met there. Justin described his conversion by saying, "Straightway a flame was kindled in my soul and a love of the prophets and those who are friends of Christ possessed me." Justin was a teacher of philosophy and engaged in debates about the truth of Christian faith. He was arrested and jailed for practicing an unauthorized religion. He refused to renounce his faith, and he and six of his students, one a woman, were beheaded.

Justin's description of early Christian worship around the year 150 is one of the foundations of the church's pattern of worship, East and West.

June 3

The Martyrs of Uganda, 1886

Christianity had been introduced to Uganda after 1877, but was made available primarily to those in the court of King Mutesa. His successor, King Mwanga, was angered by these Christian members of the court whose first allegiance was not to him but to Christ. On June 3, 1886, thirty-two young men were burned to death for refusing to renounce Christianity. Other martyrs followed. But many were impressed by the confident manner in which these Christians went to their deaths, and the persecution led to a much stronger Christian presence in the country.

June 3

John XXIII, Bishop of Rome, 1963

In his ministry as a bishop of Venice, John (then Archbishop Roncalli) was loved by his people. He visited parishes and established new ones. He had warm affection for the working class—he himself was the child of Italian peasants—and he worked at developing social-action ministries. At age seventy-seven he was elected bishop of Rome. Despite the expectation that he would be a transitional pope, he had great energy and spirit. He convened the Second Vatican Council to open the windows of the church and "let in the fresh air of the modern world." The council brought about great changes in Roman Catholic worship, changes that have influenced Lutherans and many other Protestant churches as well.

June 5

Boniface, Bishop of Mainz, missionary to Germany, martyr, 754

Boniface (his name means "good deeds") was born Wynfrith in Devonshire, England. He was a Benedictine monk who at the age of thirty was called to missionary work among the Vandal tribes in Germany. His first missionary attempt was unsuccessful, but he returned two years later and was able to plant the gospel in an area filled with superstitious and violent practices. He led large numbers of Benedictine monks and nuns in establishing churches, schools, and seminaries. Boniface was also a reformer. He persuaded two rulers to call synods to put an end to the practice of selling church offices to the highest bidder. Boniface was preparing a group for confirmation on the eve of Pentecost when he and they were killed by a band of pagans.

June 7

Seattle, chief of the Duwamish Confederacy, 1866

Noah Seattle was chief of the Suquamish tribe and later became chief of the Duwamish Confederacy, a tribal alliance. When the tribes were faced with an increasing number of white settlers, Seattle chose to live and work peacefully with them rather than engage in wars. After Seattle became a Roman Catholic, he began the practice of morning and evening prayer in the tribe, a practice that continued after his death. On the centennial of his birth, the city of Seattle—named for him against his wishes—erected a monument over his grave.

June 9

Columba, 597; Aidan, 651; Bede, 735; renewers of the church
These three monks from the British Isles were pillars among those who kept alive the light of learning and devotion during the Middle Ages. Columba founded three monasteries, including one on the island of Iona, off the coast of Scotland. That monastery was left in ruins after the Reformation but today is home to an ecumenical religious community. Aidan, who helped bring Christianity to the Northumbria area of England, was known for his pastoral style and ability to stir people to charity and good works. Bede was a Bible translator and scripture scholar. He wrote a history of the English church and was the first historian to date events *anno Domini* (A.D.), "year of our Lord." Bede is also known for his hymns, including "A Hymn of Glory Let Us Sing!" (ELW 393).

June 11

BARNABAS, APOSTLE
The Eastern church commemorates Barnabas as one of the Seventy commissioned by Jesus. Though he was not among the Twelve mentioned in the gospels, the book of Acts gives him the title of apostle. His name means "son of encouragement." When Paul came to Jerusalem after his conversion, Barnabas took him in over the fears of the other apostles, who doubted Paul's discipleship. Later, Paul and Barnabas traveled together on missions. At the Council of Jerusalem, Barnabas defended the claims of Gentile Christians in relation to the Mosaic law.

June 14

Basil the Great, Bishop of Caesarea, 379; Gregory, Bishop of Nyssa, c. 385; Gregory of Nazianzus, Bishop of Constantinople, c. 389; Macrina, theologian, c. 379
The three men in this group are known as the Cappadocian fathers; all three explored the mystery of the Holy Trinity. Basil was influenced by his sister Macrina to live a monastic life, and he settled near the family estate in Caesarea. Basil's Longer Rule and Shorter Rule for monastic life are the basis for Eastern monasticism to this day, and

express a preference for communal monastic life over that of hermits. Gregory of Nazianzus (nah-zee-AN-zus) was sent to preach on behalf of the Orthodox faith against the Arians in Constantinople, though the Orthodox did not have a church there at the time. He defended Orthodox trinitarian and Christological doctrine, and his preaching won over the city. Gregory of Nyssa (NISS-uh) was the younger brother of Basil the Great. He is remembered as a writer on spiritual life and the contemplation of God in worship and sacraments.

Macrina (muh-CREE-nuh) was the older sister of Basil and Gregory of Nyssa. She received an excellent education centered on the Bible, and when her fiancé died she devoted herself to the pursuit of Christian perfection. She was a leader of a community, based at the family estate, dedicated to asceticism, meditation, and prayer. Macrina's teaching was influential within the early church.

June 21

Onesimos Nesib, translator, evangelist, 1931

Onesimos (oh-NESS-ee-mus neh-SEEB) was born into the Oromo people of Ethiopia. He was captured by slave traders and taken from his homeland to Eritrea, where he was bought, freed, and educated by Swedish missionaries. He translated the Bible into Oromo and returned to his homeland to preach the gospel. His tombstone includes a verse from Jeremiah 22:29, "O land, land, land, hear the word of the Lord!"

June 24

John the Baptist

The birth and life of John the Baptist is celebrated exactly six months before Christmas Eve. For Christians in the Northern Hemisphere, these two dates are deeply symbolic. John said that he must decrease as Jesus increased. According to tradition, John was born as the days are longest and then steadily decrease, while Jesus was born as the days are shortest and then steadily increase. In many countries this day is celebrated with customs associated with the summer solstice.

June 25

Presentation of the Augsburg Confession, 1530

On this day in 1530 the German and Latin editions of the Augsburg Confession were presented to Emperor Charles of the Holy Roman

Empire. The Augsburg Confession was written by Philipp Melanchthon and endorsed by Martin Luther and consists of a brief summary of points in which the reformers saw their teaching as either agreeing with or differing from that of the Roman Catholic Church of the time. In 1580 when the *Book of Concord* was drawn up, the unaltered Augsburg Confession was included as the principal Lutheran confession.

June 25

Philipp Melanchthon, renewer of the church, 1560

Though he died on April 19, Philipp Melanchthon (meh-LAHNK-ton) is commemorated today because of his connection with the Augsburg Confession. Colleague and co-reformer with Martin Luther, Melanchthon was a brilliant scholar, known as "the teacher of Germany." The University of Wittenberg hired him as its first professor of Greek, and there he became a friend of Luther. Melanchthon was a popular professor—even his classes at six in the morning had as many as six hundred students. As a reformer he was known for his conciliatory spirit and for finding areas of agreement with fellow Christians. He was never ordained.

June 27

Cyril, Bishop of Alexandria, theologian, 444

Remembered as an outstanding theologian as well as a contentious personality, Cyril defended the orthodox teachings about the person of Christ against Nestorius, bishop of Constantinople. Nestorius taught that the divine and human natures of Christ were entirely distinct, and therefore Mary could not be referred to as the *theotokos*, or bearer of God. This conflict, which also had roots in a rivalry for preeminence between Alexandria and Constantinople, involved all of the major Christian leaders of the time, including the patriarchs of Rome, Antioch, and Jerusalem, and finally also the emperor. In the end it was decided that Cyril's interpretation, that Christ's person included both divine and human natures, was correct.

June 28

Irenaeus, Bishop of Lyons, c. 202

Irenaeus (ee-ren-AY-us) believed that the way to remain steadfast to the truth was to hold fast to the faith handed down from the apostles. He believed that only Matthew, Mark, Luke, and John were trustworthy gospels. Irenaeus was an opponent of gnosticism and its emphasis on dualism. As a result of his battles with the gnostics, he was one of the first to speak of the church as "catholic." By catholic he meant that local congregations did not exist by themselves but were linked to one another in the whole church. He also maintained that this church was not contained within any national boundaries. He argued that the church's message was for all people, in contrast to the gnostics and their emphasis on "secret knowledge."

June 29

Peter and Paul, Apostles

These two are an odd couple of biblical witnesses to be brought together in one commemoration. It appears that Peter would have gladly served as the editor of Paul's letters: in a letter attributed to him, Peter says that some things in Paul's letters are hard to understand. Paul's criticism of Peter is more blunt. In Galatians he points out ways that Peter was wrong. One of the things that unites Peter and Paul is the tradition that says they were martyred together on this date in 67 or 68. What unites them more closely is their common confession of Jesus Christ. In the gospel reading appointed for this day, Peter declares that Jesus is the Christ through whom the foundation of the church is established. In the second reading, we hear of Paul's faithfulness to the end, by God's help. Together Peter and Paul lay a foundation and build the framework for our lives of faith through their proclamation of Jesus Christ.

July 1

Catherine Winkworth, 1878; John Mason Neale, 1866; hymn translators

Neale was an English priest associated with the movement for church renewal at Cambridge. Winkworth lived most of her life in Manchester, where she was involved in promoting women's rights. These two hymn writers translated many hymn texts into English. Catherine Winkworth devoted herself to the translation of German hymns, nineteen of which are included in *Evangelical Lutheran Worship*; the fourteen hymn translations of John Mason Neale in the collection represent his specialization in ancient Latin and Greek hymns.

July 3

Thomas, Apostle

Thomas is perhaps best remembered as "Doubting Thomas." But alongside this doubt, the Gospel of John shows Thomas as fiercely loyal: "Let us also go, that we may die with him" (John 11:16). And John's gospel shows Thomas moving from doubt to deep faith. Thomas makes one of the strongest confessions of faith in the New Testament, "My Lord and my God!" (John 20:28). From this confession of faith, ancient stories tell of Thomas's missionary work to India, where Christian communities were flourishing a thousand years before the arrival of sixteenth-century missionaries.

The feast of St. Thomas is observed on various dates, and a long tradition in the West placed it on December 21. In 1969, however, the Roman Catholic calendar moved it to July 3 in agreement with the Syrian Church. *Evangelical Lutheran Worship* follows this ecumenical trend.

July 6

Jan Hus, martyr, 1415

Jan Hus was a Bohemian priest who spoke against abuses in the church of his day in many of the same ways Luther would a century later. He spoke against the withholding of the cup at the eucharist and because of this stance was excommunicated, not for heresy but for insubordination toward his archbishop. He preached against the selling of indulgences and was particularly mortified by the indulgence trade of two rival claimants to the papacy who were raising money for war against each other. He was found guilty of heresy by the Council of Constance and burned at the stake. The followers of Jan Hus became known as the Czech Brethren and eventually continued as the Moravian Church.

July 11

Benedict of Nursia, Abbot of Monte Cassino, c. 540

Benedict is known as the father of Western monasticism. He was educated in Rome but was appalled by the decline of life around him. He went to live as a hermit, and a community of monks came to gather around him. In the prologue of his rule for monasteries he wrote that his intent in drawing up his regulations was "to set down nothing harsh, nothing burdensome." It is that moderate spirit that characterizes his rule and the monastic communities that are formed by it. Benedict encourages a generous spirit of hospitality, saying that visitors to Benedictine communities are to be welcomed as Christ himself.

July 12

Nathan Söderblom, Bishop of Uppsala, 1931

In 1930, this Swedish theologian, ecumenist, and social activist received the Nobel Prize for peace. Söderblom (ZAY-der-blom) saw the value of the ancient worship of the church catholic and encouraged the liturgical movement. He also valued the work of liberal Protestant scholars and believed social action was a first step on the path toward a united Christianity. He organized the Universal Christian Council on Life and Work, one of the organizations that in 1948 came together to form the World Council of Churches.

July 17

Bartolomé de Las Casas, missionary to the Indies, 1566

Bartolomé de Las Casas was a Spanish priest and a missionary in the Western Hemisphere. He first came to the West while serving in the military, and he was granted a large estate that included a number of indigenous slaves. When he was ordained in 1513, he granted freedom to his servants. This act characterized much of the rest of Las Casas's ministry. Throughout the Caribbean and Central America, he worked to stop the enslavement of native people, to halt the brutal treatment of women by military forces, and to promote laws that humanized the process of colonization.

July 22

Mary Magdalene, Apostle

The gospels report Mary Magdalene was one of the women of Galilee who followed Jesus. She was present at Jesus' crucifixion and his burial. When she went to the tomb on the first day of the week to anoint Jesus' body, she was the first person to whom the risen Lord appeared. She returned to the disciples with the news and has been called "the apostle to the apostles" for her proclamation of the resurrection. Because John's gospel describes Mary as weeping at the tomb, she is often portrayed in art with red eyes. Icons depict her standing by the tomb and holding a bright red egg, symbol of the resurrection.

July 23

Birgitta of Sweden, renewer of the church, 1373

Birgitta (beer-GEE-tuh) was married at age thirteen and had four daughters with her husband. She was a woman of some standing who, in her early thirties, served as the chief lady-in-waiting to the queen of Sweden. She was widowed at the age of thirty-eight, shortly after she and her husband had made a religious pilgrimage. Following the death of her husband the religious dreams and visions that had begun in her youth occurred more regularly. Her devotional commitments led her to give to the poor and needy all that she owned, and she began to live a more ascetic life. She founded an order of monks and nuns, the Order of the Holy Savior (Brigittines), whose superior was a woman. Today the Society of St. Birgitta is a laypersons' society that continues her work of prayer and charity.

July 25

James, Apostle

James is one of the sons of Zebedee and is counted as one of the twelve disciples. Together with his brother John they had the nickname "sons of thunder." One of the stories in the New Testament tells of their request for Jesus to grant them places of honor in the kingdom. They are also reported to have asked Jesus for permission to send down fire on a Samaritan village that had not welcomed them. James was the first of the Twelve to suffer martyrdom and is the only apostle whose martyrdom is recorded in scripture. He is sometimes called James the Elder to distinguish him from James the Less, commemorated with Philip on May 1, and James of Jerusalem, commemorated on October 23.

July 28

Johann Sebastian Bach, 1750; Heinrich Schütz, 1672); George Frederick Handel, 1759; musicians

These three composers have done much to enrich the worship life of the church. Johann Sebastian Bach drew on the Lutheran tradition of hymnody and wrote about two hundred cantatas, including at least two for each Sunday and festival day in the Lutheran calendar of his day. He has been called "the fifth evangelist" for the ways he proclaimed the gospel through his music. George Frederick Handel was not primarily a church musician, but his great work *Messiah* is a musical proclamation of the scriptures. Heinrich Schütz wrote choral settings of biblical texts and paid special attention to ways his composition would underscore the meaning of the words.

July 29

Mary, Martha, and Lazarus of Bethany

Mary and Martha are remembered for the hospitality and refreshment they offered Jesus in their home. Following the characterization drawn by Luke, Martha represents the active life, Mary the contemplative. Mary is identified in the fourth gospel as the one who anointed Jesus before his passion and who was criticized for her act of devotion. Lazarus, Mary's and Martha's brother, was raised from the dead by Jesus as a sign of the eternal life offered to all believers. It was over Lazarus's tomb that Jesus wept for love of his friend.

July 29

Olaf, King of Norway, martyr, 1030

Olaf is considered the patron saint of Norway. In his early career he engaged in war and piracy in the Baltic and in Normandy. In Rouen, though, he was baptized and became a Christian. He returned to Norway, succeeded his father as king, and from then on Christianity was the dominant religion of the realm. He revised the laws of the nation and enforced them with strict impartiality, eliminating the possibility of bribes. He thereby alienated much of the aristocracy. The harshness that he sometimes resorted to in order to establish Christianity and his own law led to a rebellion. After being driven from the country and into exile, he enlisted support from Sweden to try to regain his kingdom, but he died in battle.

August 8

Dominic, founder of the Order of Preachers (Dominicans), 1221

Dominic was a Spanish priest who preached against the Albigensians, a heretical sect that held gnostic and dualistic beliefs. Dominic believed that a stumbling block to restoring heretics to the church was the wealth of clergy, so he formed an itinerant religious order, the Order of Preachers (Dominicans), who lived in poverty, studied philosophy and theology, and preached against heresy. The method of this order was to use kindness and gentle argument, rather than harsh judgment, to bring unorthodox Christians back to the fold. Dominic was opposed to burning Christians at the stake. Three times Dominic was offered the office of bishop, which he refused so that he could continue in his work of preaching.

August 10

Lawrence, deacon, martyr, 258

Lawrence was one of seven deacons of the congregation at Rome and, like the deacons appointed in Acts, was responsible for financial matters in the church and for the care of the poor. Lawrence lived during a time of persecution under the emperor Valerian. The emperor demanded that Lawrence surrender the treasures of the church. Lawrence gathered lepers, orphans, the blind and lame. He brought them to the emperor and said, "Here is the treasure of the church." This act enraged the emperor, and Lawrence was sentenced to death. Lawrence's martyrdom was one of the first to be observed by the church.

August 11

Clare, Abbess of San Damiano, 1253

At age eighteen, Clare of Assisi heard Francis preach a sermon in a church in town. From that time, she determined to follow in his example of Christian living. With Francis's help (and against the wishes of her father) she and a growing number of companions established a women's Franciscan community, called the Order of Poor Ladies, or Poor Clares. She became a confidante and advisor to Francis, and in standing up against the wishes of popes for the sake of maintaining complete poverty, she helped inspire other women to pursue spiritual goals.

August 13

Florence Nightingale, 1910; Clara Maass, 1901; renewers of society

When Florence Nightingale decided she would be a nurse, her family was horrified. In the early 1800s nursing was done by people with no training and no other way to earn a living. Florence trained at Kaiserswerth, Germany, with a Lutheran order of deaconesses. She returned home and worked to reform hospitals in England. Nightingale led a group of thirty-eight nurses to serve in the Crimean War, where they worked in appalling conditions. She returned to London as a hero and resumed her work there for hospital reform.

Clara Maass was born in New Jersey and served as a nurse in the Spanish-American War, where she encountered the horrors of yellow fever. She later responded to a call for subjects in research on yellow fever. During the experiments, which included receiving bites from mosquitoes, she contracted the disease and died. The commemoration of these women invites the church to give thanks for all who practice the arts of healing.

August 14

Maximilian Kolbe, 1941; Kaj Munk, 1944; martyrs

Father Kolbe was a Franciscan priest, born Raymond Kolbe. After spending some time working in Asia, he returned in 1936 to his native Poland, where he supervised a friary that came to house thousands of Polish war refugees, mostly Jews. The Nazis were watching, however, and he was arrested. Confined in Auschwitz, Kolbe gave generously of his meager resources and finally volunteered to be starved to death in place of another man who was a husband and father. After two weeks, he was executed by a lethal injection.

Kaj (pronounced KYE) Munk, a Danish Lutheran pastor and playwright, was an outspoken critic of the Nazis, who occupied Denmark during the Second World War. His plays frequently highlighted the eventual victory of the Christian faith despite the church's weak and ineffective witness. The Nazis feared Munk because his sermons and articles helped to strengthen the Danish resistance movement. He was executed by the Gestapo on January 5, 1944.

August 15

Mary, Mother of Our Lord

The church honors Mary with the Greek title *theotokos*, meaning God-bearer. Origen first used this title in the early church, and the councils of Ephesus and Chalcedon upheld it. Luther upheld this same title in his writings. The honor paid to Mary as *theotokos* and mother of our Lord goes back to biblical times, when Mary herself sang, "from now on all generations will call me blessed" (Luke 1:48). Mary's life revealed the presence of God incarnate, and it revealed God's presence among the humble and poor. Mary's song, the Magnificat, speaks of reversals in the reign of God: the mighty are cast down, the lowly are lifted up, the hungry are fed, and the rich are sent away empty-handed.

August 20

Bernard, Abbot of Clairvaux, 1153

Bernard was a Cistercian monk who became an abbot of great spiritual depth. He was a mystical writer deeply devoted to the humanity of Christ who emphasized the inner human experience of prayer and contemplation. He was critical of one of the foremost theologians of the day, Peter Abelard, because he believed Abelard's approach to faith was too rational and did not provide sufficient room for mystery. Bernard's devotional writings are still read today. His sermon on the Song of Solomon treats that Old Testament book as an allegory of Christ's love for humanity. Bernard wrote several hymns that are still sung today in translation, including "Jesus, the Very Thought of You" (ELW 754).

August 24

Bartholomew, Apostle

Bartholomew is mentioned as one of Jesus' disciples in Matthew, Mark, and Luke. The list in John does not include him but rather Nathanael. These two are therefore often assumed to be the same person. Except for his name on these lists of the Twelve, little is known. Some traditions say Bartholomew preached in India or Armenia following the resurrection. In art, Bartholomew is pictured holding a flaying knife to indicate the manner in which he was killed.

August 28

Augustine, Bishop of Hippo, 430

Augustine was one of the greatest theologians of the Western church. Born in North Africa, he was a philosophy student in Carthage, where he later became a teacher of rhetoric. Much of his young life was a debauched one. As an adult he came under the influence of Ambrose, the bishop of Milan, and through him came to see Christianity as a religion appropriate for a philosopher. Augustine was baptized by Ambrose at the Easter Vigil in 387. He was ordained four years later and made bishop of Hippo in 396. Augustine was a defender of the Christian faith and argued, against the Donatists, that the holiness of the church did not depend on the holiness of its members, particularly the clergy, but that holiness comes from Christ, the head of the church. Augustine's autobiography, *Confessions*, tells of his slow movement toward faith and includes the line "Late have I loved thee."

August 28

Moses the Black, monk, martyr, c. 405

A man of great strength and rough character, Moses the Black was converted to Christian faith toward the close of the fourth century. Prior to his conversion he had been a thief and a leader of a gang of robbers. The story of his conversion is unknown, but eventually he became a desert monk at Skete. The habit of his monastic community was white, though Moses is reported to have said, "God knows I am black within." The change in his heart and life had a profound impact on his native Ethiopia. He was murdered when Berber bandits attacked his monastery.

September 2

Nikolai Frederik Severin Grundtvig, bishop, renewer of the church, 1872

Grundtvig was one of two principal Danish theologians of the nineteenth century; the other was Søren Kierkegaard. Grundtvig's ministry as a parish pastor had a difficult start. He was officially censured after his first sermon, though he did receive approval a year later to be ordained. He served with his father for two years but was unable to receive a call for seven years after that. In 1826 he was forced to resign after he attacked the notion that Christianity was merely a philosophical idea rather than God's revelation made known to us in Christ and through word and sacrament. This belief would be a hallmark of Grundtvig's writing. He spent his last thirty-three years as a chaplain at a home for elderly women. From his university days he was convinced that poetry spoke to the human spirit better than prose. He wrote more than a thousand hymns, including "God's Word Is Our Great Heritage" (ELW 509).

September 9

Peter Claver, priest, missionary to Colombia, 1654

Peter Claver was born into Spanish nobility and was persuaded to become a Jesuit missionary. He served in Cartagena (in what is now Colombia) by teaching and caring for the slaves. The slaves arrived in ships, where they had been confined in dehumanizing conditions. Claver met and supplied them with medicine, food, clothing, and brandy. He learned their dialects and taught them Christianity. He called himself "the slave of the slaves forever." Claver also ministered to the locals of Cartagena who were in prison and facing death.

September 13

John Chrysostom, Bishop of Constantinople, 407

John was a priest in Antioch and an outstanding preacher. His eloquence earned him the nickname "Chrysostom" ("golden mouth"), but it also got him into trouble. As bishop of Constantinople he preached against corruption among the royal court. The empress, who had been his supporter, sent him into exile. His preaching style emphasized the literal meaning of scripture and its practical application. This interpretation stood in contrast to the common style at the time, which emphasized the allegorical meaning of the text.

September 14

Holy Cross Day

Helena, the mother of Constantine, made a pilgrimage to Israel to look for Christian holy sites. She found what she believed were the sites of the crucifixion and burial of Jesus, sites that modern archaeologists believe may be correct. Here Constantine built two churches. The celebration of Holy Cross Day originated with the dedication of the Church of the Resurrection in 335. Today the festival provides the church an opportunity to lift up the victory of the cross with a spirit of celebration that might be less suitable on Good Friday.

September 16

Cyprian, Bishop of Carthage, martyr, c. 258

Cyprian worked for the unity of the church and cared for his flock in North Africa during a time of great persecution. During Cyprian's time as bishop many people had denied the faith under duress. In contrast to some who held the belief that the church should not receive these people back, Cyprian believed they should be welcomed into full communion after a period of penance. He insisted on the need for compassion in order to preserve the unity of the church. His essay *On the Unity of the Catholic Church* stressed the role of bishops in guaranteeing the visible, concrete unity of the church. Cyprian was also concerned for the physical well-being of the people under his care. He organized a program of medical care for the sick during a severe epidemic in Carthage.

September 17

Hildegard of Bingen, abbess, 1179

Hildegard lived virtually her entire life in convents, yet was widely influential within the church. After an uneventful time as a nun, she was chosen as abbess of her community. She reformed her community as well as other convents. Around the same time, she began having visions and compiled them, as instructed, in a book she called *Scivias*. Hildegard's importance went beyond mysticism. She advised and reproved kings and popes, wrote poems and hymns, and produced treatises in medicine, theology, and natural history. She was also a musician and an artist.

September 18

Dag Hammarskjöld, renewer of society, 1961

Dag Hammarskjöld (HAH-mar-sheld) was a Swedish diplomat and humanitarian who served as secretary general of the United Nations. He was killed in a plane crash on this day in 1961, in what is now Zambia, while on he was his way to negotiate a cease-fire between the United Nations and the Katanga forces. For years Hammarskjöld had kept a private journal, and it was not until that journal was published as *Markings* that the depth of his Christian faith was known. The book revealed that his life was a combination of diplomatic service and personal spirituality, and of contemplation on the meaning of Christ in his life and action in the world.

September 21

Matthew, Apostle and Evangelist

Matthew ("Levi" in the gospels of Mark and Luke) was a tax collector for the Roman government in Capernaum. Tax collectors were distrusted because they were dishonest and worked as agents for a foreign ruler, the occupying Romans. In the gospels, tax collectors are mentioned as sinful and despised outcasts, but it was these outcasts to whom Jesus showed his love. Matthew's name means "gift of the Lord." Since the second century, tradition has attributed the first gospel to him.

September 29

Michael and All Angels

On this festival day the church ponders the richness and variety of God's created order and the limits of human knowledge of it. The scriptures speak of angels (the word means "messengers") who worship God in heaven, and in both testaments angels speak for God on earth. They are remembered most vividly as they appear to the shepherds and announce the birth of the Savior. Michael is an angel whose name appears in Daniel as the heavenly being who leads the faithful dead to God's throne on the day of resurrection. In Revelation, Michael fights in a cosmic battle against Satan.

September 30

Jerome, translator, teacher, 420

Jerome is remembered as a biblical scholar and translator. Rather than choosing classical Latin as the basis of his work, he translated the scriptures into the Latin that was spoken and written by the majority of the persons in his day. His translation is known as the Vulgate, from the Latin word for *common*. While Jerome is remembered as a saint, he could be anything but saintly. He was well known for his short temper and his arrogance, although he was also quick to admit to his personal faults. Thanks to the work of Jerome, many people received the word in their own language and lived lives of faith and service to those in need.

October 4

Francis of Assisi, renewer of the church, 1226

Francis was the son of a wealthy cloth merchant. In a public confrontation with his father, he renounced his wealth and future inheritance and devoted himself to serving the poor. Francis described this act as being "wedded to Lady Poverty." Under his leadership the Order of Friars Minor (Franciscans) was formed, and they took literally Jesus' words to his disciples that they should take nothing on their journey and receive no payment for their work. Their task in preaching was to "use words if necessary." Francis had a spirit of gladness and gratitude for all of God's creation. This commemoration has been a traditional time to bless pets and animals, creatures Francis called his brothers and sisters. A prayer and a hymn attributed to St. Francis are included in *Evangelical Lutheran Worship* (p. 87, #835).

October 4

Theodor Fliedner, renewer of society, 1864

Fliedner's (FLEED-ner) work was instrumental in the revival of the ministry of deaconesses among Lutherans. While a pastor in Kaiserswerth, Germany, he also ministered to prisoners in Düsseldorf. Through his ministry to prisoners, he came in contact with Moravian deaconesses, and it was through this Moravian influence that he was convinced that the ministry of deaconesses had a place among Lutherans. His work and writing encouraged women to care for those who were sick, poor, or imprisoned. Fliedner's deaconess motherhouse in Kaiserswerth inspired Lutherans all over the world to commission deaconesses to serve in parishes, schools, prisons, and hospitals.

October 6

William Tyndale, translator, martyr, 1536

William Tyndale was ordained in 1521, and his life's desire was to translate the scriptures into English. When his plan met opposition from King Henry VIII, Tyndale fled to Germany, where he traveled from city to city, living in poverty and constant danger. He was able to produce a New Testament in 1525. Nine years later he revised it and began work on the Old Testament, which he was unable to complete. He was captured, tried for heresy, and burned at the stake. Miles Coverdale completed Tyndale's work, and the Tyndale-Coverdale version was published as the "Matthew Bible" in 1537. For nearly four centuries the style of this translation has influenced English versions of the Bible such as the King James (Authorized Version) and the New Revised Standard Version.

October 7

Henry Melchior Muhlenberg, pastor in North America, 1787

Muhlenberg (MYOO-len-berg) was prominent in setting the course for Lutheranism in North America. He helped Lutheran churches make the transition from the state churches of Europe to a new identity on American soil. Among other things, he established the first Lutheran synod in America and developed an American Lutheran liturgy. His liturgical principles became the basis for the Common Service of 1888, used in many North American service books for a majority of the past century. That Muhlenberg and his work are remembered today was anticipated at his death. The inscription on his grave reads, in Latin, "Who and what he was, future ages will know without a stone."

October 15

Teresa of Ávila, teacher, renewer of the church, 1582

Teresa of Ávila (AH-vee-la) is also known as Teresa de Jesús. She chose the life of a Carmelite nun after reading the letters of Jerome. Frequently sick during her early years as a nun, she found that when she was sick her prayer life flowered, but when she was well it withered. Steadily her life of faith and prayer deepened, and she grew to have a lively sense of God's presence with her. She worked to reform her monastic community in Ávila, which she believed had strayed from its original purpose. Her reforms asked nuns to maintain life in the monastic enclosure without leaving it and to identify with those who are poor by not wearing shoes. Teresa's writings on devotional life have enjoyed a wide readership.

October 17

Ignatius, Bishop of Antioch, martyr, c. 115

Ignatius was the second bishop of Antioch, in Syria. It was there that the name "Christian" was first used to describe the followers of Jesus. Ignatius is known to us through his letters. In them he encouraged Christians to live in unity sustained with love while standing firm on sound doctrine. Ignatius believed Christian martyrdom was a privilege. When his own martyrdom approached, he wrote in one of his letters, "I prefer death in Christ Jesus to power over the farthest limits of the earth. . . . Do not stand in the way of my birth to real life." Ignatius and all martyrs are a reminder that even today Christians face death because of their faith in Jesus.

October 18

LUKE, EVANGELIST

St. Luke is identified by tradition as the author of both Luke and Acts. Luke is careful to place the events of Jesus' life in both their social and religious contexts. Some of the most loved parables, including the good Samaritan and the prodigal son, are found only in this gospel. Luke's gospel has also given the church some of its most beautiful songs: the Benedictus sung at morning prayer, the Magnificat sung at evening prayer, and the Nunc dimittis sung at the close of the day. These songs are powerful witnesses to the message of Jesus Christ.

October 23

James of Jerusalem, martyr, c. 62

James became an early leader of the church in Jerusalem. He is described in the New Testament as the brother of Jesus, and secular historian Josephus calls James the brother of Jesus, "the so-called Christ." Little is known about James, but Josephus reported that the Pharisees respected James for his piety and observance of the law. His enemies had him put to death.

October 26

Philipp Nicolai, 1608; Johann Heermann, 1647; Paul Gerhardt, 1676; hymnwriters

These three outstanding hymnwriters all worked in Germany during times of war and plague. When Philipp Nicolai was a pastor in Westphalia, the plague killed thirteen hundred of his parishioners. One hundred seventy people died in one week. His hymns "Wake, Awake, for Night Is Flying" (ELW 436) and "O Morning Star, How Fair and Bright!" (ELW 308) were included in a series of meditations he wrote to comfort his parishioners during the plague. The style of Johann Heermann's hymns moved away from the more objective style of Reformation hymnody toward expressing the emotions of faith. Among his hymns is the plaintive text "Ah, Holy Jesus" (ELW 349). Paul Gerhardt lost a preaching position at St. Nicholas Church in Berlin because he refused to sign a document stating he would not make theological arguments in his sermons. The author of beloved hymns such as "O Sacred Head, Now Wounded" (ELW 351), some have called Gerhardt the greatest of Lutheran hymn writers.

October 28

Simon and Jude, Apostles

Little is known about Simon and Jude. In New Testament lists of the apostles, Simon the "zealot" or Cananaean is mentioned, but he is never mentioned apart from these lists. Jude, sometimes called Thaddeus, is also mentioned in lists of the Twelve. At the last supper Jude asked Jesus why he had chosen to reveal himself to the disciples but not to the world. A traditional story about Simon and Jude says that they traveled together on a missionary journey to Persia and were both martyred there.

October 31

Reformation Day

By the end of the seventeenth century, many Lutheran churches celebrated a festival commemorating Martin Luther's posting of the Ninety-five Theses, a summary of the abuses in the church of his time. At the heart of the reform movement was the gospel, the good news that it is by grace through faith that we are justified and set free.

November 1

All Saints Day

The custom of commemorating all of the saints of the church on a single day goes back at least to the third century. All Saints celebrates the baptized people of God, living and dead, who make up the body of Christ. We remember all who have died in the faith and now serve God around the heavenly throne.

November 3

Martín de Porres, renewer of society, 1639

Martín was the son of a Spanish knight and Ana Velázquez, a freed black slave from Panama. Martín apprenticed himself to a barber-surgeon in Lima, Peru, and was known for his work as a healer. Martín was a lay brother in the Order of Preachers (Dominicans) and engaged in many charitable works. He was a gardener as well as a counselor to those who sought him out. He was noted for his care of all the poor, regardless of race. His own religious community described him as the "father of charity." His work included the founding of an orphanage, a hospital, and a clinic for dogs and cats. He is recognized as an advocate for Christian charity and interracial justice.

November 7

John Christian Frederick Heyer, 1873; Bartholomaeus Ziegenbalg, 1719; Ludwig Nommensen, 1918; missionaries

Three missionaries are commemorated on this date. Heyer was the first missionary sent out by American Lutherans. Ordained in 1820, he established Sunday schools and taught at Gettysburg College and Seminary. Heyer became a missionary in the Andhra region of India. During a break in his mission work he received the M.D. degree from what would later be Johns Hopkins University.

Bartholomaeus Ziegenbalg (ZEEG-en-balg) was a missionary to the Tamils of Tranquebar on the southeast coast of India. The first convert to Christianity was baptized about ten months after Ziegenbalg began preaching. His missionary work was opposed by the local Hindus and also by Danish authorities in that area. Ziegenbalg was imprisoned for his work on a charge of converting the natives. Today, the Tamil Evangelical Lutheran Church carries on his work.

Ludwig Ingwer Nommensen was born in Schleswig-Holstein, Germany. In the early 1860s he went to Sumatra to serve as a Lutheran missionary. His work was among the Batak people, who had previously not seen Christian missionaries. Though he encountered some initial difficulties, the missions began to succeed following the conversion of several tribal chiefs. Nommensen translated the scriptures into Batak while honoring much of the native culture.

November 11

Martin, Bishop of Tours, 397

Martin's pagan father enlisted him in the army at age fifteen. One winter day, a beggar approached Martin for aid, and he cut his cloak in half and gave a portion to the beggar. Later, Martin understood that he had seen the presence of Christ in that beggar, and this ended his uncertainty about Christianity. He soon asked for his release from his military duties, but he was imprisoned instead. After his release from prison he began preaching, particularly against the Arians. In 371 he was elected bishop of Tours. As bishop he developed a reputation for intervening on behalf of prisoners and heretics who had been sentenced to death.

November 11

Søren Aabye Kierkegaard, teacher, 1855

Kierkegaard (KEER-keh-gore), a nineteenth-century Danish theologian whose writings reflect his Lutheran heritage, was the founder of modern existentialism. Though he was engaged to a woman he deeply loved, he ended the relationship because he believed he was called to search the hidden side of life. Many of his works were published under a variety of names, so that he could reply to arguments from his own previous works. Kierkegaard's work attacked the established church of his day—its complacency, its tendency to intellectualize faith, and its desire to be accepted by polite society.

November 17

Elizabeth of Hungary, renewer of society, 1231

This Hungarian princess lived her entire life in east-central Germany, and is often called Elizabeth of Thuringia. Married to a duke, she gave large sums of money, including her dowry, for relief of the poor and sick. She founded hospitals, cared for orphans, and used the royal food supplies to feed the hungry. Though she had the support of her husband, her generosity and charity did not earn her friends within the royal court. At the death of her husband, she was driven out. She joined a Franciscan order and continued her charitable work, though she suffered abuse at the hands of her confessor and spiritual guide. Her lifetime of charity is particularly remarkable when one remembers that she died at the age of twenty-four. She founded two hospitals, and many more are named for her.

November 23

Clement, Bishop of Rome, c. 100

Clement was the third bishop of Rome and served at the end of the first century. He is best remembered for a letter he wrote to the Corinthian congregation, still having difficulty with divisions in spite of Paul's canonical letters. Clement's writing echoes Paul's. "Love . . . has no limits to its endurance, bears everything patiently. Love is neither servile nor arrogant. It does not provoke schisms or form cliques, but always acts in harmony with others." Clement's letter is also a witness to early understandings of church government and the way each office in the church works for the good of the whole.

November 23

Miguel Agustín Pro, martyr, 1927

Miguel Agustín Pro grew up among oppression in Mexico, where revolutionaries accused the church of siding with the rich. He was a Jesuit priest who served during a time of intense anticlericalism, and therefore he carried out much of his ministry in private settings. He worked on behalf of the poor and homeless. Miguel and his two brothers were arrested, falsely accused of throwing a bomb at the car of a government official, and executed by a firing squad. Just before the guns fired, he yelled, "¡Viva Cristo Rey!" which means "Long live Christ the king!"

November 24

Justus Falckner, 1723; Jehu Jones, 1852; William Passavant, 1894; pastors in North America

A native of Saxony, Falckner was the son of a Lutheran pastor and, seeing the stresses his father endured, did not plan on becoming a pastor himself, though he studied theology in Halle. Instead, he joined with his brother in the real estate business in Pennsylvania. Through this business he became acquainted with a Swedish pastor in America, and finally he decided to become ordained. He served congregations in New York and New Jersey. Not only was he the first Lutheran ordained in North America, but he published a catechism that was the first Lutheran book published on the continent.

Jones was a native of Charleston, South Carolina. Ordained by the New York Ministerium in 1832, he became the Lutheran church's first African American pastor. Upon returning to South Carolina he was arrested under a law prohibiting free blacks from reentering the state, so he was unable to join the group of Charlestonians he had been commissioned to accompany to Liberia. For nearly twenty years Jones carried out missionary work in Philadelphia in the face of many difficulties. There he led in the formation of the first African American Lutheran congregation, St. Paul's, and the construction of its church building.

William Passavant created and nurtured a new level of organized social ministry in western Pennsylvania. It was the seed of the system of social services that is now known as Lutheran Services in America. Passavant and his legacy sought to serve the poorest of the poor, providing shelter, medical, and living assistance.

November 25

Isaac Watts, hymnwriter, 1748

Isaac Watts was born in England to a family of nonconformists, people who thought the Church of England had not carried its reforms far enough. As a youth, Watts complained to his father about the quality of hymnody in the metrical psalter of his day. That was the start of his hymnwriting career. He wrote about six hundred hymns, many in a two-year period beginning when he was twenty years old. Some of Watts's hymns are based on psalms, a nonconformist tradition. When criticized for writing hymns not taken from scripture, he responded that if we can pray prayers that are not from scripture but written by us, then surely we can sing hymns that we have made up ourselves. Ten of Watts's hymn texts are in *Evangelical Lutheran Worship*, including "O God, Our Help in Ages Past" (ELW 632).

November 30

Andrew, Apostle

Andrew was the first of the Twelve. He is known as a fisherman who left his net to follow Jesus. As a part of his calling, he brought other people, including Simon Peter, to meet Jesus. The Byzantine church honors Andrew as its patron and points out that because he was the first of Jesus' followers, he was, in the words of John Chrysostom, "the Peter before Peter." Together with Philip, Andrew leads a number of Greeks to speak with Jesus, and it is Andrew who shows Jesus a boy with five barley loaves and two fish. Andrew is said to have died on a cross saltire, an X-shaped cross.

December 3

Francis Xavier, missionary to Asia, 1552

Francis Xavier (SAYV-yehr) was born in the Basque region of northern Spain. Francis's native Basque language is unrelated to any other, and Francis admitted that learning languages was difficult for him. Despite this obstacle he became a missionary to India, Southeast Asia, Japan, and the Philippines. At each point he learned the local language and, like Martin Luther, wrote catechisms for the instruction of new converts. Another obstacle Francis overcame to accomplish his mission work was a propensity to seasickness. All his travels to the Far East were by boat. Together with Ignatius Loyola and five others, Francis formed the Society of Jesus (Jesuits). Francis spoke out against the Spanish and Portuguese colonists when he discovered their oppression of the indigenous people to whom he was sent as a missionary.

December 4

John of Damascus, theologian and hymnwriter, c. 749

Born to a wealthy family in Damascus and well educated, John left a career in finance and government to become a monk in an abbey near Jerusalem. He wrote many hymns as well as theological works. Foremost among the latter is a work called *The Fount of Wisdom*, which touches on philosophy, heresy, and the orthodox faith. This summary of patristic theology remained influential for centuries.

December 6

Nicholas, Bishop of Myra, c. 342

Though Nicholas is one of the church's most beloved saints, little is known about his life. In the fourth century he was a bishop in what is now Turkey. Legends that surround Nicholas tell of his love for God and neighbor, especially the poor. One famous story tells of Nicholas secretly giving bags of gold to the three daughters of a father who was going to sell them into prostitution because he could not provide dowries for them. Nicholas has become a symbol of anonymous gift giving.

December 7

Ambrose, Bishop of Milan, c. 397

Ambrose was a governor of northern Italy and a catechumen when he was elected bishop of Milan. He was baptized, ordained, and consecrated a bishop all on the same day. While bishop he gave away his wealth and lived in simplicity. He was a famous preacher and is largely responsible for the conversion of Augustine. He is also well known for writing hymns. On one occasion, Ambrose led people in a hymn he wrote while the church in which they were secluded was threatened by attack from Gothic soldiers. The soldiers turned away, unwilling to attack a congregation that was singing a hymn. Ambrose is credited with authorship of three hymns in *Evangelical Lutheran Worship,* including "Savior of the Nations, Come" (ELW 263).

December 13

Lucy, martyr, 304

Lucy was a young Christian of Sicily who was martyred during the persecutions under Emperor Diocletian. Apparently she had decided to devote her life to God and her possessions to the poor. Beyond that, however, little is known for certain about Lucy. However, her celebration became particularly important in Sweden and Norway, perhaps because the feast of Lucia (the name means "light") originally fell on the shortest day of the year. A tradition arose of a girl in the household, wearing a crown of candles, bringing saffron rolls to her family early in the morning on the day of Lucia.

December 14

John of the Cross, renewer of the church, 1591

John was a monk of the Carmelite religious order who met Teresa of Ávila when she was working to reform the Carmelite Order and return it to a stricter observance of its rules. He followed Teresa's lead and encouraged others to follow her reform. He was imprisoned when he encountered opposition to the reform. His writings, like Teresa's, reflect a deep interest in mystical thought and meditation. In one of John's poems, "The Spiritual Canticle," he cried, "Oh, that my griefs would end! Come, grant me thy fruition full and free!"

December 20

Katharina von Bora Luther, renewer of the church, 1552

Born to an impoverished nobleman, when Katharina (Katie) was five her mother died and she was sent to live in a convent. She later took vows as a nun, but around age twenty-four she and several other nuns who were influenced by the writings of Martin Luther left the convent. Six children were born to Katie and Martin. Though initially Luther felt little affection for Katie, she proved herself a gifted household manager and became a trusted partner. She was so influential that Luther took to calling her "my lord Katie."

December 21

Evangelical Lutheran Worship moves the festival of St. Thomas to July 3 in agreement with other Western calendars.

December 26

Stephen, Deacon and Martyr

Stephen was a deacon and the first martyr of the church. He was one of those seven upon whom the apostles laid hands after they had been chosen to serve widows and others in need. Later, Stephen's preaching angered the temple authorities, and they ordered him to be put to death by stoning, with Saul (later Paul) as one of the observers. As he died, he witnessed to his faith and spoke of a vision of heaven.

December 27

John, Apostle and Evangelist

John, the son of Zebedee, was a fisherman and one of the Twelve. John, his brother James, and Peter were the three who witnessed the light of the transfiguration. John and James once made known their desire to hold positions of power in the kingdom of God. Jesus' response showed them that service to others was the sign of God's reign in the world. Tradition has attributed authorship of the gospel and the three epistles bearing his name to the apostle John. John is a saint for Christmas through his proclamation that the Word became flesh and lived among us, that the light of God shines in the darkness, and that we are called to love one another as Christ has loved us.

December 28

The Holy Innocents, Martyrs

The infant martyrs commemorated on this day were the children of Bethlehem, two years old and younger, who were killed by Herod, who worried that his reign was threatened by the birth of a new king. Augustine called these innocents "buds, killed by the frost of persecution the moment they showed themselves." Those linked to Jesus through their youth and innocence encounter the same hostility Jesus encounters later in his ministry.

Index

Cyril of Alexandria . . . . June 27
Cyril; Methodius . . . . February 14
Dominic . . . . August 8
Donne, John . . . . March 31
Dorcas . . . . January 27
Dürer, Albrecht; Grünewald, Matthias; Cranach, Lucas. . . . . April 6
Edwards, Jonathan . . . . March 22
Elizabeth of Hungary (or of Thuringia) . . . . November 17
Erik . . . . May 18
Euler, Leonhard . . . . May 24
Falckner, Justus; Jones, Jehu; Passavant, William . . . . November 24
Fedde, Elizabeth . . . . February 25
Felicity . . . . March 7
Fliedner, Theodor . . . . October 4
Francis of Assisi . . . . October 4
Gerhardt, Paul . . . . October 26
Gregory of Nazianzus . . . . June 14
Gregory of Nyssa . . . . June 14
Gregory the Great . . . . March 12
Grundtvig, Nikolai Frederik Severin . . . . September 2
Grünewald, Matthias . . . . April 6
Hammarskjöld, Dag . . . . September 18
Handel, George Frederick . . . . July 28
Hauge, Hans Nielsen . . . . March 29
Heermann, Johann . . . . October 26
Helena . . . . May 21
Henry . . . . January 19
Herbert, George . . . . March 1
Heyer, John Christian Frederick; Ziegenbalg,
Bartholomaeus; Nommensen, Ludwig . . . . November 7
Hildegard of Bingen . . . . September 17
Holy Cross Day . . . . September 14
Holy Innocents . . . . December 28
Hus, Jan . . . . July 6
Ignatius . . . . October 17
Irenaeus . . . . June 28
James (the Elder) . . . . July 25
James (the Less) . . . . May 1
James of Jerusalem . . . . October 23
Jerome . . . . September 30
John . . . . December 27

John Chrysostom . . . . September 13
John of Damascus . . . . December 4
John of the Cross . . . . December 14
John the Baptist . . . . June 24
John XXIII. . . . . June 3
Jones, Jehu . . . . November 24
Joseph, Guardian of Jesus . . . . March 19
Jude . . . . October 28
Julian of Norwich. . . . . May 8
Justin . . . . June 1
Kagawa, Toyohiko . . . . April 23
Kierkegaard, Søren Aabye. . . . . November 11
King, Martin Luther Jr.. . . . . January 15
Kolbe, Maximilian; Munk, Kaj. . . . . August 14
Las Casas, Bartolomé de . . . . July 17
Lawrence . . . . August 10
Lazarus of Bethany . . . . July 29
Loehe, Johann Konrad Wilhelm . . . . January 2
Lucy. . . . . December 13
Luke. . . . . October 18
Luther, Katharina von Bora. . . . . December 20
Luther, Martin . . . . February 18
Lydia, Dorcas, and Phoebe . . . . January 27
Maass, Clara . . . . August 13
Macrina . . . . June 14
Mark . . . . April 25
Martha of Bethany . . . . July 29
Martín de Porres. . . . . November 3
Martin of Tours . . . . November 11
Martyrs of Japan . . . . February 5
Martyrs of Uganda . . . . June 3
Mary Magdalene. . . . . July 22
Mary, Martha, and Lazarus of Bethany . . . . July 29
Mary, Mother of Our Lord . . . . August 15
Matthew. . . . . September 21
Matthias . . . . May 14
Melanchthon, Philipp . . . . June 25
Methodius . . . . February 14
Michael and All Angels. . . . . September 29
Monica. . . . . May 4
Moses the Black . . . . August 28

Sources of Prayers of the Day in *Evangelical Lutheran Worship*

This listing is intended to provide an overview of the sources of prayers of the day in Evangelical Lutheran Worship. *Many of the prayers can be traced back to multiple sources, some of which have only tangential influence on the present wording. This listing provides sources that are recognizably antecedent to the prayers in their current form. The symbols following a citation give some idea of the level of alteration that has occurred along the line from the original to its form in* Evangelical Lutheran Worship. *One asterisk indicates minor alteration (as, for instance, the addition or deletion of a single phrase), while two asterisks indicates a more extensive reworking of the prayer. Absence of a symbol indicates that the prayer is substantially unchanged from the original.*

Day	ELW #	Source
Advent 1 A	1	Gregorian Sacramentary #778*
Advent 1 B	2	Gregorian Sacramentary #778*
Advent 1 C	3	Gregorian Sacramentary #778*
Advent 2 A	4	Gelasian Sacramentary #1125**
Advent 2 B	5	Gelasian Sacramentary #1125**
Advent 2 C	6	Gelasian Sacramentary #1125**
Advent 3 A	7	Gregorian Sacramentary #894**
Advent 3 B	8	Gregorian Sacramentary #894**
Advent 3 C	9	Gregorian Sacramentary #894**
Advent 4 A	10	Gelasian Sacramentary #1121*
Advent 4 B	11	Gelasian Sacramentary #1121*
Advent 4 C	12	Gelasian Sacramentary #1121*
Nativity of Our Lord I	13	Gelasian Sacramentary #5*
Nativity of Our Lord II	14	Liturgy of the Hours*
Nativity of Our Lord III	15	Collects of Thomas Cranmer, p. 10*
1st Sunday of Christmas A	16	Gregorian Sacramentary #147*
1st Sunday of Christmas B	17	Leonine Sacramentary #1239*

Day	ELW #	Source
1st Sunday of Christmas C	18	Dawn Office of the Eastern and Leonine Churches (Westminster Collection of Christian Prayers, #97.9*)
2nd Sun of Christmas, ABC, 1	19	Gregorian Sacramentary #42**
2nd Sun of Christmas, ABC, 2	20	Evangelical Lutheran Worship
Epiphany, ABC, 1	21	Gregorian Sacramentary #87*
Epiphany, ABC, 2	22	Gelasian Sacramentary #61**
Epiphany, ABC, 3	23	Book of Common Worship (Presbyterian) 1946*
Baptism of Our Lord A	24	Book of Common Prayer (U.S.A.) 1979, p. 214*
Baptism of Our Lord B	25	Revised Common Lectionary Prayers, p. 55**
Baptism of Our Lord C	26	Book of Common Worship (Presbyterian) 1993, #178*
Epiphany 2 A	27	Anselm (Westminster Collection of Christian Prayers, #21.2**)
Epiphany 2 B	28	Richard of Chichester (Westminster Collection of Christian Prayers, #21.15*)
Epiphany 2 C	29	Lutheran Book of Worship, #12*
Epiphany 3 A	30	Gregorian Sacramentary #966**
Epiphany 3 B	31	Book of Alternative Services, p. 351
Epiphany 3 C	32	Collects of Thomas Cranmer, p. 4*
Epiphany 4 A	33	Book of Common Worship (Presbyterian) 1993, #190*
Epiphany 4 B	34	Revised Common Lectionary Prayers, p. 51*
Epiphany 4 C	35	Leonine Sacramentary #598
Epiphany 5 A	36	Gregorian Sacramentary #86*
Epiphany 5 B	37	Revised Common Lectionary Prayers, p. 62*
Epiphany 5 C	38	Sourcebook for Sundays and Seasons 1992, p. 72**
Epiphany 6 A	39	Gelasian Sacramentary #566*, Gregorian Sacramentary #86*
Epiphany 6 B	40	Gregorian Sacramentary p. 165**
Epiphany 6 C	41	Book of Alternative Services, p. 352
Epiphany 7 A	42	Lutheran Book of Worship, #18**
Epiphany 7 B	43	Book of Alternative Services, p. 356*

Day	ELW #	Source
Epiphany 7 C	44	La Clochette, 1912**
Epiphany 8 A	45	Revised Common Lectionary Prayers, p. 68**
Epiphany 8 B	46	Revised Common Lectionary Prayers, p. 68*
Epiphany 8 C	47	Evangelical Lutheran Worship
Transfiguration A	48	Latin, 15th century*
Transfiguration B	49	Ambrosian Missal**
Transfiguration C	50	Revised Common Lectionary Prayers, p. 72*
Ash Wednesday, ABC, 1	51	Collects of Thomas Cranmer, p. 32*
Ash Wednesday, ABC, 2	52	Book of Common Worship (Presbyterian) 1993, #207*
Lent 1 A	53	Lutheran Book of Worship, #25*
Lent 1 B	54	Evangelical Lutheran Worship, based on Martin Luther
Lent 1 C	55	Lutheran Book of Worship, #24*
Lent 2 A	56	Evangelical Lutheran Worship
Lent 2 B	57	Book of Common Prayer (England) 1928*
Lent 2 C	58	Evangelical Lutheran Worship
Lent 3 A	59	Columbanus (Westminster Collection of Christian Prayers, #90.3**)
Lent 3 B	60	Evangelical Lutheran Worship
Lent 3 C	61	Lutheran Book of Worship, #28*
Lent 4 A	62	Gelasian Sacramentary #1137**
Lent 4 B	63	Gelasian Sacramentary #541**
Lent 4 C	64	Revised Common Lectionary Prayers, p. 85**
Lent 5 A	65	Book of Alternative Services, p. 293*
Lent 5 B	66	Evangelical Lutheran Worship
Lent 5 C	67	Revised Common Lectionary Prayers, p. 87*
Sunday of the Passion, ABC, 1	68	Gelasian Sacramentary #329**
Sunday of the Passion, ABC, 2	69	Revised Common Lectionary Prayers, p. 91*
Sunday of the Passion, ABC, 3	70	Evangelical Lutheran Worship
Monday in Holy Week, ABC	71	Book of Common Prayer (U.S.A.) 1945, p. 138**
Tuesday in Holy Week, ABC	72	Lutheran Book of Worship, #35

Day	ELW #	Source
Wednesday in Holy Week, ABC	73	Lutheran Book of Worship, #36
Maundy Thursday, ABC, 1	74	Lutheran Book of Worship, #37*
Maundy Thursday, ABC, 2	75	Revised Common Lectionary Prayers, p. 99
Good Friday, ABC, 1	76	Gregorian Sacramentary #327*
Good Friday, ABC, 2	77	John 12:32, Revised Common Lectionary Prayers, p. 101*
Vigil of Easter, ABC, 1	78	Gelasian Sacramentary #454**
Vigil of Easter, ABC, 2	79	Evangelical Lutheran Worship
Easter Day, ABC, 1	80	Gregorian Sacramentary #324*
Easter Day, ABC, 2	81	Roman Missal, p. 270*
Easter Evening, ABC	82	Book of Common Prayer (U.S.A.) 1945, p. 166
Easter Monday, ABC	83	Gelasian Sacramentary #464*
Easter 2 A	84	Book of Alternative Services, p. 336*
Easter 2 B	85	Gregorian Sacramentary #435*
Easter 2 C	86	Evangelical Lutheran Worship
Easter 3 A	87	Book of Common Prayer (U.S.A.) 1945, p. 166
Easter 3 B	88	Evangelical Lutheran Worship
Easter 3 C	89	Evangelical Lutheran Worship
Easter 4 A	90	Revised Common Lectionary Prayers, p. 118*
Easter 4 B	91	New Zealand Prayer Book, p. 596*
Easter 4 C	92	Hebrews 13:20-21*
Easter 5 A	93	Book of Alternative Services, p. 340*
Easter 5 B	94	Evangelical Lutheran Worship; Revised Common Lectionary Prayers, p. 120**
Easter 5 C	95	Collects of Thomas Cranmer, p. 30*
Easter 6 A	96	Gregorian Sacramentary #922**
Easter 6 B	97	Gelasian Sacramentary #1178*
Easter 6 C	98	Evangelical Lutheran Worship
Ascension, ABC, 1	99	Gregorian Sacramentary #497**
Ascension, ABC, 2	100	Gelasian Sacramentary #580*
Easter 7 A	101	Revised Common Lectionary Prayers, p. 125*
Easter 7 B	102	Evangelical Lutheran Worship
Easter 7 C	103	Gelasian Sacramentary # 551*
Vigil of Pentecost, ABC	104	Gelasian Sacramentary #637, Gregorian Sacramentary #520*

Day	ELW #	Source
Day of Pentecost A	105	Gregorian Sacramentary #526*
Day of Pentecost B	106	Evangelical Lutheran Worship
Day of Pentecost C	107	Evangelical Lutheran Worship; Lutheran Book of Worship, #75**
Holy Trinity, ABC, 1	108	Leofric Missal**
Holy Trinity, ABC, 2	109	Revised Common Lectionary Prayers, p. 140*
Lectionary 8 A	45	Revised Common Lectionary Prayers, p. 68**
Lectionary 8 B	46	Revised Common Lectionary Prayers, p. 68*
Lectionary 8 C	47	Evangelical Lutheran Worship
Lectionary 9 A	110	Evangelical Lutheran Worship
Lectionary 9 B	111	Evangelical Lutheran Worship
Lectionary 9 C	112	Evangelical Lutheran Worship; Book of Common Prayer (U.S.A.) 1979, p. 337*
Lectionary 10 A	113	Evangelical Lutheran Worship
Lectionary 10 B	114	Book of Common Worship (Presbyterian) 1993, #334
Lectionary 10 C	115	Book of Alternative Services, p. 360*
Lectionary 11 A	116	Revised Common Lectionary Prayers, p. 147
Lectionary 11 B	117	Evangelical Lutheran Worship, based in part on Prayers of Catherine of Siena, #17*
Lectionary 11 C	118	Evangelical Lutheran Worship
Lectionary 12 A	119	Ignatius of Loyola*
Lectionary 12 B	120	Evangelical Lutheran Worship, based on Patrick**
Lectionary 12 C	121	Gregorian Sacramentary #150**
Lectionary 13 A	122	Evangelical Lutheran Worship
Lectionary 13 B	123	Gregorian Sacramentary #229**
Lectionary 13 C	124	Sourcebook for Sundays and Seasons 1992, p. 205*
Lectionary 14 A	125	Evangelical Lutheran Worship, based on Augustine**
Lectionary 14 B	126	Book of Common Worship (Presbyterian) 1993, #342*
Lectionary 14 C	127	Evangelical Lutheran Worship
Lectionary 15 A	128	Lutheran Book of Worship, #85

Day	ELW #	Source
Lectionary 15 B	129	Gelasian Sacramentary #1472
Lectionary 15 C	130	Jerome (Westminster Collection of Christian Prayers, #158.6**)
Lectionary 16 A	131	Revised Common Lectionary Prayers, p. 162*
Lectionary 16 B	132	Evangelical Lutheran Worship
Lectionary 16 C	133	Sourcebook for Sundays and Seasons 1992, p. 205**
Lectionary 17 A	134	Evangelical Lutheran Worship
Lectionary 17 B	135	Uniting in Worship (ldr), p. 269*
Lectionary 17 C	136	Leonine Sacramentary #917*
Lectionary 18 A	137	Revised Common Lectionary Prayers, p. 168**
Lectionary 18 B	138	Evangelical Lutheran Worship, based in part on Prayers of Catherine of Siena, #12*
Lectionary 18 C	139	Thomas à Kempis (Westminster Collection of Christian Prayers, #174.7**)
Lectionary 19 A	140	Lutheran Book of Worship, #82*
Lectionary 19 B	141	Lutheran Book of Worship, #90*
Lectionary 19 C	142	Book of Alternative Services, p. 373*
Lectionary 20 A	143	Revised Common Lectionary Prayers, p. 174*
Lectionary 20 B	144	New Zealand Prayer Book, p. 619*
Lectionary 20 C	145	Revised Common Lectionary Prayers, p. 175**
Lectionary 21 A	146	Evangelical Lutheran Worship
Lectionary 21 B	147	Evangelical Lutheran Worship
Lectionary 21 C	148	Gregorian Sacramentary #193**
Lectionary 22 A	149	Lutheran Book of Worship, #95*
Lectionary 22 B	150	Gregorian Sacramentary #202**
Lectionary 22 C	151	Leonine Sacramentary (Westminster Collection of Christian Prayers, #78.10**)
Lectionary 23 A	152	Gelasian Sacramentary #1213*
Lectionary 23 B	153	Evangelical Lutheran Worship
Lectionary 23 C	154	Gregorian Sacramentary #198*
Lectionary 24 A	155	Evangelical Lutheran Worship, based on Ambrose

Day	ELW #	Source
Lectionary 24 B	156	Revised Common Lectionary Prayers, p. 187*
Lectionary 24 C	157	Leonine Sacramentary #75**
Lectionary 25 A	158	Gregorian Sacramentary #720**
Lectionary 25 B	159	Revised Common Lectionary Prayers, p. 190*
Lectionary 25 C	160	Revised Common Lectionary Prayers, p. 183*
Lectionary 26 A	161	Gelasian Sacramentary #1213**
Lectionary 26 B	162	Evangelical Lutheran Worship
Lectionary 26 C	163	Evangelical Lutheran Worship
Lectionary 27 A	164	Gelasian Sacramentary #556*
Lectionary 27 B	165	Revised Common Lectionary Prayers, p. 196**
Lectionary 27 C	166	Martin Luther (Luther's Prayers, #138**)
Lectionary 28 A	167	Revised Common Lectionary Prayers, p. 198*
Lectionary 28 B	168	Book of Alternative Services, p. 387*
Lectionary 28 C	169	Gelasian Sacramentary #1234*
Lectionary 29 A	170	John Wesley (Westminster Collection of Christian Prayers, #21.18**)
Lectionary 29 B	171	Evangelical Lutheran Worship
Lectionary 29 C	172	Sourcebook for Sundays and Seasons 1992, p. 207*
Lectionary 30 A	173	Evangelical Lutheran Worship
Lectionary 30 B	174	Alcuin of York (Westminster Collection of Christian Prayers, #97.2**)
Lectionary 30 C	175	Evangelical Lutheran Worship
Lectionary 31 A	176	Evangelical Lutheran Worship
Lectionary 31 B	177	Book of Alternative Services, p. 365*
Lectionary 31 C	178	Evangelical Lutheran Worship
Lectionary 32 A	179	Evangelical Lutheran Worship
Lectionary 32 B	180	Gelasian Sacramentary #1198**
Lectionary 32 C	181	Evangeliebok, Church of Sweden, 1639**
Lectionary 33 A	182	Evangelical Lutheran Worship
Lectionary 33 B	183	Alternative Collects**
Lectionary 33 C	184	Gregorian Sacramentary #1158*
Christ the King A	185	Evangelical Lutheran Worship
Christ the King B	186	Roman Missal 1925**

Day	ELW #	Source
Christ the King C	187	Augustine (Westminster Collection of Christian Prayers, #106.3**)
Andrew, Apostle	188	Book of Common Prayer (U.S.A.) 1945, p. 226**
Stephen, Deacon and Martyr	189	Gregorian Sacramentary #62**
John, Apostle and Evangelist	190	Leonine Sacramentary #1283*
The Holy Innocents, Martyrs	191	Book of Common Prayer (U.S.A.) 1979, p. 238*
Name of Jesus	192	Eric Milner-White*
Confession of Peter	193	Book of Common Prayer (U.S.A.) 1979, p. 238*
Conversion of Paul	194	Gregorian Sacramentary #604**
Presentation of Our Lord	195	Gregorian Sacramentary #124*
Joseph, Guardian of Jesus	196	Book of Common Prayer (U.S.A.) 1979, p. 239*
Annunciation of Our Lord	197	Gregorian Sacramentary #143*
Mark, Evangelist	198	Gregorian Sacramentary
Philip and James, Apostles	199	Book of Common Prayer (U.S.A.) 1979*
Matthias, Apostle	200	Book of Common Prayer 1549*
Visit of Mary to Elizabeth	201	Evangelical Lutheran Worship
Barnabas, Apostle	202	Book of Common Prayer (U.S.A.) 1979, p. 241**
John the Baptist	203	Book of Common Prayer (U.S.A.) 1979, p. 241*, Lutheran Book of Worship #124*
Peter and Paul, Apostles	204	Leonine Sacramentary #280**
Thomas, Apostle	205	Book of Common Prayer 1549**
Mary Magdalene, Apostle	206	Parisian Missal, Ambrosian Missal**
James, Apostle	207	Book of Common Prayer (U.S.A.) 1979, p. 242*
Mary, Mother of Our Lord	208	Evangelical Lutheran Worship
Bartholomew, Apostle	209	Leonine Sacramentary #1273*
Holy Cross Day	210	Book of Common Prayer (U.S.A.) 1979, p. 244**
Matthew, Apostle and Evangelist	211	Parisian Missal**
Michael and All Angels	212	Gregorian Sacramentary #726*
Luke, Evangelist	213	Book of Common Prayer 1549**
Simon and Jude, Apostles	214	Book of Common Prayer (U.S.A.) 1979, p. 245

Day	ELW #	Source
Reformation Day, 1	215	Saxon Church Order 1539**
Reformation Day, 2	216	William Laud*
All Saints Day, ABC	217	Book of Common Prayer 1549*
Saints	218	Book of Common Prayer (U.S.A.) 1945, p. 258*
Martyrs	219	Lutheran Book of Worship, #138*
Missionaries	220	Book of Common Prayer (England) 1928**
Renewers of the Church	221	Lutheran Book of Worship, #140*
Renewers of Society, 1	222	Lutheran Book of Worship, #141
Renewers of Society, 2	223	Book of Common Prayer (U.S.A.) 1945, p. 44**
Pastors and Bishops, 1	224	Book of Common Worship (Church of South India)*
Pastors and Bishops, 2	225	Lutheran Book of Worship, #144
Theologians and Teachers	226	Book of Common Prayer (Canada) 1959*
Artists and Scientists	227	Lutheran Book of Worship, #146*
Day of Thanksgiving	228	Church Book 1868**
Christian Unity	229	Book of Common Prayer (U.S.A.) 1979, p. 255**
Dedication or Anniversary of a Church, 1	230	Lutheran Book of Worship, #148
Dedication or Anniversary of a Church, 2	231	Lutheran Book of Worship, #149*
Harvest	232	Church Book 1868**
Day of Penitence, 1	233	Lutheran Book of Worship, #151
Day of Penitence, 2	234	Lutheran Book of Worship, #152*
Day of Mourning, 1	235	Evangelical Lutheran Worship
Day of Mourning, 2	236	Evangelical Lutheran Worship
National Holiday	237	Lutheran Book of Worship, #153*
Peace	238	Book of Common Prayer (U.S.A.) 1979, p. 258*
Stewardship of Creation, 1	239	Book of Common Prayer (U.S.A.) 1979, p. 258*
Stewardship of Creation, 2	240	Book of Common Prayer (U.S.A.) 1979, p. 259
New Year's Eve	241	Lutheran Book of Worship, #159

Source Books for Prayers of the Day

Although some of the prayers were originally developed for provisional or trial-use materials (e.g., Liturgical Year *preceding* Book of Common Worship (Presbyterian) *or* Renewing Worship *preceding* Evangelical Lutheran Worship), *only the related final worship books are noted here and in the index above.*

Alternative Collects, 1985, The Anglican Church of Australia.

The Book of Alternative Services of The Anglican Church of Canada. Toronto: Anglican Book Centre, 1985.

Book of Common Prayer. According to the use of The Episcopal Church. New York: Church Publishing, 1979.

Book of Common Prayer (England) 1928. New York: Oxford University Press USA, 2007.

Book of Common Prayer (U.S.A.) 1945. New York: Church Pension Fund, 1945.

Book of Common Worship. Presbyterian Church (U.S.A.) and the Cumberland Presbyterian Church. Louisville: Westminster/John Knox, 1993. See also below, Daniels, *To God Alone Be Glory.*

La Clochette. Spiritual magazine published in France, first known appearance of the prayer often attributed to St. Francis. Paris: La Ligue de la Sainte-Messe, 1912.

The Collects of Thomas Cranmer. Compiled by C. Frederick Barbee and Paul F. M. Zahl. Grand Rapids: Wm. B. Eerdmans, 1999.

Daniels, Harold. *To God Alone Be Glory: The Story and Sources of the Book of Common Worship.* Louisville: Geneva Press, 2003.

Gelasian Sacramentary. *Liber Sacramentorum Romanae Aeclesiae Ordinis Anni Circuli.* Ed. Leo Cunibert Mohlberg, OSB. Rome: Herder, 1960.

Gregorian Sacramentary. *Le Sacramentaire Grégorien.* Ed. Jean Dehusses. Fribourg: Éditions Universitaires, 1979.

Leonine Sacramentary. *Sacramentarium Veronense.* Ed. Leo Cunibert Mohlberg, OSB. Rome: Herder, 1956.

Liturgy of the Hours. *Christian Prayer: The Liturgy of the Hours.* English translation prepared by the International Commission on English in the Liturgy. Boston: Daughters of St. Paul, 1976.

Lutheran Book of Worship. Minneapolis: Augsburg Publishing House; Philadelphia: Board of Publication, Lutheran Church in America; St. Louis: Concordia Publishing House; 1978.

Luther's Prayers. Ed. Herbert Brokering. Minneapolis: Augsburg, 1967.

Milner-White, Eric. *A Cambridge Bede Book.* London: Longmans, Green, 1936.

A New Zealand Prayer Book. The Anglican Church in Aotearoa, New Zealand and Polynesia. HarperSan Francisco, 1989.

The Prayers of Catherine of Siena, Second Edition. Ed. Suzanne Noffke. Mahwah, NJ: Paulist Press, 1983.

Revised Common Lectionary Prayers. Proposed by the Consultation on Common Texts (CCT). Minneapolis: Fortress, 2002.

Roman Missal. *The Sacramentary.* The Roman Missal of Pope Paul VI. English translation prepared by the International Commission on English in the Liturgy. Collegeville, MN: Liturgical Press, 1985.

Roman Missal 1925. The Missal of Pope Pius X.

Sourcebook for Sundays and Seasons, 1992. G. Thomas Ryan, principal author and compiler. Includes prayers from the International Commission on English in the Liturgy. Chicago: Liturgy Training Publications, 1992.

Uniting in Worship. Sydney: The Uniting Church in Australia, 1984.

The Westminster Collection of Christian Prayers. Compiled by Dorothy M. Stewart. Louisville: Westminster John Knox, 2002.

Index of Psalms and Psalm Refrains

Psalm	Day	Refrain
1	Oct. 23–29, Lect. 30 A	Their delight is in the law of the LORD. (v. 2)
1	Easter 7 B	The LORD knows the way of the righteous. (v. 6)
1	Sept. 18–24*, Lect. 25 B	They are like trees planted by streams of water. (v. 3)
1	Epiphany 6, Lect. 6 C	They are like trees planted by streams of water. (v. 3)
1	Sept. 4–10, Lect. 23 C	They are like trees planted by streams of water. (v. 3)
2	Transfiguration of Our Lord A	You are my son; this day have I begotten you. (v. 7)
4	Easter 3 B	The LORD does wonders for the faithful. (v. 3)
5	Martyrs	All who take refuge in you will be glad. (v. 11)
5:1-8	June 12–18*, Lect. 11 C	Lead me, LORD, in your righteousness; make your way straight before me. (v. 8)
6	Day of Penitence	Heal me, LORD, for my bones quake in terror. (v. 2)
7:1-10	James, Apostle	God is my shield and defense. (v. 10)
8	Name of Jesus	How majestic is your name in all the earth! (v. 1)
8	New Year's Eve	How majestic is your name in all the earth! (v. 1)

**denotes psalms related to the semicontinuous series of first readings in the time after Pentecost*

8	The Holy Trinity A	How majestic is your name in all the earth! (v. 1)
8	Oct. 2–8, Lect. 27 B	You crown us with glory and honor. (v. 5)
8	The Holy Trinity C	Your glory is chanted above the heavens. (v. 2)
9:1-10	Saints	Those who know your name will put their trust in you. (v. 10)
9:9-20	June 19–25*, Lect. 12 B	You, O LORD, will be a refuge in time of trouble. (v. 9)
11	Simon and Jude, Apostles	In the LORD I have taken refuge. (v. 1)
12	Bartholomew, Apostle	The words of the LORD are pure. (v. 6)
13	June 26–July 2*, Lect. 13 A	I trust in your unfailing love, O LORD. (v. 5)
14	July 24–30*, Lect. 17 B	God is in the company of the righteous. (v. 5)
14	Sept. 11–17*, Lect. 24 C	The LORD looks down from heaven upon us all. (v. 2)
15	Aug. 28–Sept. 3, Lect. 22 B	LORD, who may dwell in your tabernacle? (v. 1)
15	Epiphany 4, Lect. 4 A	LORD, who may abide upon your holy hill? (v. 1)
15	July 17–23, Lect. 16 C	LORD, who may abide upon your holy hill? (v. 1)
16	Vigil of Easter, Reading 3 ABC	You will show me the path of life. (v. 11)
16	Easter 2 A	In your presence there is fullness of joy. (v. 11)
16	Nov. 13–19, Lect. 33 B	My heart is glad and my spirit rejoices; my body shall rest in hope. (v. 9)
16	June 26–July 2, Lect. 13 C	I have set the LORD always before me. (v. 8)
16:8-11	Easter Monday ABC	My heart is glad and my spirit rejoices. (v. 9)
17:1-7, 15	July 31–Aug. 6*, Lect. 18 A	I shall see your face; when I awake, I shall be satisfied. (v. 15)
17:1-9	Nov. 6–12, Lect. 32 C	Keep me as the apple of your eye; hide me under the shadow of your wings. (v. 8)

17:1-9, 15	Stephen, Deacon and Martyr	I call upon you, O God, for you will answer me. (v. 6)
18:1-6, 16-19	Confession of Peter	My God, my rock, you are worthy of praise. (vv. 2-3)
19	Vigil of Easter, Reading 6 ABC	The statutes of the LORD are just and rejoice the heart. (v. 8)
19	Oct. 2–8*, Lect. 27 A	The statutes of the LORD are just and rejoice the heart. (v. 8)
19	Lent 3 B	The commandment of the LORD gives light to the eyes. (v. 8)
19	Sept. 11–17*, Lect. 24 B	The teaching of the LORD is perfect and revives the soul. (v. 7)
19	Epiphany 3, Lect. 3 C	The teaching of the LORD revives the soul. (v. 7)
19:1-6	Andrew, Apostle	Their sound has gone out into all lands. (v. 4)
19:7-14	Sept. 25–Oct. 1, Lect. 26 B	The commandment of the LORD gives light to the eyes. (v. 8)
20	June 12–18*, Lect. 11 B	The LORD gives victory to the anointed one. (v. 6)
20	National Holiday	The LORD gives victory to the anointed one. (v. 6)
22	Good Friday ABC	My God, my God, why have you forsaken me? (v. 1)
22:1-15	Oct. 9–15*, Lect. 28 B	My God, my God, why have you forsaken me? (v. 1)
22:19-28	June 19–25, Lect. 12 C	In the midst of the assembly I will praise you. (v. 22)
22:23-31	Lent 2 B	All the ends of the earth shall remember and turn to the LORD. (v. 27)
22:25-31	Easter 5 B	All the ends of the earth shall remember and turn to the LORD. (v. 27)
23	Easter 4 ABC	The LORD is my shepherd; I shall not be in want. (v. 1)
23	Lent 4 A	You anoint my head with oil. (v. 5)
23	Oct. 9–15, Lect. 28 A	You prepare a table before me, and my cup is running over. (v. 5)
23	July 17–23, Lect. 16 B	The LORD is my shepherd; I shall not be in want. (v. 1)

24	July 10–16*, Lect. 15 B	Lift up your heads, O gates, that the King of glory may come in. (v. 7)
24	All Saints Day B	They shall receive blessing from the God of their salvation. (v. 5)
24:7-10	Presentation of Our Lord (alt.)	Lift up your heads, O gates, that the King of glory may come in. (v. 7)
25:1-9	Sept. 25–Oct. 1, Lect. 26 A	Remember, O LORD, your compassion and love. (v. 6)
25:1-10	Lent 1 B	Your paths, O LORD, are steadfast love and faithfulness. (v. 10)
25:1-10	Advent 1 C	To you, O LORD, I lift up my soul. (v. 1)
25:1-10	July 10–16, Lect. 15 C	Show me your ways, O LORD, and teach me your paths. (v. 4)
26	Oct. 2–8*, Lect. 27 B	Your steadfast love is before my eyes; I have walked faithfully with you. (v. 3)
26:1-8	Aug. 28–Sept. 3, Lect. 22 A	Your steadfast love is before my eyes; I have walked faithfully with you. (v. 3)
27	Lent 2 C	In the day of trouble, God will give me shelter. (v. 5)
27:1, 4-9	Epiphany 3, Lect. 3 A	The LORD is my light and my salvation. (v. 1)
29	Baptism of Our Lord ABC	The voice of the LORD is upon the waters. (v. 3)
29	The Holy Trinity B	Worship the LORD in the beauty of holiness. (v. 2)
30	Epiphany 6, Lect. 6 B	My God, I cried out to you, and you restored me to health. (v. 2)
30	June 26–July 2, Lect. 13 B	I will exalt you, O LORD, because you have lifted me up. (v. 1)
30	Easter 3 C	You have turned my wailing into dancing. (v. 11)
30	June 5–11, Lect. 10 C	My God, I cried out to you, and you restored me to health. (v. 2)
30	July 3–9*, Lect. 14 C	My God, I cried out to you, and you restored me to health. (v. 2)
31:1-5, 15-16	Easter 5 A	Into your hands, O LORD, I commend my spirit. (v. 5)
31:1-5, 19-24	May 29–June 4, Lect. 9 A	Be my strong rock, a castle to keep me safe. (v. 3)

31:9-16	Sunday of the Passion ABC	Into your hands, O LORD, I commend my spirit. (v. 5)
32	Lent 1 A	Mercy embraces those who trust in the LORD. (v. 10)
32	Lent 4 C	Be glad, you righteous, and rejoice in the LORD. (v. 11)
32	June 12–18, Lect. 11 C	Then you forgave me the guilt of my sin. (v. 5)
32:1-7	Oct. 30–Nov. 5, Lect. 31 C	All the faithful will make their prayers to you in time of trouble. (v. 6)
33:1-12	June 5–11*, Lect. 10 A	Happy is the nation whose God is the LORD! (v. 12)
33:12-22	Vigil of Pentecost ABC	The LORD is our helper and our shield. (v. 20)
33:12-22	Aug. 7-13, Lect. 19 C	Let your lovingkindness be upon us, as we place our hope in you. (v. 22)
34:1-8	Aug. 7-13, Lect. 19 B	Taste and see that the LORD is good. (v. 8)
34:1-8 [19-22]	Oct. 23–29*, Lect. 30 B	Taste and see that the LORD is good. (v. 8)
34:1-9	Mary, Mother of Our Lord	Proclaim with me the greatness of the LORD. (v. 3)
34:1-10, 22	All Saints Day A	Fear the LORD, you saints of the LORD; for those who fear the LORD lack nothing. (v. 9)
34:9-14	Aug. 14-20, Lect. 20 B	Those who seek the LORD lack nothing that is good. (v. 10)
34:15-22	Aug. 21–27, Lect. 21 B	The eyes of the LORD are upon the righteous. (v. 15)
36:5-10	Epiphany 2, Lect. 2 C	We feast upon the abundance of your house, O LORD. (v. 8)
36:5-11	Monday in Holy Week ABC	All people take refuge under the shadow of your wings. (v. 7)
37:1-11, 39-40	Epiphany 7, Lect. 7 C	The lowly shall possess the land; they will delight in abundance of peace. (v. 11)
37:1-9	Oct. 2–8, Lect. 27 C	Commit your way to the LORD; put your trust in the LORD. (v. 5)
40:1-11	Epiphany 2, Lect. 2 A	I love to do your will, O my God. (v. 8)

40:5-10	Annunciation of Our Lord (alt.)	I love to do your will, O my God. (v. 8)
41	Epiphany 7, Lect. 7 B	Heal me, for I have sinned against you. (v. 4)
42 and 43	June 19–25*, Lect. 12 C	Send out your light and truth, that they may lead me. (43:3)
42 and 43	Vigil of Easter, Reading 7 ABC	I thirst for God, for the living God. (42:2)
43	Oct. 30–Nov. 5, Lect. 31 A	Send out your light and truth, that they may lead me. (v. 3)
44:1-3, 20-26	Philip and James, Apostles	Save us for the sake of your steadfast love. (v. 26)
45	Annunciation of Our Lord	I will make your name to be remembered from one generation to another. (v. 17)
45:1-2, 6-9	Aug. 28–Sept. 3*, Lect. 22 B	God has anointed you with the oil of gladness. (v. 7)
45:10-17	July 3–9*, Lect. 14 A	God has anointed you with the oil of gladness. (v. 7)
46	Vigil of Easter, Reading 2 ABC	The LORD of hosts is with us; the God of Jacob is our stronghold. (v. 7)
46	Reformation Day ABC	The LORD of hosts is with us; the God of Jacob is our stronghold. (v. 7)
46	May 29–June 4*, Lect. 9 A	The LORD of hosts is with us; the God of Jacob is our stronghold. (v. 7)
46	Christ the King, Lect. 34 C	I will be exalted among the nations. (v. 10)
47	Ascension of Our Lord ABC	God has gone up with a shout. (v. 5)
48	July 3–9*, Lect. 14 B	Great is the LORD, and highly to be praised, in the city of our God. (v. 1)
48	Missionaries	Your praise, O God, reaches to the ends of the earth. (v. 10)
49:1-12	July 31–Aug. 6, Lect. 18 C	My mouth shall speak of wisdom. (v. 3)
50:1-6	Transfiguration of Our Lord B	Out of Zion, perfect in beauty, God shines forth in glory. (v. 2)
50:1-8, 22-23	Aug. 7-13*, Lect. 19 C	To those who go the right way I will show the salvation of God. (v. 23)
50:7-15	June 5–11, Lect. 10 A	Call upon me in the day of trouble, says your God. (v. 15)

51:1-10	Sept. 11–17, Lect. 24 C	Have mercy on me, O God, according to your steadfast love. (v. 1)
51:1-12	July 31–Aug. 6*, Lect. 18 B	Have mercy on me, O God, according to your steadfast love. (v. 1)
51:1-12	Lent 5 B	Create in me a clean heart, O God. (v. 10)
51:1-17	Ash Wednesday ABC	Have mercy on me, O God, according to your steadfast love. (v. 1)
52	July 17–23*, Lect. 16 C	I am like a green olive tree in the house of God. (v. 8)
54	Sept. 18–24, Lect. 25 B	God is my helper; it is the Lord who sustains my life. (v. 4)
56	Matthias, Apostle	I am bound by the vow I made to you, O God. (v. 12)
57	Mark, Evangelist	I will give you thanks among the peoples, O LORD. (v. 9)
62:5-12	Epiphany 3, Lect. 3 B	God alone is my rock and my salvation. (v. 6
63:1-8	Lent 3 C	O God, eagerly I seek you; my soul thirsts for you. (v. 1)
65	Oct. 23–29*, Lect. 30 C	Your paths overflow with plenty. (v. 11)
65	Day of Thanksgiving A	You crown the year with your goodness, and your paths overflow with plenty. (v. 11)
65	Harvest	You crown the year with your goodness, and your paths overflow with plenty. (v. 11)
65:[1-8] 9-13	July 10–16, Lect. 15 A	Your paths overflow with plenty. (v. 11)
66:1-9	July 3–9, Lect. 14 C	All the earth bows down before you and sings out your name. (v. 4)
66:1-12	Oct. 9–15*, Lect. 28 C	God has kept us among the living. (v. 9)
66:8-20	Easter 6 A	Bless our God, you peoples; let the sound of praise be heard. (v. 8)
67	Conversion of Paul	Let all the peoples praise you, O God. (v. 3)

67	Aug. 14-20, Lect. 20 A	Let all the peoples praise you, O God. (v. 3)
67	Easter 6 C	Let the nations be glad and sing for joy. (v. 4)
68:1-10, 32-35	Easter 7 A	Sing to God, who rides upon the clouds. (v. 4)
69:7-10 [11-15] 16-18	June 19–25, Lect. 12 A	Answer me, O LORD, for your love is kind. (v. 16)
70	Wednesday in Holy Week ABC	Be pleased, O God, to deliver me. (v. 1)
70	Nov. 6–12, Lect. 32 A	You are my helper and my deliverer; O LORD, do not tarry. (v. 5)
71:1-6	Epiphany 4, Lect. 4 C	From my mother's womb you have been my strength. (v. 6)
71:1-6	Aug. 21–27*, Lect. 21 C	From my mother's womb you have been my strength. (v. 6)
71:1-14	Tuesday in Holy Week ABC	From my mother's womb you have been my strength. (v. 6)
72:1-7, 10-14	Epiphany of Our Lord ABC	All kings shall bow down before him. (v. 11)
72:1-7, 18-19	Advent 2 A	May the righteous flourish; let there be an abundance of peace. (v. 7)
73:23-28	Mary Magdalene, Apostle	I have made you my refuge, Lord GOD, to tell of all your works. (v. 28)
77:1-2, 11-20	June 26–July 2*, Lect. 13 C	By your strength you have redeemed your people. (v. 15)
78:1-2, 34-38	Holy Cross Day (alt.)	God was their rock and the Most High God their redeemer. (v. 35)
78:1-4, 12-16	Sept. 25–Oct. 1*, Lect. 26 A	We will recount to generations to come the power of the LORD. (v. 4)
78:1-7	Nov. 6–12*, Lect. 32 A	We will recount to generations to come the power of the LORD. (v. 4)
78:23-29	July 31–Aug. 6, Lect. 18 B	God rained down manna from heaven; so mortals ate the bread of angels. (vv. 24, 25)
79:1-9	Sept. 18–24*, Lect. 25 C	Deliver us and forgive our sins, for your name's sake. (v. 9)
80:1-2, 8-19	Aug. 14-20*, Lect. 20 C	Look down from heaven, O God; behold and tend this vine. (vv. 14, 15)

87:1-3, 5-7	Peter and Paul, Apostles	Glorious things are spoken of you, O city of our God. (v. 3)
89:1-4, 15-18	June 26–July 2, Lect. 13 A	Your love, O LORD, forever will I sing. (v. 1)
89:1-4, 19-26	Advent 4 (alt.) B	Your love, O LORD, forever will I sing. (v. 1)
89:1-29	Joseph, Guardian of Jesus	Your steadfast love, O LORD, is established forever. (v. 2)
89:20-37	July 17–23*, Lect. 16 B	Your love, O LORD, forever will I sing. (v. 1)
90:1-6, 13-17	Oct. 23–29*, Lect. 30 A	Show your servants your works, and your splendor to their children. (v. 16)
90:1-8 [9-11] 12	Nov. 13–19, Lect. 33 A	So teach us to number our days that we may apply our hearts to wisdom. (v. 12)
90:12-17	Oct. 9–15, Lect. 28 B	So teach us to number our days that we may apply our hearts to wisdom. (v. 12)
91:1-2, 9-16	Lent 1 C	God will give the angels charge over you, to guard you in all your ways. (v. 11)
91:1-6, 14-16	Sept. 25–Oct. 1*, Lect. 26 C	You are my refuge and my stronghold, my God in whom I put my trust. (v. 2)
91:9-16	Oct. 16–22, Lect. 29 B	You have made the LORD your refuge, and the Most High your habitation. (v. 9)
92:1-4, 12-15	June 12–18, Lect. 11 B	The righteous shall spread abroad like a cedar of Lebanon. (v. 12)
92:1-4, 12-15	Epiphany 8, Lect. 8 C	The righteous shall flourish like a palm tree. (v. 12)
92:1-4, 12-15	May 24–28, Lect. 8 C	The righteous shall flourish like a palm tree. (v. 12)
93	Ascension of Our Lord (alt.) ABC	Ever since the world began, your throne has been established. (v. 2)
93	Christ the King, Lect. 34 B	Ever since the world began, your throne has been established. (v. 2)
94:1-15	Renewers of Society	You will not abandon your people, O LORD. (v. 14)
95	Lent 3 A	Let us shout for joy to the rock of our salvation. (v. 1)

95:1-7a	Christ the King, Lect. 34 A	We are the people of God's pasture and the sheep of God's hand. (v. 7)
96	Christmas I ABC	Let the heavens rejoice and the earth be glad. (v. 11)
96	May 29–June 4*, Lect. 9 C	Ascribe to the LORD honor and power. (v. 7)
96	Artists and Scientists	Worship the LORD in the beauty of holiness. (v. 9)
96:1-9	May 29–June 4, Lect. 9 C	Declare the glory of the LORD among the nations. (v. 3)
96:1-9 [10-13]	Oct. 16–22, Lect. 29 A	Ascribe to the LORD honor and power. (v. 7)
97	Christmas II ABC	Light dawns for the righteous, and joy for the honest of heart. (v. 11)
97	Easter 7 C	Rejoice in the LORD, you righteous. (v. 12)
98	Christmas III ABC	All the ends of the earth have seen the victory of our God. (v. 3)
98	Vigil of Easter, Reading 9 ABC	Lift up your voice, rejoice, and sing. (v. 4)
98	Easter 6 B	Shout with joy to the LORD, all you lands. (v. 4)
98	Nov. 13–19, Lect. 33 C	In righteousness will the LORD judge the world. (v. 9)
98	Nov. 6–12*, Lect. 32 (alt.) C	In righteousness will the LORD judge the world. (v. 9
98:1-4	Holy Cross Day ABC	The LORD has done marvelous things. (v. 1)
99	Transfiguration A (alt.) C	Proclaim the greatness of the LORD; worship upon God's holy hill. (v. 9)
99	Oct. 16–22*, Lect. 29 A	Proclaim the greatness of the LORD our God. (v. 5)
100	June 12–18, Lect. 11 A	We are God's people and the sheep of God's pasture. (v. 3)
100	Christ the King*, Lect. 34 A	We are God's people and the sheep of God's pasture. (v. 3)
100	Day of Thanksgiving C	Enter God's gates with thanksgiving. (v. 4)
103:[1-7] 8-13	Sept. 11–17, Lect. 24 A	LORD, you are full of compassion and mercy. (v. 8)
103:1-8	Aug. 21–27, Lect. 21 C	The LORD crowns you with mercy and steadfast love. (v. 4)

103:1-13, 22	Epiphany 8, Lect. 8 B	LORD, you are full of compassion and mercy. (v. 8)
103:1-13, 22	May 24–28, Lect. 8 B	LORD, you are full of compassion and mercy. (v. 8)
103:1-5, 20-22	Michael and All Angels	Bless the LORD, you angels, all you hosts of God. (vv. 20, 21)
104:1, 13-23	Stewardship of Creation	O LORD, how manifold are your works! (v. 24)
104:1-9, 24, 35b	Oct. 16–22*, Lect. 29 B	O LORD, how manifold are your works! In wisdom you have made them all. (v. 24)
104:24-34, 35b	Day of Pentecost ABC	Send forth your Spirit and renew the face of the earth. (v. 30)
104:24-35	Stewardship of Creation	O LORD, how manifold are your works! (v. 24)
105:1-6, 16-22, 45b	Aug. 7-13*, Lect. 19 A	Make known the deeds of the LORD among the peoples. Hallelujah! (vv. 1, 45)
105:1-6, 23-26, 45b	Aug. 28–Sept. 3*, Lect. 22 A	Make known the deeds of the LORD among the peoples. Hallelujah! (vv. 1, 45)
105:1-6, 37-45	Sept. 18–24*, Lect. 25 A	Make known the deeds of the LORD among the peoples. Hallelujah! (vv. 1, 45)
105:1-11, 45b	July 24–30*, Lect. 17 A	Make known the deeds of the LORD among the peoples. Hallelujah! (vv. 1, 45)
106:1-6, 19-23	Oct. 9–15*, Lect. 28 A	Remember, O LORD, the favor you have for your people. (v. 4)
107:1-3, 17-22	Lent 4 B	You deliver your people from their distress. (v. 19)
107:1-3, 23-32	June 19–25, Lect. 12 B	You stilled the storm and silenced the waves of the sea. (v. 29)
107:1-7, 33-37	Oct. 30–Nov. 5*, Lect. 31 A	We give thanks to you, LORD, for your wonderful works. (v. 8)
107:1-9, 43	July 31–Aug. 6*, Lect. 18 C	We give thanks to you, LORD, for your wonderful works. (v. 8)
111	Epiphany 4, Lect. 4 B	The fear of the LORD is the beginning of wisdom. (v. 10)
111	Aug. 14-20*, Lect. 20 B	The fear of the LORD is the beginning of wisdom. (v. 10)

111	Oct. 9–15, Lect. 28 C	I will give thanks to the LORD with my whole heart. (v. 1)
112	Aug. 28–Sept. 3, Lect. 22 C	The righteous are merciful and full of compassion. (v. 4)
112	Barnabas, Apostle	Happy are they who fear the LORD. (v. 1)
112:1-9 [10]	Epiphany 5, Lect. 5 A	Light shines in the darkness for the upright. (v. 4)
113	Sept. 18–24, Lect. 25 C	The LORD lifts up the poor from the ashes. (v. 7)
113	Visit of Mary to Elizabeth	Let the name of the LORD be blessed from this time forth forevermore. (v. 2)
114	Easter Evening ABC	Tremble, O earth, at the presence of the LORD. (v. 7)
114	Sept. 11–17*, Lect. 24 A	Tremble, O earth, at the presence of the LORD. (v. 7)
116:1-2, 12-19	Maundy Thursday ABC	I will lift the cup of salvation and call on the name of the LORD. (v. 13)
116:1-2, 12-19	June 12–18*, Lect. 11 A	I will call on the name of the LORD. (v. 13)
116:1-4, 12-19	Easter 3 A	I will call on the name of the LORD. (v. 13)
116:1-9	Sept. 11–17, Lect. 24 B	I will walk in the presence of the LORD. (v. 9)
116:12-19	John, Apostle and Evangelist	Precious in your sight, O LORD, is the death of your servants. (v. 15)
118:1-2, 14-24	Easter Day ABC	This is the day that the LORD has made; let us rejoice and be glad in it. (v. 24)
118:14-29	Easter 2 C	You are my God, and I will exalt you. (v. 28)
119:1-8	Epiphany 6, Lect. 6 A	Happy are they who follow the teaching of the LORD. (v. 1)
119:1-8	Oct. 30–Nov. 5, Lect. 31 B	Happy are they who seek the LORD with all their hearts. (v. 2)
119:9-16	Lent 5 (alt.) B	I treasure your promise in my heart. (v. 11)
119:33-40	Epiphany 7, Lect. 7 A	Teach me, O LORD, the way of your statutes. (v. 33)

119:33-40	Sept. 4–10, Lect. 23 A	I desire the path of your commandments. (v. 35)
119:33-40	Matthew, Apostle and Evangelist	Teach me, O LORD, the way of your statutes. (v. 33)
119:89-104	Theologians and Teachers	Your words are sweet to my taste, sweeter than honey to my mouth. (v. 103)
119:97-104	Oct. 16–22*, Lect. 29 C	Your words are sweet to my taste, sweeter than honey to my mouth. (v. 103)
119:105-112	July 10–16*, Lect. 15 A	Your word is a lamp to my feet and a light upon my path. (v. 105)
119:129-136	July 24–30, Lect. 17 A	When your word is opened, it gives light and understanding. (v. 130)
119:137-144	Oct. 30–Nov. 5*, Lect. 31 C	Grant me understanding, that I may live. (v. 144)
121	Lent 2 A	I lift up my eyes to the hills; my help comes from the LORD. (vv. 1, 2)
121	Oct. 16–22, Lect. 29 C	My help comes from the LORD, the maker of heaven and earth. (v. 2)
122	Advent 1 A	I was glad when they said to me, "Let us go to the house of the LORD." (v. 1)
123	Nov. 13–19*, Lect. 33 A	Our eyes look to you, O God, until you show us your mercy. (v. 2)
123	July 3–9, Lect. 14 B	Our eyes look to you, O God, until you show us your mercy. (v. 2)
124	Aug. 21–27*, Lect. 21 A	We have escaped like a bird from the snare of the fowler. (v. 7)
124	Sept. 25–Oct. 1*, Lect. 26 B	We have escaped like a bird from the snare of the fowler. (v. 7)
124	The Holy Innocents, Martyrs	We have escaped like a bird from the snare of the fowler. (v. 7)
124	Luke, Evangelist	Our help is in the name of the LORD. (v. 8)
125	Sept. 4–10*, Lect. 23 B	Those who trust in the LORD stand fast forever. (v. 1)
126	Advent 3 B	The LORD has done great things for us. (v. 3)
126	Day of Thanksgiving B	The LORD has done great things for us, and we are glad indeed. (v. 3)

126	Lent 5 C	Those who sowed with tears will reap with songs of joy. (v. 5)
126	Oct. 23–29, Lect. 30 B	Those who sowed with tears will reap with songs of joy. (v. 5)
127	Nov. 6–12*, Lect. 32 B	Children are a heritage from the LORD. (v. 3)
128	July 24–30*, Lect. 17 (alt.) A	Happy are they who follow in the ways of God. (v. 1)
130	Vigil of Pentecost (alt.) ABC	There is forgiveness with you. (v. 4)
130	Lent 5 A	I wait for you, O LORD; in your word is my hope. (v. 5)
130	June 5–11, Lect. 10 B	Wait for the LORD, for with the LORD there is steadfast love. (v. 7)
130	June 26–July 2*, Lect. 13 B	Out of the depths I cry to you, O LORD. (v. 1)
130	Aug. 7-13*, Lect. 19 B	Out of the depths I cry to you, O LORD. (v. 1)
131	Epiphany 8, Lect. 8 A	Like a child upon its mother's breast, my soul is quieted within me. (v. 2)
131	May 24–28, Lect. 8 A	Like a child upon its mother's breast, my soul is quieted within me. (v. 2)
132:1-12 [13-18]	Christ the King*, Lect. 34 B	Let your faithful people sing with joy. (v. 9)
133	Aug. 14-20, Lect. 20 A*	How good and pleasant it is to live together in unity. (v. 1)
133	Easter 2 B	How good and pleasant it is to live together in unity. (v. 1)
133	June 19–25*, Lect. 12 (alt.) B	How good and pleasant it is to live together in unity. (v. 1)
133	Christian Unity	How good and pleasant it is to live together in unity. (v. 1)
136:1-4, 23-26	Thomas, Apostle	God's mercy endures forever. (v. 1)
136:1-9, 23-26	Vigil of Easter, Reading 1 ABC	God's mercy endures forever. (v. 1)
137	Oct. 2–8*, Lect. 27 (alt.) C	Remember the day of Jerusalem, O LORD. (v. 7)
138	Aug. 21–27, Lect. 21 A	O LORD, your steadfast love endures forever. (v. 8)
138	June 5–11*, Lect. 10 B	Your love endures forever; do not abandon the works of your hands. (v. 8)

138	Epiphany 5, Lect. 5 C	I will bow down toward your holy temple. (v. 2)
138	July 24–30, Lect. 17 C	Your steadfast love endures forever; do not abandon the works of your hands. (v. 8)
139:1-6, 13-18	Epiphany 2, Lect. 2 B	You have searched me out and known me. (v. 1)
139:1-6, 13-18	May 29–June 4*, Lect. 9 B	You have searched me out and known me. (v. 1)
139:1-6, 13-18	Sept. 4–10, Lect. 23 C	You have searched me out and known me. (v. 1)
139:1-12, 23-24	July 17–23*, Lect. 16 A	You have searched me out and known me. (v. 1)
140	Day of Mourning	You, O GOD, are the strength of my salvation. (v. 7)
141	John the Baptist	My eyes are turned to you, Lord GOD. (v. 8)
143	Vigil of Easter, Reading 8 ABC	Revive me, O LORD, for your name's sake. (v. 11)
145:1-5, 17-21	Nov. 6–12*, Lect. 32 C	Great is the LORD and greatly to be praised! (v. 3)
145:1-8	Sept. 18–24, Lect. 25 A	The LORD is slow to anger and abounding in steadfast love. (v. 8)
145:8-9, 14-21	July 31–Aug. 6, Lect. 18 A	You open wide your hand and satisfy the desire of every living thing. (v. 16)
145:8-14	July 3–9, Lect. 14 A	The LORD is gracious and full of compassion. (v. 8)
145:10-18	July 24–30, Lect. 17 B	You open wide your hand and satisfy the desire of every living thing. (v. 16)
146	Sept. 4–10, Lect. 23 B	I will praise the LORD as long as I live. (v. 2)
146	Oct. 30–Nov. 5*, Lect. 31 B	The LORD lifts up those who are bowed down. (v. 8)
146	Nov. 6–12, Lect. 32 B	The LORD lifts up those who are bowed down. (v. 8)
146	June 5–11*, Lect. 10 C	The LORD lifts up those who are bowed down. (v. 8)
146	Sept. 25–Oct. 1, Lect. 26 C	The LORD gives justice to those who are oppressed. (v. 8)

Wisdom 6:17-20	Nov. 6–12, Lect. 32 (alt.) A	The beginning of wisdom is the most sincere desire for instruction. (v. 17)
Wisdom 7:26—8:1	Sept. 11–17*, Lect. 24 (alt.) B	God loves nothing so much as the person who lives with wisdom. (7:28)
Song of the Three 35-65	Vigil of Easter, Reading 12 ABC	Praise and magnify the Lord forever. (v. 35)
Luke 1:46b-55	Advent 3 (alt.) A	My spirit rejoices in God my Savior. (v. 47)
Luke 1:46b-55	Advent 3 (alt.) B	You, Lord, have lifted up the lowly. (v. 52)
Luke 1:46b-55	Advent 4 B	You, Lord, have lifted up the lowly. (v. 52)
Luke 1:46b-55	Advent 4 C	You, Lord, have lifted up the lowly. (v. 52)
Luke 1:68-79	Advent 2 C	In the tender compassion of our God the dawn from on high shall break upon us. (v. 78)
Luke 1:68-79	Christ the King*, Lect. 34 C	You have raised up for us a mighty savior. (v. 69)

**denotes psalms related to the semicontinuous series of first readings in the time after Pentecost*

APPENDIX D

Index of Gospel Acclamations in *Evangelical Lutheran Worship*

Gospel Acclamation	Sunday, Festival, Commemoration, Occasion
Exodus 15:1-2	Vigil of Easter ABC
Deuteronomy 30:14	July 10–16, Lect. 15 A
1 Samuel 2:8	November 6–12, Lect. 32 B
Psalm 67:4, 5	National Holiday
Psalm 85:7	Advent 1 AB
Psalm 90:1	Day of Penitence
Psalm 90:1	New Year's Eve
Psalm 98:3	Christmas 2 ABC
Psalm 98:7, 8	Stewardship of Creation
Psalm 103:20	Michael and All Angels
Psalm 119:135	September 4–10, Lect. 23 C
Psalm 130:5	August 7–13, Lect. 19 A
Isaiah 6:3	The Holy Trinity ABC
Isaiah 25:9	October 9–15, Lect. 28 A
Isaiah 52:7	Bartholomew, Apostle
Isaiah 52:7	Luke, Evangelist
Isaiah 55:11	July 17–23, Lect. 16 A
Jeremiah 1:7, 8	Epiphany 4, Lect. 4 C
Jeremiah 15:16	Artists and Scientists
Lamentations 3:22	Epiphany 8, Lect. 8 A
Lamentations 3:22	May 24–28, Lect. 8 A
Joel 2:13	Ash Wednesday ABC
Matthew 1:23	Advent 4 A
Matthew 2:2	Epiphany of Our Lord ABC
Matthew 3:17	Baptism of Our Lord, Lect. 1 ABC
Matthew 4:4	Lent 1 ABC
Matthew 4:4	July 31–August 6, Lect. 18 AB
Matthew 4:14	Epiphany 6, Lect. 6 A

Matthew 4:16	Epiphany 4, Lect. 4 B
Matthew 4:17	Lent 3 C
Matthew 4:19	Epiphany 5, Lect. 5 C
Matthew 4:23	Epiphany 3, Lect. 3 A
Matthew 4:23	August 14–20, Lect. 20 A
Matthew 5:3	October 9–15, Lect. 28 B
Matthew 5:3	July 31–August 6, Lect. 18 C
Matthew 5:10	Stephen, Deacon and Martyr
Matthew 5:10	The Holy Innocents, Martyrs
Matthew 5:10	John the Baptist
Matthew 5:10	James, Apostle
Matthew 5:12	Epiphany 4, Lect. 4 A
Matthew 5:16	Renewers of Society
Matthew 8:11	July 24–30, Lect. 17 A
Matthew 8:17	Epiphany 5, Lect. 5 B
Matthew 11:10	Advent 3 ABC
Matthew 11:25	July 3–9, Lect. 14 A
Matthew 11:29	August 28–September 3, Lect. 22 C
Matthew 16:16	August 21–27, Lect. 21 A
Matthew 23:10, 11	October 30–November 5, Lect. 31 A
Matthew 24:42, 44	November 6–12, Lect. 32 A
Matthew 24:42, 44	August 7–13, Lect. 19 C
Matthew 28:19, 20	Ascension of Our Lord ABC
Mark 1:15	June 12–18, Lect. 11 A
Mark 1:15	Epiphany 3, Lect. 3 B
Mark 2:17	Epiphany 8, Lect. 8 B
Mark 2:17	May 24–28, Lect. 8 B
Mark 10:45	October 16–22, Lect. 29 B
Mark 11:9	Christ the King, Lect. 34 ABC
Luke 1:28, 35	Annunciation of Our Lord
Luke 1:28, 35	Mary, Mother of Our Lord
Luke 1:38	Advent 4 BC
Luke 1:47	Visit of Mary to Elizabeth
Luke 2:10-11	Nativity of Our Lord I ABC
Luke 2:10-11	Nativity of Our Lord III ABC
Luke 2:30-31	Presentation of Our Lord
Luke 3:4, 6	Advent 2 ABC
Luke 3:17	August 21–27, Lect. 21 C
Luke 4:15, 17	Epiphany 6, Lect. 6 B
Luke 4:18	June 5–11, Lect. 10 A
Luke 4:18	Epiphany 7, Lect. 7 B

John 12:26	Saints
John 12:31, 32	June 5–11, Lect. 10 B
John 13:34	Maundy Thursday ABC
John 13:35	Easter 5 C
John 14:6	Easter 5 A
John 14:18	Easter 7 ABC
John 14:23	Easter 6 ABC
John 14:27	Peace
John 15:4, 5	November 13–19, Lect. 33 A
John 15:5	Easter 5 B
John 15:16	October 2–8, Lect. 27 A
John 15:26, 27	June 19–25, Lect. 12 A
John 17:7	May 29–June 4, Lect. 9 B
John 17:7	September 25–October 1, Lect. 26 B
John 20:29	Easter 2 ABC
Acts 1:8	Andrew, Apostle
Acts 1:8	Confession of Peter
Acts 1:8	Philip and James, Apostles
Acts 1:8	Matthias, Apostle
Acts 1:8	Thomas, Apostle
Acts 1:8	Matthew, Apostle and Evangelist
Acts 1:8	Simon and Jude, Apostles
Acts 2:24	Easter Monday ABC
Acts 2:32	Conversion of Paul
Acts 2:32	Mark, Evangelist
Acts 2:32	Barnabas, Apostle
Acts 2:32	Peter and Paul, Apostles
Acts 2:32	Mary Magdalene, Apostle
Romans 1:16	May 29–June 4, Lect 9 A
1 Corinthians 1:18	Missionaries
1 Corinthians 1:18	Renewers of the Church
1 Corinthians 1:18	Pastors and Bishops
1 Corinthians 1:23, 24	Lent 3 B
1 Corinthians 5:7, 8	Easter Day ABC
2 Corinthians 1:3, 4	Day of Mourning
2 Corinthians 5:1	Joseph, Guardian of Jesus
2 Corinthians 5:1	Dedication/Anniversary of a Church
2 Corinthians 5:19	September 4–10, Lect. 23 A
2 Corinthians 6:2	June 19–25, Lect. 12 B
2 Corinthians 8:9	September 25–October 1, Lect. 26 C
2 Corinthians 9:8	Day of Thanksgiving ABC

Traditional	Nativity of Our Lord III (alt.) ABC
Traditional	Vigil of Pentecost ABC
Traditional	Day of Pentecost ABC
Traditional	September 18–24, Lect. 25 A

Offering Canticles for Use with *Evangelical Lutheran Worship*

According to the notes in Evangelical Lutheran Worship, "Assembly song or other music may accompany or follow the gathering of the offering" (AE p. 106). Although proper texts are not provided for each Sunday and festival, the following texts as well as others chosen locally may serve as the basis for offering canticles sung by choir or cantor.

ADVENT

Many will come from east and west, and from north and south, and will eat in the kingdom of God. Blessed are they who eat bread in the kingdom of God. (Luke 13:29; 14:15)

The LORD says, I will make a covenant of peace with them; it shall be an everlasting covenant with them. My dwelling-place shall be with them; and I will be their God, and they shall be my people. (Ezek. 37:26, 27)

Who is like the LORD our God,
 who sits enthroned on high,
but stoops to behold
 the heavens and the earth?
The Lord takes up the weak out of the dust,
 and lifts up the poor from the ashes,
enthroning them with the rulers,
 with the rulers of the people. (Ps. 113:5-8)

CHRISTMAS, EPIPHANY

The people who walked in darkness
 have seen a great light;

those who dwelt in a land of deep darkness—
    on them light has shined.
For a child has been born for us,
    a son given to us;
authority rests on his shoulders;
    and he is named
Wonderful Counselor, Mighty God,
    Everlasting Father, Prince of Peace. (Isa. 9:2, 6)

The Lord said to me, You are my son;
    this day have I begotten you.
Princely state has been yours
    from the day of your birth.
In holiness have I begotten you,
    like dew from the womb of the morning. (Ps. 2:7; Ps. 110:3)

The Lord said to me, You are my son;
    this day have I begotten you.
Ask me, and I will make the nations your inheritance,
    and the ends of the earth your possession. (Ps. 2:7-8)

In the beginning was the Word, and the Word was with God, and the Word was God. And the Word became flesh and lived among us, and we have seen his glory, the glory as of a father's only son, full of grace and truth. (John 1:1, 14)

Arise, shine; for your light has come,
    and the glory of the Lord has risen upon you.
They shall bring gold and frankincense,
    and shall proclaim the praise of the Lord.
We have seen his star in the East
    and have come to pay him homage. (Isa. 60:1, 6; Matt. 2:2)

TIME AFTER EPIPHANY

When you pass through the waters, I will be with you;
    and through the rivers, they shall not overwhelm you;
when you walk through fire you shall not be burned,
    and the flame shall not consume you.

For I am the LORD your God,
  the Holy One of Israel, your Savior. (Isa. 43:2-3)

Let your face shine on your servant;
  save me in your steadfast love!
Oh, how abundant is your goodness,
  which you have laid up for those who fear you,
which you have done in the sight of all
  for those who put their trust in you. (Ps. 31:16, 19)

You are a chosen race, a royal priesthood, a holy nation, God's own people, that you may proclaim the mighty acts of the one who called you out of darkness into God's marvelous light. Once you were not a people, but now you are God's people; once you had not received mercy, but now you have received mercy. (1 Peter 2:9-10)

Blessed are the poor in spirit,
  for theirs is the kingdom of heaven.
Blessed are the meek,
  for they shall inherit the earth.
Blessed are those who hunger and thirst for righteousness,
  for they shall be satisfied. (Matt. 5:3, 5-6)

I appeal to you, therefore, by the mercies of God, to present your bodies as a living sacrifice, holy and acceptable to God, which is your spiritual worship. Do not be conformed to this world, but be transformed by the renewing of your minds, that you may discern what is the will of God—what is good and acceptable and perfect. (Rom. 12:1-2)

LENT

Create in me a clean heart, O God,
  and renew a right spirit within me.
Cast me not away from your presence,
  and take not your Holy Spirit from me.
Restore to me the joy of your salvation,
  and uphold me with your free Spirit. (Ps. 51:10-12)

God so loved the world that he gave his only Son, so that whoever believes in him may not perish but may have eternal life. (John 3:16)

Repent and turn from all your sins, lest iniquity be your ruin. Cast away from you all the sins that you have committed against me, and get yourselves a new heart and a new spirit! For I have no pleasure in the death of anyone, says the Lord God, so turn to me and live. (Ezek. 18:30-32)

The Lord, the Lord,
a God merciful and gracious,
slow to anger,
and abounding in steadfast love and faithfulness,
keeping steadfast love for thousands,
forgiving iniquity and transgression and sin. (Exod. 34:6-7)

Remember Jesus Christ, raised from the dead, a descendant of David. If we have died with him, we shall also live with him; if we endure, we shall also reign with him; if we are faithless, he remains faithful—for he cannot deny himself. (2 Tim. 2:8, 11-13)

Christ Jesus emptied himself and became obedient to the point of death—even death on a cross. Therefore God also highly exalted him and gave him the name that is above every name, so that at the name of Jesus every knee should bend, and every tongue should confess that Jesus Christ is Lord, to the glory of God the Father. (Phil. 2:7-11)

Very truly, I tell you, unless a grain of wheat falls into the earth and dies, it remains just a single grain; but if it dies, it bears much fruit. Whoever serves me must follow me, and where I am, there will my servant be also. Whoever serves me, the Father will honor. (John 12:24, 26)

EASTER

Alleluia, alleluia, alleluia.
Cleanse out the old yeast to make yourselves fresh dough, new unleavened bread! For Christ our Passover Lamb has been sacrificed. Therefore let us celebrate the feast with the unleavened bread of sincerity and truth. Alleluia, alleluia, alleluia. (1 Cor. 5:7-8)

Alleluia, alleluia, alleluia.
If you have been raised with Christ, seek the things that are above, where Christ is, seated at the right hand of God. When Christ who is your life is revealed, then you also will be revealed with him in glory.
Alleluia, alleluia, alleluia. (Col. 3:1, 4)

Alleluia, alleluia, alleluia.
The Lord GOD says, I myself will search for my sheep and will seek them out. As shepherds seek out their flocks when some of their sheep have been scattered abroad, so will I seek out my sheep. I will bring them out from the peoples, and I will feed them on the mountains of Israel.
Alleluia, alleluia, alleluia. (Ezek. 34:11-13)

Alleluia, alleluia, alleluia.
Truly, truly, I say to you, those who believe in me will also do the works that I do; and greater works than these will they do, because I go to the Father. I will do whatever you ask in my name, so that the Father may be glorified in the Son. If you ask anything in my name, I will do it.
Alleluia, alleluia, alleluia. (John 14:12-14)

Alleluia, alleluia, alleluia.
Worthy is the Lamb who was slain, to receive power and wealth and wisdom and might and honor and glory and blessing! To the one seated on the throne and to the Lamb be blessing and honor and glory and might forever and ever! Amen!
Alleluia, alleluia, alleluia. (Rev. 5:12-14)

PENTECOST

Be careful, then, how you live, not as unwise but as wise; be filled with the Spirit, as you sing psalms and hymns and spiritual songs, singing and making melody to the Lord in your hearts, giving thanks to God the Father at all times and for everything in the name of our Lord Jesus Christ. (Eph. 5:15, 18-20)

TIME AFTER PENTECOST

Go therefore and make disciples of all nations, baptizing them in the name of the Father and of the Son and of the Holy Spirit, and teaching them to obey everything that I have commanded you. And remember, I am with you always, to the end of the age. (Matt. 28:19-20)

They devoted themselves to the apostles' teaching and fellowship, to the breaking of bread and the prayers. And day by day, attending the temple together and breaking bread in their homes, they ate their food with glad and generous hearts. (Acts. 2:42, 46)

Come to me, all you that are weary and are carrying heavy burdens, and I will give you rest. Take my yoke upon you, and learn from me; for I am gentle and humble in heart, and you will find rest for your souls. For my yoke is easy, and my burden is light. (Matt. 11:28-30)

I will wash my hands in innocence, O LORD,
  that I may go in procession round your altar,
singing aloud a song of thanksgiving,
  and recounting all your wonderful deeds.
LORD, I love the house in which you dwell,
  and the place where your glory abides. (Ps. 26:6-8)

Even the sparrow has found a home,
  and the swallow a nest
  where she may lay her young,
by the side of your altars, O LORD of hosts,
  my king and my God.
Happy are those who dwell in your house!
  They will always be praising you. (Ps. 84:3-4)

From your dwelling on high, you water the mountains;
  the earth is filled with the fruit of your work.
You make grass grow for the cattle,
and plants to serve humankind,
  that we may bring forth food from the earth,
wine to gladden our hearts,

oil to make the face shine,
and bread to strengthen the human heart. (Ps. 104:13-15)

Do not worry, saying, "What will we eat?" or "What will we drink?" or "What will we wear?" Your heavenly Father knows that you need all these things. But strive first for the kingdom of God and his righteousness, and all these things will be given to you as well. (Matt. 6:31-33)

This is the bread that comes down from heaven, that one may eat of it and not die. I am the living bread that came down from heaven. Whoever eats of this bread will live forever; and the bread that I will give for the life of the world is my flesh. (John 6:50-51)

Do not lag in zeal, be ardent in spirit, serve the Lord. Rejoice in hope, be patient in suffering, persevere in prayer. Contribute to the needs of the saints, offer hospitality to strangers. (Rom. 12:11-13)

Those who observe the day, observe it in honor of the Lord. Also those who eat, eat in honor of the Lord, since they give thanks to God. We do not live to ourselves, and we do not die to ourselves. If we live, we live to the Lord, and if we die, we die to the Lord; so then, whether we live or whether we die, we are the Lord's. (Rom. 14:6-8)

Supplemental Psalms for Daily Prayer

One or more of the listed psalms may be used to supplement the psalms appointed in the Daily Lectionary, AE p. 1121.

	Th	F	Sa	Su	M	Tu	W
ADVENT							
Morning	18:1-19; 147:12-21	102, 148	90, 149	24, 150	122, 145	33, 146	50, 147:1-11
Evening	126, 62	130, 16	80, 72	25, 110	40, 67	85, 94	53, 17

CHRISTMAS				
	December 24		*December 31*	
	Evening Prayer	132, 114	Morning Prayer	98, daily psalm*
			Evening Prayer	45, 96
	December 25		*January 1*	
	Morning Prayer	2, daily psalm*	Morning Prayer	98, daily psalm*
	Evening Prayer	98, 96	Evening Prayer	99, 8
	December 26		*January 2*	
	Morning Prayer	116, daily psalm*	Morning Prayer	48, daily psalm*
	Evening Prayer	119:1-24; 27	Evening Prayer	9, 29
	December 27		*January 3*	
	Morning Prayer	34, daily psalm*	Morning Prayer	111, daily psalm*
	Evening Prayer	19, 121	Evening Prayer	107, 15
	December 28		*January 4*	
	Morning Prayer	2, daily psalm*	Morning Prayer	20, daily psalm*
	Evening Prayer	110, 111	Evening Prayer	93, 97
	December 29		*January 5*	
	Morning Prayer	96, daily psalm*	Morning Prayer	99, daily psalm*
	Evening Prayer	132, 97	Evening Prayer	96, 110
	December 30		*January 6*	
	Morning Prayer	93, daily psalm*	Morning Prayer	72, daily psalm*
	Evening Prayer	89:1-18; 89:19-52	Evening Prayer	100, 67

*Daily psalms for Morning Prayer:
Thursday—147:12-21; Friday—148; Saturday—149; Sunday—150; Monday—145; Tuesday—146; Wednesday—147:1-11

TIME AFTER EPIPHANY – *see General below*							
	Th	F	Sa	Su	M	Tu	W
LENT							
Morning	27, 147:12-21	22, 148	43, 149	84, 150	119:73-80; 145	34, 146	5, 147:1-11
Evening	126, 102	105, 130	31, 143	42, 32	121, 6	25, 91	27, 51
EASTER							
Morning	47, 147:12-21	96, 148	92, 149	93, 150	97, 145	98, 146	99, 147:1-11
Evening	68, 113	49, 138	23, 114	137, 117	124, 115	66, 116	9, 118
TIME AFTER PENTECOST – *see General below*							
GENERAL							
Week 1							
Morning	97, 147:12-21	51, 148	104, 149	103, 150	5, 145	42, 146	89:1-18; 147:1-11
Evening	16, 62	142, 65	138, 98	117, 139	82, 29	102, 133	1, 33
Week 2							
Morning	36, 147:12-21	130, 148	56, 149	19, 150	135, 145	123, 146	15, 147:1-11
Evening	80, 27	32, 139	118, 111	81, 113	97, 112	30, 86	48, 4
Week 3							
Morning	143, 147:12-21	88, 148	122, 149	67, 150	57, 145	54, 146	65, 147:1-11
Evening	81, 116	6, 20	100, 63	46, 93	85, 47	28, 99	125, 91
Week 4							
Morning	116, 147:12-21	84, 148	63, 149	108, 150	62, 145	12, 146	96, 147:1-11
Evening	26, 130	25, 40	125, 90	66, 23	73, 9	36, 7	132, 134

APPENDIX G

Chanted Collects for Night Prayer

These are simple chant settings of the prayers that appear in text-only form in Night Prayer, AE pp. 325–326 (LE pp. 724–725)

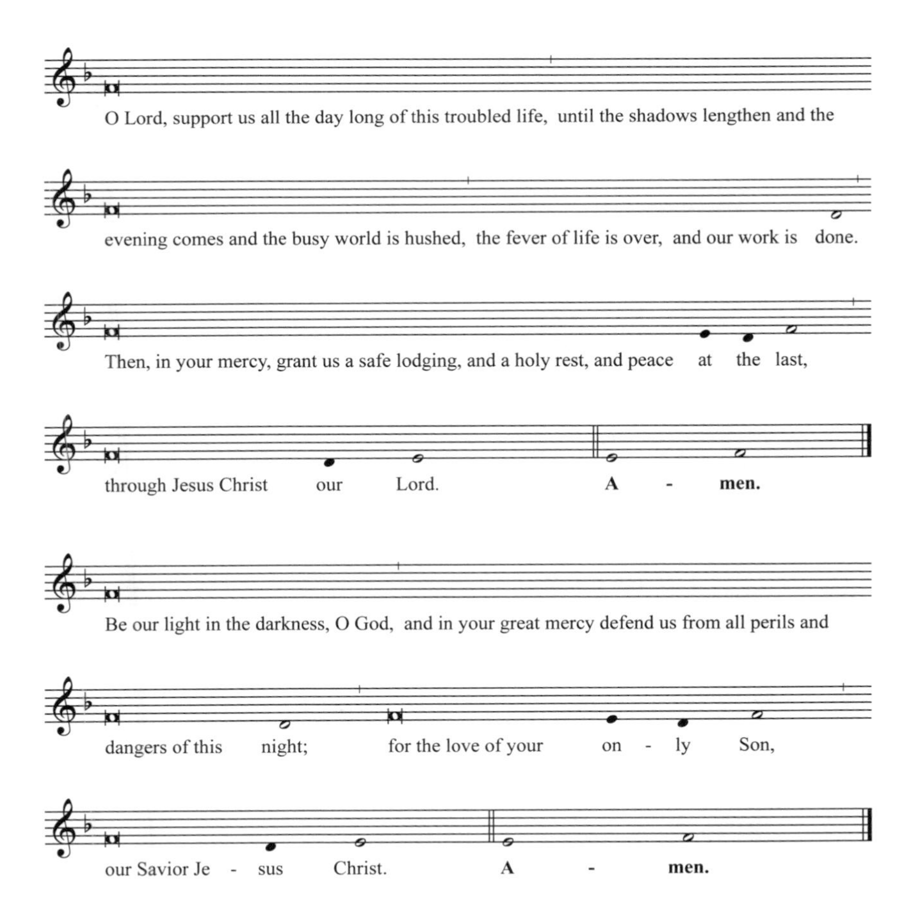

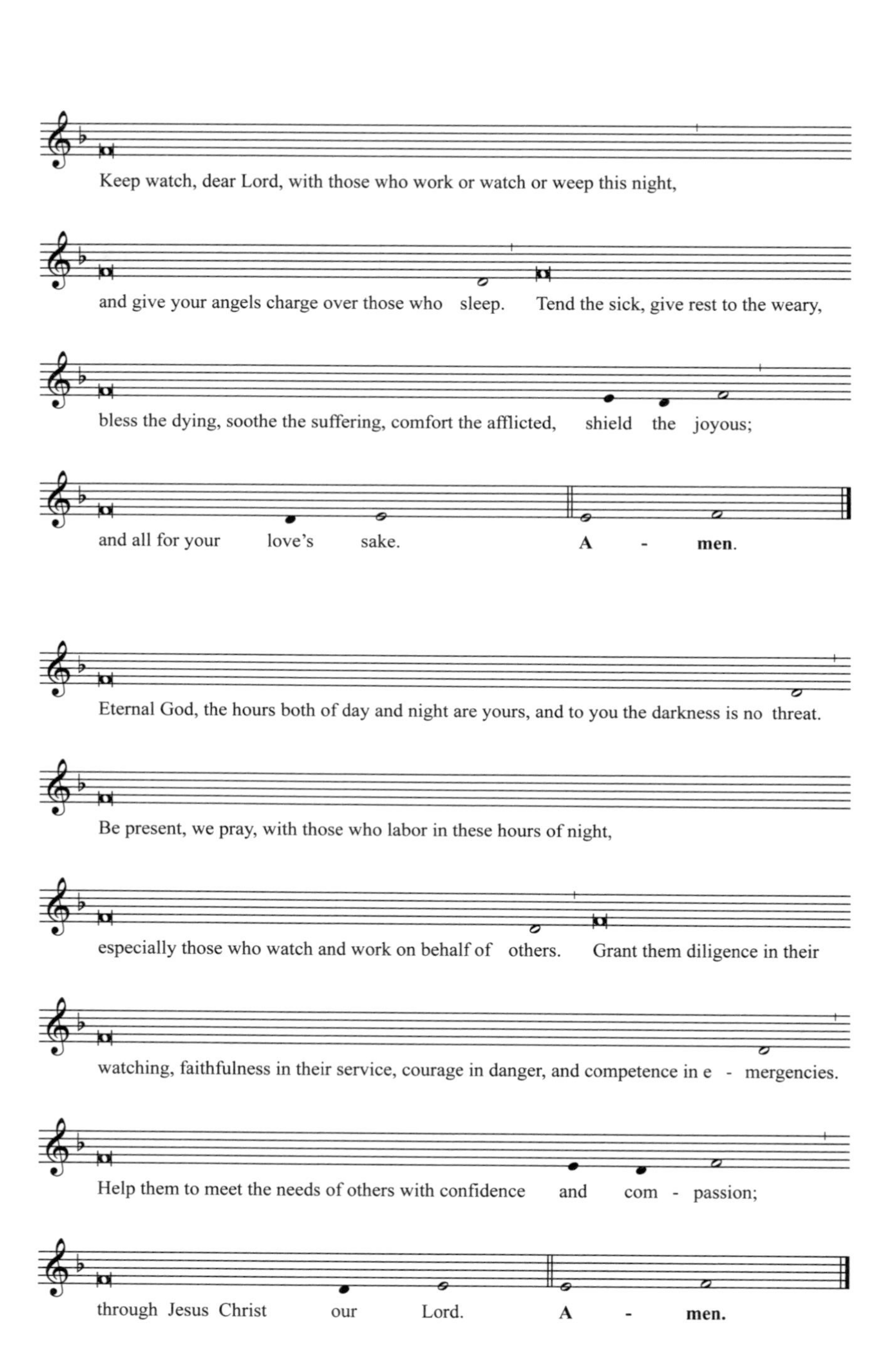
Keep watch, dear Lord, with those who work or watch or weep this night,
and give your angels charge over those who sleep. Tend the sick, give rest to the weary,
bless the dying, soothe the suffering, comfort the afflicted, shield the joyous;
and all for your love's sake. A - men.
Eternal God, the hours both of day and night are yours, and to you the darkness is no threat.
Be present, we pray, with those who labor in these hours of night,
especially those who watch and work on behalf of others. Grant them diligence in their
watching, faithfulness in their service, courage in danger, and competence in e - mergencies.
Help them to meet the needs of others with confidence and com - passion;
through Jesus Christ our Lord. A - men.

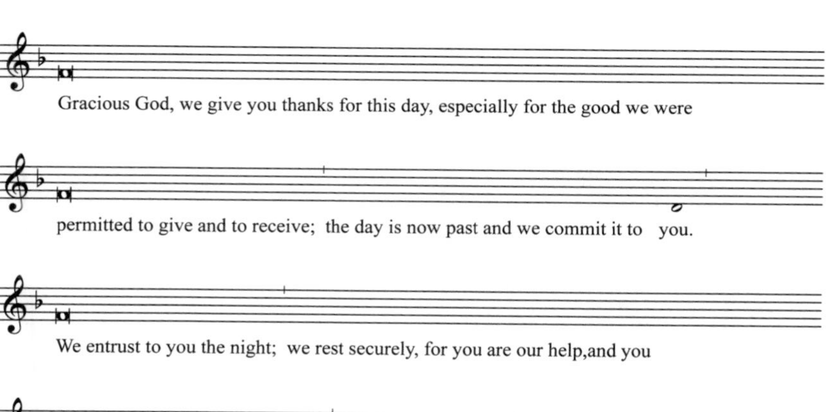
Gracious God, we give you thanks for this day, especially for the good we were
permitted to give and to receive; the day is now past and we commit it to you.
We entrust to you the night; we rest securely, for you are our help,and you
neither slum - ber nor sleep; through Jesus Christ our Lord. A - men.

Endnotes

Chapter One

1 James White. *Documents of Christian Worship* (Louisville: Westminster John Knox Press, 1992), 19.

2 Gerhard Frost. *Law Perfect: Ten Studies on the Commandments* (Minneapolis: Augsburg Publishing House, 1952), 26.

3 Gordon Lathrop. *Holy Things: A Liturgical Theology* (Minneapolis: Fortress Press, 1993). Lathrop explores the patterns of Sunday and the week in more detail in a section titled "The Ordo of Seven Days and the Eighth Day," 36–43.

4 Dorothy Bass. *Receiving the Day: Christian Practices for the Opening the Gift of Time* (San Francisco: Jossey-Bass, 2000), 47. Bass quotes Moltmann in discussion of the third commandment, keeping the Sabbath holy.

5 Cheslyn Jones, Geoffrey Wainwright, Edward Yarnold, SJ, and Paul Bradshaw. *The Study of Liturgy* [rev. ed.] (New York: Oxford University Press, 1992), 457.

6 Lathrop in *Holy Things* juxtaposes Pascha and the days of the year in a more expansive way in a section titled "The Ordo of the Year and Pascha," 68–79.

7 Walter Abbott, SJ. *The Documents of Vatican II* (Chicago: Follett Publishing, 1966), 169.

8 Bass, 76–77.

9 For ideas of how to use worship space imaginatively and inexpensively, see the short chapter, "Worship in Space," in the book of essays titled *With A Voice of Singing* (Minneapolis: Kirk House Publishers, 2007), 129–137.

10 Evangelical Lutheran Church in America, *Principles for Worship* (Minneapolis: Augsburg Fortress, 2002), 68. This helpful essay was part of the process of preparing *Evangelical Lutheran Worship.*

11 Abbott, 144.

12 Cheslyn Jones, Geoffrey Wainwright, Edward Yarnold, SJ, and Paul Bradshaw, eds., *The Study of the Liturgy* [rev. ed.] (New York: Oxford University Press, 1992), 537.

13 1 Cor. 12:12-13.

Chapter Three

1 Gordon W. Lathrop, *Central Things: Worship in Word and Sacrament* (Minneapolis: Augsburg Fortress, 2005).

2 For discussions of the development of Christmas, see Susan K. Roll, "The Origins of Christmas: The State of the Question," *Between Memory and Hope: Readings on the Liturgical Year,* ed. Maxwell E. Johnson (Collegeville: The Liturgical Press, 1991), 273–290; and Thomas J. Talley, *The Origins of the Liturgical Year,* Second Edition (Collegeville: The Liturgical Press, 1991), 79–162.

3 *Egeria: Diary of a Pilgrimage*, tr. George A. Gingras (New York: Newman Press, 1970), 111.

4 Asterius of Amasea, "Homily 19," in *The Paschal Mystery: Ancient Liturgies and Patristic Texts*, ed. A. Hamman (Staten Island, NY: Alba House, 1969), 109–110.

5 The text of the Song of the Three and a musical setting are provided in *Psalter for Worship,* Evangelical Lutheran Worship Edition (Minneapolis: Augsburg Fortress, 2006-2008).

6 John Chrysostom, "Easter Homily," in Gabe Huck, *The Three Days: Parish Prayer in the Paschal Triduum* (Chicago: Liturgy Training Publications, 1981), 80.

Chapter Four

1 Robert Kolb and Timothy J. Wengert, eds., *The Book of Concord: The Confessions of the Evangelical Lutheran Church*, (Minneapolis: Fortress Press, 2000), 399:92.

2 Kolb and Wengert, 58:1–2.

3 Geddes MacGregor, *The Rhythm of God: A Philosophy of Worship* (New York: Seabury Press, 1974), 15.

4 Philip H. Pfatteicher, *New Book of Festivals and Commemorations: A Proposed Common Calendar of Saints* (Minneapolis: Fortress Press, 2008).

5 *Bread for the Day: Daily Bible Readings and Prayers* (Minneapolis: Augsburg Fortress, annual).

Chapter Five

1 Paul Bradshaw, ed., *The New Westminster Dictionary of Liturgy & Worship* (Louisville: Westminster John Knox Press, 2002). The eleven-page article on "Daily Prayer" (pp. 140–150) gives a quick overview of developments of daily prayer and their use in various denominations.

2 Alan Hugh M'Neile, *The Gospel According to St. Matthew* (London: MacMillan, 1957), 267.

3 Eugene Lipman, *The Mishnah* (New York: Schocken Books, 1970), 37.

4 TJ, Ber. 4:3, 8a in *Encyclopaedia Judaica* (Jerusalem: MacMillan, 1971), vol. 11, 392.

5 *The Didache*, commentary by Kurt Niederwimmer, trans. by Linda M. Maloney and edited by Harold W. Attridge in the *Hermeneia* series (Minneapolis: Fortress Press, 1998), 134.

6 Robert Taft, *The Liturgy of the Hours in East and West: The Origins of the Divine Office and Its Meaning for Today* (Collegeville, MN: Liturgical Press, 1986), 351.

7 Taft, 357.

8 George Guiver, *Company of Voices: Daily Prayer and the People of God* (Norwich: Canterbury Press, 2001), 53. Guiver's work seeks to renew daily prayer in a context where he knows it has been discarded by many. He imaginatively suggests ways to revive and renew prayer patterns for our contemporary setting.

9 Paul F. Bradshaw, *Two Ways of Praying* (Nashville: Abingdon, 1995).

10 Heinrich Bornkamm, *Luther's World of Thought*, trans. Martin H. Bertram (Saint Louis: Concordia Publishing House, 1958), 81.

11 *Luther's Works, vol. 43: Devotional Writings II* , ed. Gustav K. Wiencke (Philadelphia: Fortress Press, 1968), 198.

12 *Program Book and Festival Guide* (Minneapolis: Augsburg Publishing House, 1983) for the Festival of Worship and Witness (June 20–24, 1983).

13 Paul Bradshaw, *The Search for the Origins of Christian Worship* (New York: Oxford Press, 1992), 189.

14 J. Gordon Davies, *Worship and Mission* (London: SCM Press, 1966), 114.

15 Gail Ramshaw, ed., *Between Sundays: Daily Bible Readings Based on the Revised Common Lectionary* (Minneapolis: Augsburg Fortress, 1997).

16 *Revised Common Lectionary Daily Readings: Proposed by the Consultation on Common Texts* (Minneapolis: Fortress Press, 2005).

17 Dietrich Bonhoeffer, *Prayerbook of the Bible* in *Dietrich Bonhoeffer Works*, vol. 5 (Minneapolis: Fortress Press, 1996), 147. The editor of the English edition, Geoffrey B. Kelly, states that Bonhoeffer's ultimate aim in writing the *Prayerbook* was "to assist people to pray the Psalms in union with Jesus Christ" (154).

18 Walter Huffman, *The Prayer of the Faithful: Understanding and Creatively Using the Prayer of the Church* (Minneapolis: Augsburg Fortress, 1986), 29.

19 Daniel Stevick, *The Crafting of the Liturgy: A Guide for Preparers* (New York: Church Hymnal Corporation), 1990, 130.

20 For additional guidance on clothing for the liturgy, see *The Sunday Assembly* (Using *Evangelical Lutheran Worship,* vol. 1), pp. 91–99.

Chapter Six

1 Eric Milner-White and George Wallace Briggs, *Daily Prayer* (London: Oxford, 1941), p. 14.

Chapter Seven

1 Ibid.

Chapter Eight

1 Dietrich Bonhoeffer, *Life Together, Prayerbook of the Bible* in *Dietrich Bonhoeffer Works,* vol. 5, trans. Daniel W. Bloesch and James H. Burtness (Minneapolis: Fortress Press, 1996), 108.

Bibliography

Adam, Adolf, *The Liturgical Year: Its History and Its Meaning after the Reform of the Liturgy.* Collegeville, MN: The Liturgical Press, 1981.

Bass, Dorothy C. *Receiving the Day: Christian Practices for Opening the Gift of Time.* San Francisco: Jossey-Bass, 2000.

Bonhoeffer, Dietrich. *Life Together and Prayerbook of the Bible.* Dietrich Bonhoeffer Works, vol. 5. Minneapolis: Fortress Press, 1996.

Bower, Peter C., ed., *Handbook for the Revised Common Lectionary.* Louisville: Westminster John Knox Press, 1996.

Bradshaw, Paul. *Daily Prayer in the Early Church.* New York: Oxford University Press, 1982.

Bradshaw, Paul, and Lawrence Hoffman, eds, *Passover and Easter: Origin and History to Modern Times.* South Bend, IN: University of Notre Dame Press, 1999.

Bradshaw, Paul, ed. *The New Westminister Dictionary of Liturgy & Worship.* Louisville: Westminster John Knox Press, 2002.

Bread for the Day: Daily Bible Readings and Prayers. Annual resource. Minneapolis: Augsburg Fortress.

Brugh, Lorraine S., and Gordon W. Lathrop. *The Sunday Assembly.* Using *Evangelical Lutheran Worship*, vol. 1. Minneapolis: Augsburg Fortress, 2007.

Bushkofsky, Dennis, and Craig Satterlee. *The Christian Life.* Using *Evangelical Lutheran Worship,* vol. 2. Minneapolis: Augsburg Fortress, 2008.

Chupungco, Ansgar, *Shaping the Easter Feast.* Washington, D.C.: Pastoral Press, 1992.

The Church's Year: Propers and Seasonal Rites. Renewing Worship 8. Minneapolis: Augsburg Fortress, 2004.

Dahill, Lisa E. *Truly Present: Practicing Prayer in the Liturgy.* Minneapolis: Augsburg Fortress, 2005.

Daily Prayer. Renewing Worship 7. Minneapolis: Augsburg Fortress, 2004.

Evangelical Lutheran Worship. Pew Edition and Leaders Edition. Minneapolis: Augsburg Fortress. 2006.

Gallagher, Nora. *Things Seen and Unseen: A Year Lived in Faith.* New York: Vintage Books, 1998.

Guiver, George. *Company of Voices: Daily Prayer and the People of God*. Second edition. Norwich: Canterbury Press, 2001.

Highben, Zebulon M., and Kristine M. Langlois, ed. *With a Voice of Singing*. Minneapolis: Kirk House, 2007.

Huffman, Walter C. *Prayer of the Faithful: Understanding and Creatively Leading Corporate Intercessory Prayer*. Revised edition. Minneapolis: Augsburg Fortress, 1992.

Huffman, Walter C., and S. Anita Stauffer. *Where We Worship*. Philadelphia: Board of Publication of the Lutheran Church in America, 1987.

Indexes to Evangelical Lutheran Worship. Minneapolis: Augsburg Fortress, 2007.

Johnson, Donald W. *Praying the Catechism*. Revised edition. Evangelical Lutheran Church in Canada, 1998.

Johnson, Maxwell, Jr., ed. *Between Memory and Hope: Readings on the Liturgical Year*. Collegeville, MN: The Liturgical Press, 2000.

Lathrop, Gordon W. *Holy Things: A Liturgical Theology*. Minneapolis: Fortress Press, 1993.

Lutheran Book of Worship. Pew Edition and Ministers Edition. Minneapolis: Augsburg Publishing House; Philadelphia: Board of Publication, Lutheran Church in America; St. Louis: Concordia Publishing House; 1978.

Peterson, Eugene H. *Answering God: The Psalms as Tools for Prayer*. New York: Harper & Row, 1989.

Pfatteicher, Philip H., ed. *The Daily Prayer of the Church*. Minneapolis: Lutheran University Press, 2005.

Pfatteicher, Philip H., and Carlos Messerli. *Manual on the Liturgy*. Minneapolis: Augsburg Publishing House, 1979.

Pfatteicher, Philip H. *New Book of Festivals and Commemorations: A Proposed Common Calendar of Saints*. Minneapolis: Fortress Press, 2008.

Principles for Worship. Renewing Worship 2. Minneapolis: Augsburg Fortress, 2002.

Ramshaw, Gail. *A Three-Year Banquet: The Lectionary for the Assembly*. Minneapolis: Augsburg Fortress 2004.

———. *The Three-Day Feast: Maundy Thursday, Good Friday, Easter*. Minneapolis: Augsburg Fortress, 2004.

Schattauer, Thomas W., ed. *Inside Out: Worship in an Age of Mission*. Minneapolis: Fortress Press, 1999.

Schmit, Clayton J. *Public Reading of Scripture: A Handbook*. Nashville: Abingdon Press, 2002.

Schumacher, Frederick, ed. *For All the Saints: A Prayer Book for and by the Church*. Four volumes. Delhi, NY: American Lutheran Publicity Bureau, 1994, 1995, 1996.

Stevick, Daniel. *The Crafting of the Liturgy: A Guide for Preparers*. New York: Church Hymnal Corporation, 1990.

Stookey, Laurence Hull. *Calendar: Christ's Time for the Church*. Nashville: Abingdon, 1996.

Sundays and Seasons. Annual guide to worship planning. Minneapolis: Augsburg Fortress.

Taft, Robert, S.J. *The Liturgy of the Hours in East and West: The Origins of the Divine Office and Its Meaning for Today.* Collegeville, MN: The Liturgical Press, 1986.

Talley, Thomas J., *The Origins of the Liturgical Year.* Collegeville, MN: The Liturgical Press, 1986.

Tickle, Phyllis. *The Divine Hours: Prayers for Autumn and Wintertime.* Garden City, NY: Doubleday, 2000.

———. *The Divine Hours: Prayers for Springtime: A Manual for Prayer.* Garden City, NY: Doubleday, 2001.

———. *The Divine Hours: Prayers for Summertime.* Garden City, NY: Doubleday, 2000.

West, Fritz. *Scripture and Memory: The Ecumenical Hermeneutic of the Three-Year Lectionaries.* Collegeville, MN: The Liturgical Press, 1997.

White, James F. *Documents of Christian Worship: Descriptive and Interpretative Sources.* Nashville: Abingdon Press, 1992.

———. *Introduction to Christian Worship.* Third Edition, revised and expanded. Nashville: Abingdon Press, 2000.

Index